THE EVERYTHING®
VEGETARIAN PRESSURE COOKER COOKBOOK

Dear Reader,

Take a step inside your grocery store or browse the menu at local restaurants and you'll see that exciting vegetarian options are everywhere. But, the bar has been raised and serving healthful but boring vegetarian food is not enough. With a variety of meat substitutes, innovative cooking techniques, and exciting recipes, many vegetarians won't settle for anything less than a flavorful meal every time they eat—including us!

We won't compromise on flavor but we do know how to be flexible. Justin is a long time professional cook who is vegetarian, and Amy is an animal activist and food writer who is vegan. Almost all of the recipes we use at home must accommodate both diets and we're giving you the same flexible options in this book. Every recipe can be made vegan or vegetarian and thanks to the speedy cooking times provided by a pressure cooker, most can be made in mere minutes. And if your house is anything like ours, we don't always have every ingredient on hand, so we've included tips for substitutions and have noted ingredients that can be left out in a pinch.

If you're not vegetarian but are trying to eat more fast, meat-free meals, the easy but full-flavored recipes in this book will be right for you.

Amy & Justin

Welcome to the EVERYTHING® Series!

These handy, accessible books give you all you need to tackle a difficult project, gain a new hobby, comprehend a fascinating topic, prepare for an exam, or even brush up on something you learned back in school but have since forgotten.

You can choose to read an *Everything®* book from cover to cover or just pick out the information you want from our four useful boxes: e-questions, e-facts, e-alerts, and e-ssentials.

We give you everything you need to know on the subject, but throw in a lot of fun stuff along the way, too.

We now have more than 400 *Everything®* books in print, spanning such wide-ranging categories as weddings, pregnancy, cooking, music instruction, foreign language, crafts, pets, New Age, and so much more. When you're done reading them all, you can finally say you know *Everything®*!

QUESTION
Answers to common questions

FACT
Important snippets of information

ALERT
Urgent warnings

ESSENTIAL
Quick handy tips

PUBLISHER Karen Cooper

DIRECTOR OF ACQUISITIONS AND INNOVATION Paula Munier

MANAGING EDITOR, EVERYTHING® SERIES Lisa Laing

COPY CHIEF Casey Ebert

ACQUISITIONS EDITOR Katrina Schroeder

ASSOCIATE DEVELOPMENT EDITOR Hillary Thompson

EDITORIAL ASSISTANT Ross Weisman

EVERYTHING® SERIES COVER DESIGNER Erin Alexander

LAYOUT DESIGNERS Colleen Cunningham, Elisabeth Lariviere, Ashley Vierra, Denise Wallace

Visit the entire Everything® series at *www.everything.com*

THE EVERYTHING®

VEGETARIAN PRESSURE COOKER COOKBOOK

Amy Snyder and Justin Snyder

Adamsmedia
Avon, Massachusetts

To our baby boy. You may not be here yet,
but already you are an inspiration to us.

An Everything® Series Book.
Everything® and everything.com® are registered
trademarks of F+W Media, Inc.

Contains material adapted and abridged from
The Everything® Pressure Cooker Cookbook,
by Pamela Rice Hahn, copyright © 2009
by F+W Media, Inc., ISBN 10: 1-4405-0017-7,
ISBN 13: 978-1-4405-0017-6.

Nutrition statistics run by B. E. Horton, MS, RD

Published by Adams Media,
a division of F+W Media, Inc.
57 Littlefield Street, Avon, MA 02322 U.S.A.
www.adamsmedia.com

ISBN 10: 1-4405-0672-8
ISBN 13: 978-1-4405-0672-7
eISBN 10: 1-4405-0673-6
eISBN 13: 978-1-4405-0673-4

Printed in the United States of America.

10 9 8 7 6 5 4 3 2 1

This publication is designed to provide accurate
and authoritative information with regard to the subject matter covered. It is sold with the understanding
that the publisher is not engaged in rendering legal,
accounting, or other professional advice. If legal advice
or other expert assistance is required, the services of a
competent professional person should be sought.

—From a *Declaration of Principles* jointly adopted
by a Committee of the American Bar Association
and a Committee of Publishers and Associations

Many of the designations used by manufacturers and
sellers to distinguish their products are claimed as
trademarks. Where those designations appear in this
book and Adams Media was aware of a trademark
claim, the designations have been printed with initial
capital letters.

This book is available at quantity discounts
for bulk purchases.
For information, please call 1-800-289-0963.

Library of Congress Cataloging-in-Publication Data
Snyder, Amy R.
The everything vegetarian pressure cooker cookbook
/ Amy Snyder and Justin Snyder.
p. cm. — (Everything series)
"Contains material adapted and abridged from The
Everything pressure cooker cookbook, by Pamela
Rice Hahn, copyright © 2009 by F+W Media"—Prelim.
Includes index.
ISBN 978-1-4405-0672-7
1. Vegetarian cooking. 2. Pressure cooking. I. Sny-
der, Justin. II. Hahn, Pamela Rice. Everything pressure
cooker cookbook. III. Title.
TX837.S675 2010
641.5'636—dc22
                    2010022577

Contents

Introduction

WITH MORE THAN 8 million vegetarians in the United States and even more of the population describing themselves as vegetarian-inclined, the necessity for meat-free cookbooks is on the rise. However, simply leaving the meat out of dishes is no longer enough for some conscientious consumers. Veganism, defined as avoiding all animal products, including dairy, eggs, honey, and meat, is also gaining in popularity. Even those who are not vegetarian or vegan may eat vegetarian one or two days per week. These people do so because of the health benefits provided by eating more nutrient-rich fruits and vegetables, instead of cholesterol- and fat-heavy meats and cheese. Many households must now accommodate meat-eaters, vegetarians, and vegans alike. All of today's diet options mean the home cook needs to be flexible, and recipes must be adaptable. The recipes in this cookbook provide vegan ingredient alternatives. Certain brands are suggested, to achieve specific consistencies and results, but can be replaced with other similar ingredients.

Also on the rise today is the consumption of fast food and restaurant-prepared meals, which can contain more fat, salt, and sugar than home-made meals. Many families do not think they have the time to prepare nutritious meals at home, but with the use of a pressure cooker, your next healthy meal may only be minutes away. This lesser-known appliance is making a comeback in kitchens across the country because it cooks ingredients in a fraction of the time a stovetop or oven would, and it helps retain key nutrients.

Pressure cookers date back to the 1600s, when the first was invented by Frenchman Denis Papin. Pressure cookers work by allowing water to boil under pressure at higher temperatures than the normal 212°F, and locking the steam produced from the liquid in an airtight container. The hotter water and resultant steam cook foods faster. It was not until the 1940s post–World War II era that pressure cookers became popular in the United States because of their convenience—but along with the boom came the horror stories of pressure cooker accidents. The modern pressure cooker has safety mechanisms in place to prevent the seemingly common accidents that once plagued pressure cookers, and users need not be worried.

Just because you might be looking for healthy vegetarian or vegan recipes that can be prepared quickly does not mean you have to sacrifice flavor or variety. *The Everything® Vegetarian Pressure Cooker Cookbook* is full of easily adaptable recipes that suit a variety of tastes. Many of the cookbook's 300 recipes, which feature global cuisine such as Mexican, Thai, Indian, Middle Eastern, and African, are naturally vegan, and for those that are not there are tips for easily making the recipe vegan. Many of the recipes will turn out well even if you don't have all of the ingredients on hand. If you only have dried basil on hand for the pasta dish that calls for oregano, no problem! The recipes in this book are flexible, so have fun with them.

Each chapter, from appetizers and sauces to entrées and desserts, begins with the basics, and then moves into more complex variations within that category. Most chapters end with a variety of ethnic recipes and mouthwatering regional American dishes. Whether the recipe is simple, or exotic and complex, the flavors are full-bodied and will not leave you missing the meat.

CHAPTER 1

An Introduction to Pressure Cooking and Vegetarianism

Pressure cookers might not be as commonly used as microwave ovens are today, but they are nearly as easy to use as other popular appliances. Once you factor in the nutritional benefits of using a pressure cooker to prepare vegetarian meals, as opposed to a microwave, stovetop, or oven, it becomes clear that this handy appliance deserves a starring role in your kitchen. Almost any vegetarian or vegan recipes can be made in a pressure cooker—even cakes!

Operating Your Pressure Cooker

The pressure cooker you can purchase today and the one sitting on your grandmother's kitchen counter for the last twenty-five years are two very different appliances. Newer pressure cookers can be made for the stovetop or electric range, and can vary in capacity from a few quarts to over ten.

FACT

Large pressure cookers with the capacity to hold jars used in home canning are called pressure canners. Laboratories and hospitals sterilize materials using a type of pressure cooker known as an autoclave. Pressure cookers used in the food industry are often referred to as retorts.

Depending on which route you're going, old school or new, the instructions for operating your pressure cooker may vary. The manual that came with your pressure cooker will be the best resource on how to operate it, but there are some useful tips that can be applied to all pressure cookers.

Don't Ignore Liquid Recommendations

Some pressure cookers come complete with recommendations for the minimum and maximum amount of liquid that should be used in the appliance. This warning should not be ignored. Using too little liquid may result in burnt food and the inability to build pressure properly, while too much will result in longer cook times. In addition to not adding too much liquid, you should be sure to never overfill your pressure cooker. A general rule is that half full is the maximum for liquids and two-thirds full is the maximum for all other foods.

Stand Guard

Gone are the days of "exploding" pressure cookers, because today's models come equipped with built-in safety features. One common feature is that you cannot remove the lid until all pressure has been released, but if you are using a vintage model be sure to use extra caution. Others have release valves that allow for the escape of excess pressure when needed.

Even with these features in place to protect, you should never leave a pressure cooker unattended. Stand guard while it's in use.

Pressure Release Methods

There are three methods used to release pressure from a cooker—natural, quick, and cold water—and choosing the right method for each recipe is an important part of using a pressure cooker. The natural-release method will help retain the most nutrients, but takes longer than other methods. Food continues to slowly cook during the release time, so it is not appropriate for all recipes. Use this method for tougher, denser items, or those that will be enhanced with a longer cook time.

ALERT

The cold water release method isn't suggested in any of the recipes in this book; however, if you find that your pressure cooker retains too much heat after the quick-release method when you prepare foods that only require a short cooking time—like certain vegetables, risotto, or polenta—try using the cold water release method the next time you prepare that food.

If you need to release pressure rapidly because of a delicate ingredient or the need to add more ingredients, use the quick-release method. Depending on your model of pressure cooker, there will be a knob or a button for the quick-release method. Finally, the cold water method is used when you need to release pressure and reduce heat quickly. As the name implies, you do this by running cold water over the pressure cooker.

Advantages of Using a Pressure Cooker

The lure of making a meal in mere minutes is enough for some to try a pressure cooker, but there are other reasons to invest in this appliance. In addition to saving time for busy families, pressure cookers are excellent at retaining nutrients sometimes lost during the cooking process. They're also great at helping you keep a little extra cash in your wallet because they may help reduce the cost of utilities associated with cooking.

Speed

Speed is without a doubt the main reason people decide to use a pressure cooker. Dried beans can be soaked in one hour and then cooked in a matter of minutes. Soups and stews that normally take hours to develop flavors can be done in fifteen minutes or less. Nearly an hour to cook brown rice is not needed when using a pressure cooker—it's done in fifteen minutes. The amount of time saved when using a pressure cooker is drastic and can really add up when a pressure cooker is used consistently. That means more time for your friends, family, work, and favorite activities, instead of hovering over a hot stove.

Health

Fast cooking times produced by a pressure cooker may limit the number of weekly trips you make to fast food joints or restaurants, which will naturally make your diet more healthful. Meals cooked at home often contain less fat and salt than versions of the same meal prepared at a restaurant. Foods prepared in a pressure cooker may also retain more nutrients than those prepared using other methods. Pressure cookers use the steam from liquid to cook food, and this limited amount of liquid may help keep vitamins locked in.

Money

It's known that pressure cookers cut back on cooking times, but did you know they may also cut back your monthly utility costs? Shorter cooking times required when using a pressure cooker also mean a shorter period of time your stovetop needs to be on, heating up your kitchen. On a hot summer day, your air conditioner will thank you. For some recipes, using a pressure cooker can shave up to 45 minutes off of the time you need to have your stove on, which can add up to significant savings throughout the course of a month.

Adapting Recipes for Your Pressure Cooker

Once you know the basic steps for operating your pressure cooker, you're ready to explore the plethora of diverse vegetarian and vegan recipes in this book, or create your own. Adapting recipes written for a stovetop or oven is easy, even if they contain meat. Just remember these four tips for easy adapting.

Know Your Cooking Times

The first step in adapting a recipe to a pressure cooker recipe is determining the cooking time of your main ingredient. Depending on the ingredient, cooking times will vary dramatically and should always be researched before you start. For example, a few stalks of asparagus are not going to take nearly as long as one cup of dried black beans, so be sure to check. There are several online resources that list the cooking times for almost all common ingredients used in American cooking. Refer to Appendix C for a list of some of the most popular websites.

Some Techniques Should Be Avoided

Once you have determined the cooking time of your main ingredient, think about which steps of your recipe are best suited for a pressure cooker and which should be completed in the oven or on the stove. Some techniques should be avoided in a pressure cooker. Deep frying is one of them. Every pressure cooker comes with a recommendation for the maximum amount of oil you should use in the pressure cooker and that amount should not be ignored. Typically the quantity is small, about ¼ cup, and will not allow for frying. Be sure to read your instruction manual to find out the maximum amount of oil for your appliance. Also, remember that the size of your pressure cooker will impact which recipes you can prepare in it, so make sure that a recipe will work for your appliance before you get started. Don't let this scare you away from trying to adapt your own recipes however, because there are many techniques that are appropriate for pressure cookers. Try boiling, steaming, braising, and even baking.

Flavors Don't Change

Now that your cooking times and techniques have been determined, move on to the fun part—flavor. Certain preparation techniques enhance flavors. Think of how pine nuts develop their rich nutty flavor after you toast them in the oven, or sauces come to life after they have been simmered over low heat for hours on end. Knowing how to prepare each ingredient can enhance the flavor. However, the basics of combining flavors will not change just because you are using a pressure cooker. For each of the recipes you are creating you should consider how much fat, salt, acid, sweetness, and herbs are needed to bring the best results. Typically, this will not be very different than if you had prepared the dish on the stovetop or in the oven instead of in your pressure cooker, so there is no need to stress over how a pressure cooker will change your flavors.

Experiment

You've heard it before: Practice makes perfect, and cooking is no exception. The first recipe you adapt for a pressure cooker probably won't be a masterpiece, but if you experiment you might get there.

Adjust the cooking times, techniques, flavors, and types of recipes you are preparing in your pressure cooker until you reach optimal results, and just have fun with it!

ESSENTIAL

As you prepare the dishes in this cookbook or adapt other recipes for your pressure cooker, make notes about which ones you, your family, and your friends preferred and don't rely on your memory. If you think a recipe in this book would benefit by adding a bit more seasoning, then note that in the margin. Making notes and writing down *your* version of recipes now will make future experiments in the kitchen even easier.

Vegetarian 101

A vegetarian is usually defined as one who does not consume animal flesh, including fish and other seafood. Most people who refer to themselves as vegetarian do eat eggs and dairy products, and may still wear animal products such as fur, leather, and wool. Those who take their stance against cruelty to animals a step further and avoid all animal products, including meat, eggs, dairy, and honey are called vegans. In many cases, this lifestyle choice does not apply only to food but is also reflected in their choice of clothing, makeup, and household products. In most cases, vegans try to live a 100 percent cruelty-free lifestyle.

Vegetarianism and veganism are rapidly gaining in popularity across the United States, but the reason for going meat-free varies greatly from person to person. For some, the decision is reached after watching graphic footage of how animals are housed and then slaughtered on modern factory farms and in slaughterhouses. Some people realize that they can no longer contribute to the routine cruelty they've witnessed. The decision may be based on the many health benefits of choosing a meat-free diet, or the desire to try to undo the environmental harm caused by the meat industry. For others, the decision may be based on religion, upbringing, or other personal factors.

If you are considering making the switch to a vegetarian or vegan diet, there are three compelling reasons to do so now:

1. Cruelty to animals
2. Health
3. Environment

Cruelty to Animals

Imagine spending your entire life stuffed into a cramped shed or cage, with barely enough room to turn around, and being fed to grow so large your legs cannot withstand the weight of your body. The only escape from this suffering is when you are en route to being slaughtered using a cruel and outdated method that does not allow you to quickly escape the painful world in which you live, but often prolongs the agony. This is the life of millions of animals, such as chickens, cows, and pigs, on today's modern factory farms and in slaughterhouses. Most animals are not kept in the sunny pastures or on quaint family farms you see on television or in ads. Instead, they are treated as objects so that companies can maximize their profits at the expense of an animal's well-being. The conditions are no better for dairy cows and egg-laying hens. They too suffer on factory farms, and when they can no longer produce as expected, are slaughtered.

QUESTION

Isn't cruelty to animals illegal?
While some federal laws exist to protect animals on factory farms, they are inadequate and often poorly enforced. Many industry standards that result in suffering, such as debeaking without painkillers and overcrowding animals, are not covered.

Several animal rights groups have released undercover video exposés that show what really happens to animals when people think no one else is looking. Visit PETA.org to watch video footage online and to learn more about these issues.

The only way to avoid contributing to the cruelty to animals described here is by not eating animals. Choosing a vegetarian diet will alleviate some of the suffering experienced by chickens, pigs, cows, and fish every day, but the only way to be sure that you are not contributing to any cruelty to farmed animals is by going vegan.

Health

Eating meat is not only contributing to cruelty to animals, but it may be harming your health. Meat and dairy products contain unhealthy saturated fat and cholesterol, and by eliminating them from your diet you are one step closer to a healthy heart and trim waistline. Cholesterol is known to clog arteries, and this buildup can lead to heart disease. But did you know that plant-based foods (vegan foods) contain no cholesterol? Research has shown that those who eat a cholesterol- and cruelty-free diet are 50 percent less likely to develop heart disease than meat-eaters. In addition, meat-free diets are also higher in fiber and can be lower in fat, which helps keep vegetarians and vegans slimmer, on average, than their meat-eating counterparts.

Environment

When thinking of ways to help the environment, many people decide to recycle, carry reusable bags to the grocery store, or drive a hybrid car, but the most effective way to help may be by changing what's on your dinner plate. A United Nations report states that "the livestock sector emerges as one of the top two or three most significant contributors to the most serious environmental problems, at every scale from local to global." Eating meat leads to land degradation, climate change and air pollution, and water shortage and water pollution; but by choosing a vegetarian diet instead you can help stop this environmental harm.

FACT

Eating meat means wasting an essential resource—water. The average vegetarian diet takes 300 gallons of water per day to produce, while the average meat-filled diet takes more than 4,000 gallons of water to produce.

Finding the ingredients to help you fuel your vegetarian or vegan diet is now easier than ever before. Many national grocery store chains carry popular mock meats, such as the Boca and Morningstar Farms brands. Several even have health food sections that are stocked with vegan mayonnaise, tofu, and soymilk. Better yet, many of the products sitting in your cupboards right now might be "accidentally vegan." Popular items such as Bisquick, some Duncan Hines cake mixes, and even some flavors of Jell-O brand instant pudding are all vegan if you prepare them with vegan products. For those items that aren't quite as easy to find, refer to Appendix C for a list of online vegan retailers.

In addition to online vegan specialty stores that sell food products, there are a multitude of other resources online that will help with your transition to a vegetarian or vegan diet. Groups such as People for the Ethical Treatment of Animals (PETA) offer free vegetarian starter kits, recipes, lists of "accidentally vegan" food items, information on animal rights, and much more. Refer to Appendix C for a list of additional online resources.

Vegetarian Nutrition

What do vegans eat? Where do vegetarians get their protein? Are you worried about becoming anemic? These are common questions many vegans and vegetarians face, but they are largely unfounded. Vegan and vegetarian diets are loaded with essential nutrients and, if done right, can be healthier than a diet full of meat and cheese. As with any diet, the key is to choose healthful foods and limit your consumption of fatty, sugar- or sodium-heavy, and overly processed foods to a minimum. When choosing the healthiest foods the majority of the time, vegan and vegetarian diets can be full of protein, iron, calcium, and other vital nutrients.

Protein

Protein is a required nutrient for maintaining a healthy body. Luckily, many foods considered the staple of a meat-free diet are rich with protein, but contain none of the fat and cholesterol found in meat. The real protein powerhouse is the soybean. This powerful bean contains a whopping 28.62 grams of protein per cup. Soybeans are commonly used in mock meats and vegan dairy products, but they can also be cooked and prepared in other recipes, so getting your daily requirement of protein should not be a problem if soy is a part of your plan.

▼ **TABLE 1-1: HEALTHY PROTEIN SOURCES**

Ingredient	Grams of Protein
Soybean, boiled (1 cup)	28.62
Lentils, boiled (1 cup)	17.9
Pinto beans, boiled (1 cup)	15.4
Black beans, boiled (1 cup)	15.2
Chickpeas, boiled (1 cup)	14.5
Soymilk, unfortified (1 cup)	8.0
Roasted peanuts (1 ounce)	8.0
Spinach, boiled (1 cup)	7.6
Couscous, cooked (1 cup)	6.0
Broccoli, cooked (1 cup)	5.7
Whole wheat bread (1 slice)	4.1

Source: USDA.gov

Another benefit to consuming plant-based proteins over animal proteins is that these ingredients typically contain fiber and complex carbohydrates that are not found in animal products. For example, lentils, which contain 17.9 grams of protein per cup, also contain 15.6 grams of fiber!

Iron

Anemia is a common concern of some new vegans and vegetarians and it can be caused by iron deficiency. People worry that if they leave meat off their plate, they won't be able to reach the daily recommended intake. However, a study in the *American Journal of Clinical Nutrition* states that there is no significant difference in anemia levels between vegetarians and meat-eaters. Vegetarian foods are loaded with iron, and according to the USDA's National Nutrient Database, some of the most iron-rich foods are vegetarian. Several cereals top the USDA's list, along with Cream of Wheat, soybeans, some canned beans, lentils, and more. Iron deficiency is a very real concern, but not more so for vegetarians and vegans than for meat-eaters.

Calcium

Cows produce milk to nourish their young and provide all of the nutrients they need to grow strong, just as humans do. But no other mammals drink the milk of another species—except humans. Humans consume cow's milk throughout their lifetime even though it is the number-one cause of food allergies in infants and children, and millions of people around the world suffer from lactose intolerance. Many plant-based foods are an alternative source of calcium that don't come with the health problems associated with drinking cow's milk. Many soymilks and brands of orange juice are fortified with calcium but it is also found naturally in several items. Collard greens, rhubarb, spinach, and soybeans are just a few of the rich sources of plant-based calcium.

Protein, iron, and calcium are just some of the nutrients you find naturally in vegan and vegetarian foods, but there are a couple that may be best consumed through a supplement or other method. For example, you may prefer to get your daily dose of vitamin D from basking in the sun, but you can also get it through items such as fortified soymilk. However, vitamin

B12 is not found naturally in plant-based foods and must be obtained through a supplement, such as a multivitamin. Just be sure to read the label and make sure it contains B12.

ESSENTIAL

As with any diet, eating a variety of fresh and healthy foods is the key to optimal nutrition. Vegetarians should focus on consuming a variety of "whole foods," such as beans, nuts, whole grains, fruits, and vegetables. This, paired with supplements for any vitamins you may be missing, will put you one step closer to a healthier you.

Adapting Recipes for Your Vegetarian Diet

As with adapting recipes for your pressure cooker, adapting recipes for your vegan or vegetarian diet can be easy, healthy, and tasty. Some adaptations will include replacing an animal product with a cruelty-free alternative, but others will involve finding a new and exciting approach to food. Instead of always trying to find a way to make your dish taste as if it contains meat, dairy, or eggs, there are many ways of adding rich flavors. Remember the same four tips for easy recipe adapting to get started.

Know Your Cooking Times

Faux meats and soy cheeses may offer flavors similar to animal products but they are very different than "the real thing." Many mock meats require a much shorter cooking time than animal flesh and conversely, vegan cheeses often take much longer to melt. When replacing the flesh or by-product of an animal with a cruelty-free version, remember to read the package instructions and adjust your cooking times accordingly.

Some Techniques Should Be Avoided

When reading the packaging for many faux meats you will also find that certain techniques for preparation should be avoided. Some brands of veggie hot dogs or sausages can be prepared on the open flame of a grill, but not all. Cooking on a grill may lead to an overly done and tough veggie dog. For others, baking in the oven may not lead to optimal results. Be sure to read the package instructions before proceeding.

Flavors Don't (Have to) Change

If you are replacing chicken flesh with a vegan product, such as Morningstar Farms Meal Starter Chik'n Strips, you can build the flavors in your recipe around it just as you would real chicken. The accompanying flavors in your recipe do not need to be adjusted just because you're ditching the meat. You can, however, take this opportunity to explore a diverse world of new flavors. A meal does not have to be centered around meat for the protein—beans, tempeh, and tofu are great alternatives that are rich in protein, and will bring new tastes and textures to your cooking.

One of the best parts of trying a new diet is that you get to experiment with new recipes and foods! Ethnic cuisines, such as Indian, Japanese, and Middle Eastern, can be more vegetarian-friendly than traditional American fare because of the diverse proteins used in their recipes. Experiment with recipes from around the world to find your favorites, or experiment with "veganizing" your family's favorite recipes.

Experiment

Finding vegetarian and vegan versions of your favorite products is easier than ever before; just check out all of the options at your local grocery store or natural health-food store. For any products that are hard to find in your area, try ordering online. Refer to Appendix C for a listing of online stores. And for more information on how to replace specific animal products in your recipe, see Appendix B for a list of common substitutions.

CHAPTER 2

Appetizers and Snacks

Baba Gannouj

Serve with toasted pita chips or as a vegetable dip.

INGREDIENTS | **YIELDS 1½ CUPS**

1 tablespoon olive or sesame oil
1 large eggplant
4 cloves garlic, peeled and minced
½ cup water
3 tablespoons fresh parsley
½ teaspoon salt
2 tablespoons fresh lemon juice
2 tablespoons tahini
1 tablespoon extra-virgin olive oil

1. Add the olive or sesame oil to the pressure cooker and bring to temperature over medium heat. Peel and dice the eggplant and add it to the pressure cooker. Sauté the eggplant in the oil until it begins to get soft. Add the garlic and sauté for 30 seconds. Add the water.

2. Lock on the lid. Bring to high pressure; maintain pressure for 4 minutes. Remove the pan from the heat, quick-release the pressure, and remove the lid.

3. Strain the cooked eggplant and garlic and add to a food processor or blender along with the parsley, salt, lemon juice, and tahini. Pulse to process. Scrape down the side of the food processor or blender container if necessary. Add the extra-virgin olive oil and process until smooth.

PER ¼ CUP SERVING
Calories: 90 | Fat: 7g | Protein: 2g | Sodium: 200mg | Carbohydrates: 7g | Fiber: 3g

Black Bean Dip

To give this dip a little kick, you can substitute canned jalapeño peppers for the mild green chilies or add 2 teaspoons of chipotle powder.

INGREDIENTS | SERVES 12

1 cup dried black beans

2 cups water

1 tablespoon olive oil

1 small onion, peeled and diced

3 cloves garlic, peeled and minced

1 14½-ounce can diced tomatoes

2 4-ounce cans mild green chilies, finely chopped

1 teaspoon chili powder

½ teaspoon dried oregano

¼ cup fresh cilantro, finely chopped

Salt, to taste

1 cup Monterey jack cheese, grated, or vegan Monterey jack cheese, such as Follow Your Heart Monterey Jack Cheese Alternative

Other Bean Options

Bean dips are delicious when made with a variety of dried beans. To complement the flavors in this recipe, use black beans, pinto beans, or white beans. If you're pressed for time, use canned beans instead of dried beans, but be sure to drain the liquid first.

1. Add the beans and water to a container; cover and let the beans soak 8 hours at room temperature.

2. Add the oil and the onions to the pressure cooker; sauté for 3 minutes or until the onion is soft. Add the garlic and sauté for 30 seconds.

3. Drain the beans and add them to the pressure cooker along with the tomatoes, chilies, chili powder, and oregano. Stir well. Lock the lid into place. Bring to high pressure; maintain pressure for 12 minutes. Remove from heat and allow pressure to release naturally for 10 minutes.

4. Quick-release any remaining pressure. Remove the lid. Transfer the cooked beans mixture to a food processor or blender. Add the cilantro and process until smooth. Taste for seasoning; add salt if desired.

5. Transfer the dip to a bowl. Stir in the cheese. Serve warm.

PER SERVING
Calories: 120 | Fat: 4g | Protein: 6g | Sodium: 85mg | Carbohydrates: 14g | Fiber: 3g

Hummus

Hummus can come in a wide variety of flavors. Add roasted red peppers, roasted garlic, or sun-dried tomatoes to spice up this basic recipe.

INGREDIENTS | YIELDS 2 CUPS

1 cup dried chickpeas
8 cups water
¼ cup plus 1 tablespoon olive oil
2 teaspoons cumin
¾ teaspoon pepper
¾ teaspoon salt
⅓ cup lemon juice
1 teaspoon garlic
⅓ cup tahini

1. Add the chickpeas and 4 cups water to the pressure cooker. Lock the lid into place; bring to high pressure for 1 minute. Remove from the heat and quick-release the pressure.

2. Drain the water, rinse the beans, and add to the pressure cooker again with the remaining 4 cups water. Let soak for 1 hour.

3. Add 1 tablespoon olive oil. Lock the lid into place; bring to high pressure and maintain for 20 minutes. Remove from heat and allow pressure to release naturally. Drain beans and water.

4. Place all the ingredients, including the drained and cooked chickpeas, in a food processor and blend until mixture has achieved a creamy texture. Serve chilled or at room temperature.

PER ¼ CUP SERVING
Calories: 230 | Fat: 15g | Protein: 7g | Sodium: 230mg | Carbohydrates: 18g | Fiber: 4g

Stuffed Grape Leaves

*A medium (about 5-ounce) lemon will yield about
2 teaspoons of lemon zest and 2–3 tablespoons of juice.*

INGREDIENTS | SERVES 16

⅓ cup olive oil
4 scallions, minced
⅓ cup fresh mint, minced
⅓ cup fresh parsley, minced
3 cloves garlic, peeled and minced
1 cup long-grain white rice
2 cups vegetable broth
1 teaspoon salt
¼ teaspoon freshly ground black pepper
½ teaspoon lemon zest, grated
1 16-ounce jar grape leaves
2 cups water
½ cup fresh lemon juice

Dolmades

Stuffed grape leaves are often referred to as dolmades. Some versions call for spiced ground lamb or other ground meat to be added to the filling, but you can make them vegetarian with a rice and herb filling.

1. Bring the oil to temperature in the pressure cooker over medium-high heat. Add the scallions, mint, and parsley; sauté for 2 minutes or until the scallions are soft. Add the garlic and sauté for an additional 30 seconds. Add the rice and stir-fry in the sautéed vegetables and herbs for 1 minute. Add the broth, salt, pepper, and lemon zest; stir to mix. Lock the lid into place. Bring to high pressure; maintain pressure for 8 minutes.

2. Quick-release the pressure. Remove lid and transfer the rice mixture to a bowl.

3. Drain the grape leaves. Rinse them thoroughly in warm water and then arrange them rib-side up on a work surface. Trim away any thick ribs. Spoon about 2 teaspoons of the rice mixture on each grape leaf; fold the sides of each leaf over the filling and then roll it from the bottom to the top. Repeat with each leaf. Pour the water into the pressure cooker. Place a steamer basket in the pressure cooker and arrange the stuffed grape leaves seam-side down in the basket. Pour the lemon juice over the stuffed grape leaves and then press heavy plastic wrap down around them.

4. Lock the lid into place. Bring to high pressure; maintain pressure for 10 minutes.

5. Quick-release the pressure. Remove the lid. Lift the steamer basket out of the pressure cooker and, leaving the plastic in place, let the stuffed grape leaves rest for 5 minutes. Serve hot or cold.

PER SERVING
Calories: 120 | Fat: 5g | Protein: 3g | Sodium: 220mg |
Carbohydrates: 16g | Fiber: 4g

Chickpea-Parsley-Dill Dip

Try any combination of fresh herbs, such as basil,
thyme, or mint, in this versatile dip.

INGREDIENTS | YIELDS 2 CUPS

1 cup dried chickpeas
8 cups water
3 tablespoons olive oil
2 garlic cloves, minced
⅛ cup fresh parsley
⅛ cup fresh dill
1 tablespoon fresh lemon juice
2 tablespoons water
¾ teaspoon salt

1. Add the chickpeas and 4 cups water to the pressure cooker. Lock the lid into place; bring to high pressure for 1 minute. Remove from the heat and quick-release the pressure.

2. Drain the water, rinse the chickpeas, and add to the pressure cooker again with the remaining 4 cups of water. Let soak for 1 hour.

3. Add 1 tablespoon olive oil. Lock the lid into place; bring to high pressure and maintain for 20 minutes. Remove from the heat and allow pressure to release naturally. Drain chickpeas and water.

4. Add the drained, cooked chickpeas, garlic, parsley, dill, lemon juice, and water to a food processor or blender. Blend for about 30 seconds.

5. With the lid still in place, slowly add the remaining oil while still blending, then add the salt.

PER ¼ CUP SERVING
Calories: 130 | Fat: 6g | Protein: 5g | Sodium: 220mg |
Carbohydrates: 15g | Fiber: 3g

Jalapeño Cheese Dip

*To eliminate the spice, just leave the pickled
jalapeños out of this recipe.*

INGREDIENTS | SERVES 12

2 tablespoons butter, or vegan margarine

2 tablespoons flour

1 cup milk, or vegan soymilk

8 ounces shredded Cheddar cheese, or vegan Cheddar such as Daiya Chedder Style Shreds

8 ounces shredded Colby cheese, or more vegan Cheddar

½ cup canned tomatoes

½ cup pickled jalapeños

2 tablespoons lemon juice

Salt and pepper, to taste

1. In the pressure cooker, soften butter over medium-high heat and gradually add flour until you have a paste. Add milk and stir until it has thickened and there are no lumps. Bring the mixture to a boil.

2. Add the cheeses and stir until smooth. Add the tomatoes and jalapeños and secure the lid on the pressure cooker. Cook on medium until the pressure-indicator rises. Lower heat and cook for 3 minutes. Allow the pressure to release and remove the lid. Add the lemon juice, salt, and pepper.

PER SERVING
Calories: 180 | Fat: 14g | Protein: 10g | Sodium: 280mg | Carbohydrates: 4g | Fiber: 0g

Texas Caviar

*Prepare this dip up to 2 days in advance and store
in a covered container in the refrigerator.*

INGREDIENTS | YIELDS 5 CUPS

1 cup dried black-eyed peas

8 cups water

1 pound cooked corn kernels

½ onion, diced

½ bell pepper, diced

1 pickled jalapeño, finely chopped

1 medium tomato, diced

2 tablespoons fresh cilantro

¼ cup red wine vinegar

2 tablespoons olive oil

1 teaspoon salt

½ teaspoon ground black pepper

½ teaspoon ground cumin

1. Rinse and soak the black-eyed peas in 4 cups of water for 1 hour. Drain and rinse.

2. Add the black-eyed peas and remaining 4 cups of water to the pressure cooker. Lock the lid into place; bring to high pressure and maintain for 11 minutes. Remove from the heat and allow pressure to release naturally.

3. Pour the drained black-eyed peas into a large mixing bowl; add all remaining ingredients and stir until combined. Refrigerate 1–2 hours before serving.

PER ¼ CUP SERVING
Calories: 70 | Fat: 1.5g | Protein: 3g | Sodium: 125mg | Carbohydrates: 11g | Fiber: 2g

Warm Spinach-Artichoke Dip

*Serve with toasted pita points
or slices of warm baguette.*

INGREDIENTS | YIELDS 4 CUPS

1 medium-sized artichoke

2 cups water

1 teaspoon lemon juice

1 tablespoon butter, or vegan margarine, such as Earth Balance

1 cup thawed, chopped frozen spinach

8 ounces cream cheese, softened, or soy cream cheese

16 ounces sour cream, or soy sour cream

⅓ cup grated Parmesan, or vegan Parmesan

¼ teaspoon garlic powder

¼ teaspoon salt

Serving Options

This recipe calls for serving the dip warm, but chilling the dip and serving cool is also delicious. After cooking, let the dip cool to room temperature, then store in the refrigerator in an airtight container. Let cool for at least 3 hours before serving.

1. Trim the sharp points off the artichoke and cut the end of the stem off.

2. Put the metal rack in the bottom of the pressure cooker. Add water and lemon juice.

3. Lock the lid into place; bring to high pressure and maintain for 6–8 minutes. Remove from the heat and allow pressure to release naturally.

4. Remove the artichoke and coarsely chop.

5. In a large saucepan over medium heat, melt the butter, then add the spinach and chopped artichoke hearts.

6. Add all remaining ingredients, stir, and let cook for 5 minutes. Serve warm.

PER ¼ CUP SERVING
Calories: 130 | Fat: 12g | Protein: 3g | Sodium: 140mg | Carbohydrates: 3g | Fiber: <1g

Tomatillo Salsa

*Serve with corn tortilla chips or as an accompaniment
to Black Bean Dip (page 16).*

INGREDIENTS | SERVES 8

1 pound tomatillos, paper removed

Water, as needed

2 jalapeños, stemmed, seeded, and chopped

½ onion, chopped

½ cup cold water

½ cup chopped cilantro

2 teaspoons salt

Tomatillo

Tomatillo is the small yellowish or green fruit of a Mexican ground cherry. Surprisingly, it is not a variety of tomato.

1. Cut the tomatillos in half and then place in the pressure cooker. Add enough water to cover the tomatillos.

2. Lock the lid into place; bring to high pressure and maintain for 2 minutes. Remove from the heat and allow pressure to release naturally.

3. Add the drained, cooked tomatillos, jalapeños, onion, and cold water to a food processor or blender. Blend until well combined. Add the cilantro and salt and pulse until combined. Chill the salsa before serving.

PER SERVING
Calories: 20 | Fat: 0.5g | Protein: 1g | Sodium: 600mg | Carbohydrates: 4g | Fiber: 1g

Roasted Garlic Spread

*Garlic is known for being pungent, but a lesser-known quality
is that it may be able to help prevent heart disease and cancer.*

INGREDIENTS | YIELDS ½ CUP

2 whole heads garlic

1 cup water

½ cup butter, softened, or vegan margarine such as Earth Balance

2 tablespoons fresh basil

2 tablespoons fresh oregano

½ teaspoon salt

1. Cut the tops off each head of garlic. Pour water into the pressure cooker, then add the steamer basket. Add the garlic. Lock the lid into place; bring to high pressure and maintain for 2 minutes. Remove from the heat and allow pressure to quick-release.

2. Once the garlic has cooled, peel away the paper until you are left with only the cloves. In a small bowl, mash the cloves then add the butter, basil, oregano, and salt. Refrigerate for 1 hour before serving.

PER 1 TABLESPOON SERVING
Calories: 110 | Fat: 11g | Protein: 1g | Sodium: 150mg | Carbohydrates: 2g | Fiber: 0g

Steamed Spring Rolls

Serve with Spicy Peanut Sauce (page 54) or a sweet and sour dipping sauce.

INGREDIENTS | SERVES 12

1 cup cabbage, shredded

1 cup bamboo shoots, sliced

¼ cup cilantro, chopped

2 cloves garlic, minced

5 shiitake mushrooms, sliced

2 carrots, grated

1 teaspoon soy sauce

1 teaspoon rice wine vinegar

12 spring roll wrappers

2 cups water

Spring Roll Wrappers

Spring roll wrappers are also known as rice paper because they are made from rice flour, and rolled into thin, translucent sheets. Before using you must briefly soak the papers in water so they become soft and pliable for rolling up the spring roll filling.

1. Combine the cabbage, bamboo shoots, cilantro, garlic, mushrooms, carrots, soy sauce, and rice wine vinegar in a medium bowl. Stir until just combined.

2. Place the spring roll wrappers on a flat surface.

3. Top each wrapper with an equal amount of the cabbage mixture, making a row down the center. Roll up the wrappers, tuck in the ends, and place side by side in the pressure cooker steamer basket.

4. Add water to the pressure cooker and lower in the steamer basket.

5. Lock the lid into place. Bring to high pressure; maintain pressure for 3 minutes. Quick-release the pressure, then remove the lid.

PER SERVING
Calories: 40 | Fat: 0g | Protein: 2g | Sodium: 80mg | Carbohydrates: 8g | Fiber: 1g

Dhal

Serve spread on toasted flatbread or as a vegetable dip.

INGREDIENTS | YIELDS 2 CUPS

1 tablespoon olive oil

1 teaspoon unsalted butter, or vegan margarine

1 small onion, peeled and diced

2 teaspoons fresh ginger, grated

1 serrano chili pepper, seeded and finely diced

1 clove garlic, peeled and minced

½ teaspoon garam masala

¼ teaspoon ground turmeric

½ teaspoon dry mustard

1 cup dried yellow split peas

2 cups water

¼ cup plain yogurt or sour cream, or soy sour cream, such as Tofutti Sour Supreme

2 tablespoons fresh cilantro, minced

1. Add the oil and butter to the pressure cooker and bring to temperature over medium heat. Add the onion, ginger, and chili pepper; sauté for 3 minutes or until soft. Add the garlic, garam masala, turmeric, and dry mustard; sauté for an additional minute. Stir in the split peas. Pour in the water.

2. Lock on the lid. Bring the pressure cooker to high pressure; maintain for 8 minutes. Remove from the heat and allow pressure to release naturally. Transfer the cooked split-pea mixture to a bowl; stir until cooled.

3. Add the yogurt or sour cream; whisk until smooth. Stir in the cilantro.

PER ¼ CUP SERVING
Calories: 120 | Fat: 2.5g | Protein: 7g | Sodium: 5mg | Carbohydrates: 18g | Fiber: 0g

Sweet and Sour "Meatballs"

Worcestershire sauce typically contains anchovies, but some grocery store brands omit this ingredient, making it vegetarian.

INGREDIENTS | YIELDS 12 "MEATBALLS"

½ cup white sugar

2 tablespoons pineapple juice

⅓ cup white vinegar

⅔ cup water

2 tablespoons soy sauce

2 tablespoons vegetarian Worcestershire sauce

1 tablespoon ketchup

2 tablespoons cornstarch

1 pound vegetarian ground beef, such as Gimme Lean Beef

½ onion, diced

1 clove garlic, minced

½ cup panko bread crumbs

Panko Bread Crumbs

Panko is a type of bread crumb made from white bread without crusts. It typically creates a crispier texture when used as the coating on food than regular bread crumbs. To make your own, bake crustless white bread crumbs until they are dry, but not browned.

1. In the pressure cooker, bring the sugar, pineapple juice, vinegar, water, soy sauce, Worcestershire sauce, ketchup, and cornstarch to a boil over high heat. Stir continuously until the mixture has thickened, then remove from heat.

2. In a large mixing bowl, combine the vegetarian ground beef, onion, garlic, and bread crumbs, and mix until well combined. (Using your hands is the easiest method.)

3. Roll the "beef" mixture into 12 meatballs; add them to the sauce in the pressure cooker.

4. Lock the lid into place. Bring to high pressure; maintain pressure for 5 minutes. Quick-release the pressure, then remove the lid. Serve warm.

PER "MEATBALL"
Calories: 110 | Fat: 0g | Protein: 7g | Sodium: 400mg | Carbohydrates: 20g | Fiber: <1g

Baked Potato Skins

Steaming and then baking the potato skins, instead of frying, gives you a healthier version of this popular appetizer. Use the excess potato for a side of mashed potatoes.

INGREDIENTS | SERVES 6

6 Idaho potatoes

2 cups water

1 tablespoon vegetable oil

8 ounces shredded Cheddar cheese, or vegan Cheddar, such as Daiya Cheddar Style Shreds

⅛ cup soy bacon bits, such as Bac-Os

4 tablespoons thinly sliced scallions

¼ cup sour cream, or soy sour cream

1. Preheat the oven to 400°F.

2. Wash the potatoes, then slice each in half lengthwise. Pour 2 cups water into the pressure cooker. Add the steamer basket and arrange the potatoes in one or two layers.

3. Lock the lid into place. Bring to high pressure; maintain pressure for 10 minutes. Quick-release the pressure, then remove the lid.

4. Remove the potatoes from the pressure cooker and scoop out the inside, leaving a ¼"-thick shell.

5. Brush the scooped-out shell of each potato with oil and arrange on an ungreased baking sheet.

6. Cook the potato skins for 15 minutes, or until the edges begin to brown, then remove from the oven.

7. Fill the potato skins with the cheese and bake for an additional 5–10 minutes, or until the cheese has melted.

8. Top each skin with soy bacon bits, sliced scallions, and a dollop of sour cream.

PER SERVING (2 FILLED POTATO SKINS)
Calories: 310 | Fat: 18g | Protein: 15g | Sodium: 310mg | Carbohydrates: 28g | Fiber: 3g

Boiled Peanuts

Use "green" raw peanuts, not cooked or dried nuts.

INGREDIENTS | SERVES 16

2 pounds raw peanuts

12 cups water

⅓ cup salt

Cajun Peanuts

Add a little flavor to plain boiled peanuts by adding Cajun seasoning to the water when boiling. Try a preblended seasoning or make your own by combining red pepper, black pepper, cayenne pepper, garlic powder, and salt.

1. Rinse the peanuts under cold water then place in the pressure cooker. Add the water and salt.

2. Lock the lid in place; bring to 10 pounds of pressure, or a medium setting, and cook for 45 minutes. Remove from the heat and allow pressure to release naturally.

3. Let the peanuts cool in the water, then drain.

PER 2-OUNCE SERVING
Calories: 320 | Fat: 28g | Protein: 15g | Sodium: 2310mg | Carbohydrates: 9g | Fiber: 5g

CHAPTER 3

Soups

Vegetable Stock

Save scraps of vegetables to use to make a homemade stock.

INGREDIENTS | YIELDS 4 CUPS

2 large onions, peeled and halved

2 medium carrots, cleaned and cut into large pieces

3 stalks celery, cut in half

1 whole bulb garlic

10 peppercorns

1 bay leaf

4½ cups water

1. Add the onions, carrots, and celery to the pressure cooker. Break the bulb of garlic into individual cloves; peel and add to the pressure cooker. Add the peppercorns, bay leaf, and water to completely cover the vegetables. Lock the lid into place and bring to low pressure; maintain pressure for 10 minutes. Remove from the heat and allow pressure to release naturally.

2. Strain the stock through a fine-mesh strainer. Store in the refrigerator for 2–3 days, or freeze for up to 3 months.

PER CUP
Calories: 35 | Fat: 0g | Protein: 1g | Sodium: 30mg | Carbohydrates: 8g | Fiber: 2g

Mushroom Broth

Fresh broth can be refrigerated for 2 or 3 days or frozen for 3 months.

INGREDIENTS | YIELDS 8 CUPS

4 carrots, washed and cut into large pieces

2 large leeks, well cleaned and cut into large pieces

2 large onions, peeled and quartered

1 celery stalk, chopped

5 whole cloves

Pinch dried red pepper flakes

2 cups fresh mushrooms, sliced

8½ cups water

1. Put all ingredients in the pressure cooker. Lock the lid into place and bring to low pressure; maintain pressure for 15 minutes.

2. Remove from the heat and allow pressure to release naturally. Strain for a clear stock.

PER CUP
Calories: 25 | Fat: 0g | Protein: 1g | Sodium: 15mg | Carbohydrates: 6g | Fiber: 1g

Mushroom Varieties

You can use button mushrooms for a mellow flavor, or for a more intense flavor, try portobello mushroom caps cleaned of the black gills. You could also try wild mushrooms like chanterelles or shiitake.

Minestrone

Minestrone is filled with nutrients and is substantial enough to stand on its own as a light meal.

INGREDIENTS | SERVES 6

2 tablespoons olive oil

1 large onion, peeled and diced

2 cloves garlic, peeled and minced

2 large carrots, peeled and diced

2 leeks, white part only, cleaned and diced

½ head cabbage, cored and roughly chopped

2 stalks celery, diced

2 14½-ounce cans diced tomatoes

¼ teaspoon dried rosemary

1 teaspoon dried parsley

¼ teaspoon dried oregano

4½ cups Vegetable Stock (page 29)

½ cup dried elbow macaroni

½ cup Arborio rice

Salt and freshly ground black pepper, to taste

1. Add the olive oil to the pressure cooker over medium heat. Add the onion and sauté for 3 minutes or until the onion is soft. Stir in the garlic, carrots, leeks, cabbage, celery, undrained tomatoes, rosemary, parsley, oregano, and Vegetable Stock.

2. Lock the lid into place and bring to low pressure; maintain pressure for 5 minutes. Remove from the heat and quick-release the pressure.

3. Stir in the macaroni and rice.

4. Lock the lid into place and bring to high pressure; maintain pressure for 7 minutes. Remove from the heat and naturally release the pressure. Remove the lid.

5. Taste for seasoning and add salt, pepper, and additional herbs if needed.

PER SERVING
Calories: 220 | Fat: 5g | Protein: 5g | Sodium: 560mg | Carbohydrates: 40g | Fiber: 7g

Fresh Tomato Soup

This soup celebrates the simple, yet wondrous, summery taste of fresh vine-ripened tomatoes. You can add sautéed onion or shallots and herbs if you wish.

INGREDIENTS | SERVES 4

8 medium fresh tomatoes

¼ teaspoon sea salt

1 cup water

½ teaspoon baking soda

2 cups milk, half-and-half, or heavy cream, or unsweetened soymilk

Freshly ground black pepper, to taste

Choosing the Right Tomato

Most types of tomatoes will work in tomato soup; the key is to find tomatoes that are fresh. If you have your pick of tomatoes, try a combination of roma and beefsteak.

1. Wash, peel, seed, and dice the tomatoes. Add them and any tomato juice you can retain to the pressure cooker. Stir in the salt and water. Lock the lid into place. Place the pressure cooker over medium heat and bring to low pressure; maintain for 2 minutes. Quick-release the pressure and remove the lid.

2. Stir the baking soda into the tomato mixture. Once it's stopped bubbling and foaming, stir in your choice of milk, half-and-half, or cream. Cook and stir until the soup is brought to temperature. Add pepper, to taste.

PER SERVING
Calories: 140 | Fat: 5g | Protein: 6g | Sodium: 360mg | Carbohydrates: 20g | Fiber: 2g

White Bean with Garlic and Kale Soup

This soup is best enjoyed during the winter, when kale is in peak season.

INGREDIENTS | SERVES 8

2 cups dried cannellini beans

Water, as needed

2 tablespoons olive oil

½ cup onion, thinly sliced

6 garlic cloves, thinly sliced

2 teaspoons dried oregano

1 6-ounce can tomato paste

2 tablespoons red wine vinegar

8 cups Vegetable Stock (page 29)

3 cups kale, chopped

Salt and pepper, to taste

1. Rinse the cannellini; soak for 8 hours in enough water to cover them by more than 1". Drain. Bring the oil to temperature in the pressure cooker over medium heat. Add the onion and sauté until golden brown. Add the garlic and sauté for about 1 minute. Add the rest of the ingredients.

2. Lock the lid into place and bring to high pressure. Cook for about 10 minutes. Remove from the heat and allow pressure to release naturally. Taste for seasoning and add more salt and pepper if needed.

PER SERVING
Calories: 260 | Fat: 4g | Protein: 14g | Sodium: 780mg | Carbohydrates: 45g | Fiber: 9g

Italian Pasta and Bean Soup

Experiment with the types of grains and beans in this soup.
Smaller pastas and couscous work well in this soup.

INGREDIENTS | SERVES 10

1 pound dried cannellini beans

Water, as needed, plus 6 cups

1 tablespoon extra-virgin olive oil

4 medium carrots, peeled and diced

2 stalks celery, diced

2 medium onions, peeled and diced

3 cloves garlic, peeled and minced

1 teaspoon dried basil

1 teaspoon dried oregano

1 bay leaf

1 teaspoon dried parsley

4 cups Vegetable Stock (page 29) or Mushroom Broth (page 29)

1½ cups small macaroni or small shell pasta

Salt and freshly ground black pepper, to taste

1. Rinse the cannellini; soak for 8 hours in enough water to cover them by more than 1". Drain.

2. Bring the oil to temperature in the pressure cooker over medium heat. Add the carrots and celery; sauté for 3 minutes. Add the onion; sauté for 3 minutes or until the vegetables are soft. Add the garlic, basil, and oregano; sauté for 30 seconds.

3. Add 6 cups water, beans, and bay leaf. Lock the lid into place and bring to high pressure; maintain pressure for 10 minutes. Remove from the heat and allow pressure to release naturally.

4. Remove and discard the bay leaf. Add the parsley, and Vegetable Stock or Mushroom Broth. Return to the heat and bring to a boil; stir in the macaroni or shells. Cook pasta to al dente according to package directions. Taste for seasoning and add salt and pepper if needed.

PER SERVING
Calories: 260 | Fat: 2g | Protein: 13g | Sodium: 270mg | Carbohydrates: 48g | Fiber: 9g

Creamy White Bean and Garlic Soup

White bean purée is a great alternative for achieving a creamy texture in soups.

INGREDIENTS | SERVES 8

2 cups dried great northern beans
Water, as needed
3 tablespoons olive oil
1 onion, sliced
6 cloves garlic, minced
6 cups Vegetable Stock (page 29)
1 bay leaf
1 tablespoon rosemary, chopped
1 teaspoon lemon juice
Salt and pepper, to taste

1. Rinse the beans; soak for 8 hours in enough water to cover them by more than 1". Drain.

2. Bring the oil to temperature in the pressure cooker over medium heat. Add the onion and sauté until golden brown. Add the garlic and sauté for about 1 minute.

3. Add the Vegetable Stock, bay leaf, and the rosemary.

4. Lock the lid into place and bring to high pressure. Cook for 10 minutes. Remove from the heat and allow pressure to release naturally.

5. Remove the bay leaf. Purée the soup in a food processor or blender. Add the lemon juice. Taste for seasoning and add salt and pepper if needed.

PER SERVING
Calories: 230 | Fat: 6g | Protein: 10g | Sodium: 450mg | Carbohydrates: 36g | Fiber: 10g

Mushroom-Barley Soup

The portobello cap will bring umami, the fifth flavor, to this soup.

INGREDIENTS | SERVES 6

2 tablespoons butter, or vegan margarine such as Earth Balance

1 tablespoon olive or vegetable oil

2 stalks celery, diced

1 large carrot, peeled and diced

1 large sweet onion, peeled, halved, and sliced

2 cloves garlic, peeled and minced

1 portobello mushroom cap, diced

8 ounces button mushrooms, cleaned and sliced

1 bay leaf

½ cup pearl barley

6 cups water

2 tablespoons vermouth or brandy, optional

Salt and freshly ground black pepper, to taste

1. Melt the butter and bring the oil to temperature in the pressure cooker over medium heat. Add the celery and carrot; sauté for 2 minutes. Add the onion and sauté for 3 minutes or until the onion is soft and transparent. Stir in the garlic and mushrooms; sauté for 5 minutes or until the mushrooms release their moisture and the onion begins to turn golden.

2. Stir in the bay leaf, barley, water, and vermouth or brandy (if using). Lock the lid into place and bring to high pressure; maintain pressure for 20 minutes. Remove from the heat and allow pressure to release naturally.

3. Remove the lid. Remove and discard the bay leaf. Taste for seasoning and add salt and pepper if needed. Serve.

PER SERVING
Calories: 150 | Fat: 6g | Protein: 4g | Sodium: 25mg | Carbohydrates: 20g | Fiber: 4g

Pearl Barley

Pearl barley is the type of barley that has the outer hull and the bran layer removed. It is one of the most commonly used varieties, but not the most nutritious.

Lentil Soup

Any color lentils—red, yellow, brown, or green—will work in lentil soup.

INGREDIENTS | SERVES 4–6

1 tablespoon olive oil

1 yellow onion, sliced

4 garlic cloves, minced

1 carrot, sliced

5 plum tomatoes, chopped

2 teaspoons dried tarragon

1 teaspoon dried thyme

1 teaspoon paprika

6 cups Vegetable Stock (page 29)

2 cups lentils

2 bay leaves

Salt and pepper, to taste

1. Heat the olive oil in the pressure cooker; add the onions and sauté until they begin to turn golden. Add the garlic and carrots and sauté for 2–3 minutes.

2. Add the remaining ingredients except salt and pepper. Lock the lid into place and bring to high pressure. Once the pressure is achieved, turn the heat to low and cook for 8 minutes. Remove from the heat and allow pressure to release naturally. Remove the bay leaves and season to taste with salt and pepper.

PER SERVING
Calories: 470 | Fat: 3.5g | Protein: 31g | Sodium: 900mg | Carbohydrates: 84g | Fiber: 15g

Old Fashioned Potato Soup

Top with soy bacon bits and shredded cheese to turn this into a baked potato soup.

INGREDIENTS | SERVES 4

¼ cup extra-virgin olive oil

½ cup onion, diced

½ cup celery, sliced

4 cups potatoes, peeled and diced

3 cups Vegetable Stock (page 29)

2 cups vegan Béchamel Sauce (page 48)

Salt and pepper, to taste

Chopped chives or parsley, optional

1. Add the oil to the pressure cooker and sauté the onion and celery over medium-high heat for 5 minutes. Add potatoes and stock. Lock the lid into place and bring to high pressure. Once pressure is achieved, turn the heat to low and cook for 8–10 minutes. Remove from the heat and release pressure naturally for 20 minutes. Quick-release any remaining pressure. Remove the lid.

2. Bring the soup to a simmer in the pressure cooker and slowly stir in the Béchamel Sauce to thicken. Taste for seasoning and add salt and pepper if needed. Garnish with chives or parsley.

PER SERVING
Calories: 520 | Fat: 30g | Protein: 10g | Sodium: 920mg | Carbohydrates: 54g | Fiber: 4g

French Onion Soup

Red wine can be used as a substitute for beef broth,
an ingredient typically found in French onion soup.

INGREDIENTS | SERVES 4

¼ cup extra-virgin olive oil

4 Vidalia onions, sliced

4 cloves garlic, minced

1 tablespoon dried thyme

1 cup red wine

4 cups Vegetable Stock (page 29)

Salt and pepper, to taste

4 ounces Swiss cheese, or vegan cheese such as Daiya Mozzarella Style Shreds

4 slices French bread

Extra Herbs

To add even more flavor to this rich, brothy soup, use a bouquet garni instead of thyme. Bouquet garni is a small bundle of parsley, thyme, and bay leaf tied together. Remove the entire bouquet from the soup before serving.

1. Pour the extra-virgin olive oil into the pressure cooker and sauté the onions over medium-high heat until golden brown. Add the garlic and sauté for 1 minute. Add the thyme, red wine, and Vegetable Stock.

2. Lock the lid into place and bring to high pressure. Once the pressure is achieved, turn the heat to low and cook for 8–10 minutes. Remove from the heat and allow pressure to release naturally for 20 minutes. Quick-release any remaining pressure and remove the lid.

3. Taste for seasoning, and add salt and pepper if needed.

4. Preheat the oven to the broiler setting. Lightly toast the slices of French bread. To serve, ladle the soup into a broiler-safe bowl, place a slice of the toasted French bread on top of the soup, put a slice of the Swiss cheese on top of the bread, and place the soup under the broiler until the cheese has melted.

PER SERVING
Calories: 550 | Fat: 24g | Protein: 15g | Sodium: 1040mg | Carbohydrates: 59g | Fiber: 4g

Creamy Lima Bean Soup

Be very careful when blending hot soups. Do not overfill the blender, and be sure to use a kitchen towel to hold the lid in place during blending.

INGREDIENTS | SERVES 4–6

2 cups dried lima beans

Water, as needed, plus ½ cup

1 tablespoon olive oil

1 small onion, diced

1 clove garlic, minced

2 cups Vegetable Stock (page 29)

Salt and pepper, to taste

2 tablespoons chives, sliced

1. Rinse the lima beans; soak for 8 hours in enough water to cover them by more than 1". Drain.

2. Heat the oil in the pressure cooker and sauté the onion until golden brown. Add the garlic and cook for 1 minute more.

3. Add the stock, ½ cup water, and lima beans. Lock the lid into place and bring to high pressure. Cook for 6 minutes. Remove from the heat and allow pressure to release naturally.

4. Purée the soup in a food processor or blender.

5. Season with salt and pepper, then garnish with chives before serving.

PER SERVING
Calories: 350 | Fat: 4g | Protein: 19g | Sodium: 310mg | Carbohydrates: 61g | Fiber: 17g

Corn Chowder

For an extra kick, drain and dice 2 4-ounce cans of green chilies and add them to the chowder.

INGREDIENTS | SERVES 6

2 tablespoons butter, or vegan margarine, such as Earth Balance

4 large leeks

4 cups Vegetable Stock (page 29)

2 cups water

6 medium russet or Idaho baking potatoes, peeled and diced

1 bay leaf

Salt and freshly ground black pepper, to taste

1½ cups fresh or frozen corn

½ teaspoon dried thyme

Pinch sugar

½ cup heavy cream, or unsweetened soymilk

What Is Chowder?

Chowder originally indicated a thick soup made with chunks of seafood, but the meaning has been expanded to include other main ingredients, like vegetables such as corn.

1. Melt the butter in the pressure cooker over medium heat. Cut off the root end of the leeks and discard any bruised outer leaves. Slice the leeks. Add to the pressure cooker and sauté for 2 minutes. Stir in the stock, water, and potatoes. Add the bay leaf, salt, and pepper.

2. Lock the lid into place and bring to high pressure; maintain pressure for 4 minutes. Quick-release the pressure and remove the lid. Remove and discard the bay leaf.

3. Stir in the corn, thyme, sugar, and cream. Bring to temperature, stirring occasionally.

PER SERVING
Calories: 360 | Fat: 12g | Protein: 7g | Sodium: 430mg | Carbohydrates: 60g | Fiber: 6g

Creamy Asparagus Soup

To sneak protein into this soup, try adding 1 cup cooked navy beans to the soup before blending.

INGREDIENTS | SERVES 4–6

2 pounds asparagus

2 tablespoons butter, or vegan margarine, such as Earth Balance

1 large onion, diced

1½ teaspoons salt

⅛ teaspoon cayenne pepper

5 cups Vegetable Stock (page 29)

¼ cup milk, or unsweetened soymilk

1 teaspoon lemon juice

Peak Season

Asparagus is in peak season during the spring, and during this time there are plenty of the flavorful stalks for sale at grocery stores or farmers' markets. Use asparagus in a soup, grilled or baked, or even battered and fried.

1. Trim the hard ends off the asparagus and cut it into 1" pieces. Add the butter to the pressure cooker and sauté the onion until golden brown. Add the asparagus, salt, and cayenne pepper and sauté for about 5 minutes.

2. Add the Vegetable Stock. Lock the lid into place and bring to high pressure. Once the pressure is achieved, turn the heat to low and cook for about 5 minutes. Remove from the heat and allow pressure to release naturally.

3. Add the milk and lemon juice to the soup and purée in a food processor or blender.

PER SERVING
Calories: 160 | Fat: 6g | Protein: 6g | Sodium: 1620mg | Carbohydrates: 22g | Fiber: 5g

Curry Chickpea Bisque

Make this Middle Eastern soup as spicy or as mild as you'd like.

INGREDIENTS | SERVES 8

2 cups dried chickpeas

Water, as needed

3 tablespoons extra-virgin olive oil

½ onion, diced

2 cloves garlic, minced

1 teaspoon fresh ginger

1 teaspoon garam masala

2–3 teaspoons curry powder

2 cups Vegetable Stock (page 29)

1 14-ounce can coconut milk

Salt and pepper, to taste

1. Rinse the chickpeas; soak for 8 hours in enough water to cover them by more than 1". Drain.

2. Add the oil to the pressure cooker and sauté the onions until they are golden brown. Add the garlic, ginger, garam masala, and curry powder, and sauté for an additional minute.

3. Add the stock and coconut milk. Lock the lid into place and bring to high pressure. Maintain for 20 minutes and then remove from the heat. Allow pressure to release naturally.

4. Purée the soup in a food processor or blender. Taste for seasoning and add salt and pepper, if needed.

PER SERVING
Calories: 330 | Fat: 18g | Protein: 11g | Sodium: 160mg | Carbohydrates: 34g | Fiber: 7g

Cream of Mushroom Soup

Puréed potatoes help to thicken creamy soups.

INGREDIENTS | SERVES 4

¼ cup butter, or vegan margarine, such as Earth Balance

1 yellow onion, diced

2 cups white mushrooms, sliced

2 potatoes, peeled and diced

2 cloves garlic, minced

¼ cup white wine

3 cups milk, or unsweetened soymilk

1 teaspoon dried thyme

1 cup Béchamel Sauce (see page 48), or vegan version of Béchamel Sauce

Salt and pepper, to taste

Variations

This soup has mild flavors that are perfect as a base for additional flavors. Try adding vegetables, such as steamed green bean pieces or spinach, or chunks of vegetarian chicken for a cream of chicken soup.

1. Add the butter to the pressure cooker and sauté the onions until golden brown. Add the mushrooms, potatoes, and garlic and continue sautéing for about 5 minutes more.

2. Add the white wine, soymilk, thyme, and Béchamel Sauce.

3. Lock the lid into place and bring to high pressure. Once the pressure is achieved, turn the heat to low and cook for about 8 minutes. Remove from the heat and allow pressure to release naturally.

4. Purée the soup in a food processor or blender. Taste for seasoning and add salt and pepper if needed.

PER SERVING
Calories: 360 | Fat: 19g | Protein: 13g | Sodium: 310mg | Carbohydrates: 35g | Fiber: 3g

Posole

Posole is a traditional Mexican soup that has corn as the main ingredient.

INGREDIENTS | SERVES 8

2 cups hominy

8 cups water

2 tablespoons olive oil

½ onion, diced

2 yellow squash, diced

2 zucchini, diced

2 cloves garlic, minced

1 cup tomato, diced

2 dried Ancho chilies

2 bay leaves

8 cups Vegetable Stock (page 29)

2 teaspoons dried oregano

1 teaspoon dried thyme

1 teaspoon saffron

1 teaspoon salt

1 tablespoon lime juice

1 avocado, pitted and sliced

1. Add the hominy and 4 cups water to the pressure cooker. Lock the lid into place; bring to high pressure for 1 minute. Remove from the heat and quick-release the pressure.

2. Drain the water, rinse the hominy, and add to the pressure cooker again with the remaining 4 cups water. Let soak for 1 hour. Drain and set aside.

3. Add the olive oil to the empty pressure cooker and bring to medium heat. Add the onion, squash, and zucchini; sauté for 5 minutes. Add the garlic and sauté for an additional 30 seconds.

4. Add all remaining ingredients except for the avocado; stir. Lock the lid into place; bring to high pressure and maintain for 20 minutes. Remove from the heat and allow pressure to release naturally.

5. Spoon into serving bowls and top each with ⅛ of the sliced avocado.

PER SERVING
Calories: 280 | Fat: 8g | Protein: 6g | Sodium: 890mg | Carbohydrates: 49g | Fiber: 6g

Tortilla Soup

Turn this soup into a complete meal by adding pieces of cooked vegetarian chicken, such as Morningstar Farms Meal Starters Chik'n Strips or Gardein Seasoned Bites.

INGREDIENTS | SERVES 6–8

2 tablespoons olive oil

1 large onion, chopped

2 cloves garlic, minced

2 tablespoons soy sauce

7 cups Vegetable Stock (page 29)

12 ounces firm silken tofu, crumbled

2 cups tomato, diced

1 cup corn kernels

1 teaspoon chipotle powder

1 teaspoon cayenne pepper

2 teaspoons ground cumin

2 teaspoons salt

1 teaspoon dried oregano

10 small corn tortillas, sliced

8 ounces shredded Monterey jack cheese, or vegan cheese, such as Daiya Mozzarella Style Shreds

Chipotle Powder

Chipotle powder is made from ground chipotle peppers, a type of dried jalapeño. They bring a smoky spiciness to dishes but can be replaced with cayenne pepper or chili powder.

1. Add the olive oil to the pressure cooker and bring to medium heat. Sauté the onions until just soft, about 3 minutes. Add the garlic and sauté for an additional 30 seconds.

2. Add the soy sauce, stock, tomato, corn, chipotle, cayenne, cumin, salt, and oregano; stir.

3. Lock the lid into place; bring to medium pressure and maintain for 15 minutes. Remove from the heat and quick-release the pressure.

4. While the soup is cooking, slice the corn tortillas into thin strips and place on an ungreased baking sheet. Bake in a 450°F oven for about 10 minutes, or until they turn golden brown. Remove from heat and set aside.

5. Use an immersion blender or a regular blender to purée the soup.

6. Serve with cooked tortilla strips and 1 ounce of shredded cheese on each bowl of soup.

PER SERVING
Calories: 400 | Fat: 19g | Protein: 18g | Sodium: 2050mg | Carbohydrates: 41g | Fiber: 5g

Split Pea Dhal

*If you don't have allspice on hand, it's alright to
omit the spice from this recipe.*

INGREDIENTS | SERVES 6

2 cups dried green split peas

Water, as needed, plus 4 cups

4 cups Vegetable Stock (page 29)

2 medium potatoes, diced

2 large carrots, chopped

3 stalks celery, chopped

2 cloves garlic, minced

2 teaspoons dry mustard

⅛ teaspoon allspice

1 teaspoon cumin

1 teaspoon sage

1 teaspoon thyme

2 bay leaves

Salt and pepper, to taste

1. Rinse the green split peas; soak overnight in enough water to cover them by more than 1". Drain.

2. Add 4 cups water to the pressure cooker, then add all remaining ingredients except salt and pepper. Lock the lid into place and bring to high pressure; maintain pressure for 15 minutes. Remove from the heat and allow pressure to release naturally. Quick-release any remaining pressure and remove the lid.

3. Remove the bay leaves. Purée the soup in a food processor or blender until smooth, and then serve. Taste for seasoning, and add salt and pepper if needed.

PER SERVING
Calories: 300 | Fat: 1g | Protein: 18g | Sodium: 440mg | Carbohydrates: 57g | Fiber: 19g

Thai Carrot Soup

Carrots are loaded with vitamin A and help maintain good vision.

INGREDIENTS | SERVES 4

1 tablespoon olive oil

1 onion, diced

2 cloves garlic, minced

3 teaspoons curry powder

1 bay leaf

1 pound carrots, peeled and chopped

2 cups Vegetable Stock (page 29)

1 cup coconut milk

Salt and pepper, to taste

¼ cup basil

Chiffonade

Chiffonade is a technique for cutting herbs and greens. To chiffonade basil, stack the cleaned and dried leaves, roll the leaves loosely, and slice from end to end. You'll be left with thin ribbons of basil.

1. Add the olive oil to the pressure cooker and sauté the onions until golden brown. Add the garlic and curry powder and sauté for an additional 30 seconds.

2. Add the bay leaf, carrots, and Vegetable Stock. Lock the lid into place and bring to high pressure. Once the pressure is achieved, turn the heat to low and cook for about 5 minutes. Remove from the heat and allow pressure to release naturally.

3. Remove the bay leaf. Pour the soup into a food processor or blender. Purée the soup while slowly adding the coconut milk. Taste for seasoning, and add salt and pepper if needed. Chiffonade basil to garnish.

PER SERVING
Calories: 230 | Fat: 16g | Protein: 4g | Sodium: 360mg | Carbohydrates: 21g | Fiber: 5g

CHAPTER 4

Sauces

Espagnole

Espagnole is one of the "mother sauces," and is used as the foundation for other sauces in this book.

INGREDIENTS | YIELDS 3 CUPS

1 small carrot, chopped

1 medium white onion, chopped

¼ cup butter, or vegan margarine, such as Earth Balance

¼ cup flour

4 cups hot Vegetable Stock, preferably vegan beef flavor

¼ cup canned tomato purée

2 large garlic cloves, chopped

1 celery rib, chopped

½ teaspoon whole black peppercorns

1 bay leaf

What Is a Roux?

A roux is a blend of equal parts fat, such as butter, margarine, or oil, and flour that is used to thicken sauces. It's cooked over various levels of heat and different lengths of time to achieve either a white, blond, or brown roux.

1. Sauté the carrot and onion in the butter over medium-high heat in the pressure cooker until golden. Add the flour and whisk to form a roux. Continue to cook, stirring continuously, until the roux is medium brown, about 30 minutes. While whisking, add the hot stock, being sure to prevent lumps. Add the tomato purée, garlic, celery, peppercorns, and bay leaf.

2. Lock the lid into place and bring to high pressure. Once the pressure is achieved, turn the heat to low and cook for about 5 minutes. Remove from the heat and allow pressure to release naturally.

3. Bring the sauce to a simmer; cook, uncovered, until reduced to 3 cups, stirring frequently. Remove the solids from the sauce before serving.

PER CUP
Calories: 240 | Fat: 15g | Protein: 2g | Sodium: 820mg | Carbohydrates: 25g | Fiber: 2g

Béchamel Sauce

*Béchamel is one of the most commonly used "mother sauces,"
and is the foundation for an alfredo sauce.*

INGREDIENTS | YIELDS 3 CUPS

½ cup butter, or vegan margarine, such as Earth Balance

½ cup all-purpose flour

4 cups milk, heated, or unsweetened soymilk

1 teaspoon salt

1 teaspoon pepper

1. Soften the butter over medium heat in the pressure cooker. Add flour and stir to create a roux. Gradually whisk in the warm milk until there are no lumps.

2. Lock the lid into place and bring to high pressure. Once the pressure is achieved, turn the heat to low and allow to cook for about 5 minutes, or until the sauce has thickened. Remove from the heat and allow pressure to release naturally.

3. Season with salt and pepper.

PER CUP
Calories: 460 | Fat: 31g | Protein: 85g | Sodium: 920mg | Carbohydrates: 33g | Fiber: <1g

Au Jus

*Try Better Than Bouillon, No Beef Base instead of
plain Vegetable Stock in this rich sauce.*

INGREDIENTS | YIELDS 1½ CUPS

1 tablespoon butter, or vegan margarine, such as Earth Balance

1 shallot, minced

1 tablespoon flour

2 cups faux-beef stock or Vegetable Stock (page 29)

1 cup red wine

¼ teaspoon liquid smoke

1 teaspoon salt

1 teaspoon pepper

1. Add the butter to the pressure cooker and sauté the shallots over medium-high heat until golden brown. Stir in the flour to create a roux. Add the stock, red wine, liquid smoke, salt, and pepper to the roux.

2. Lock the lid into place and bring to high pressure. Once the pressure is achieved, turn the heat to low and cook for about 5 minutes. Allow pressure to release naturally. Remove lid and continue to simmer over low heat until the sauce has reduced by half.

PER RECIPE
Calories: 410 | Fat: 12g | Protein: 4g | Sodium: 3530mg | Carbohydrates: 37g | Fiber: 1g

Beurre Blanc

*Try adding a variety of ingredients to this basic beurre blanc—
herbs, spices, or even fruit!*

INGREDIENTS | YIELDS 1 CUP

2 cups white wine

1 tablespoon shallot, minced

2 cups butter, cold, or vegan margarine, such as Earth Balance

1 teaspoon salt

1. Heat the wine and shallots in the pressure cooker and bring to a simmer. Let the wine reduce to half.

2. While the wine is reducing, begin cutting the butter into medium cubes. Once reduced, begin whisking the cubes of butter in a few at a time, in order to create an emulsion. Once all the butter has been whisked into the sauce, lock the lid into place and bring to high pressure. When pressure is achieved, turn the heat to low and cook for 5 minutes. Quick-release the pressure and remove the lid. Season with salt.

PER CUP
Calories: 3540 | Fat: 363g | Protein: 5g | Sodium: 2400mg | Carbohydrates: 6g | Fiber: 0g

Garden Marinara Sauce

Serve warmed sauce over pasta, rice, or vegetables.

INGREDIENTS | SERVES 4–6

2 tablespoons olive oil

1 large sweet onion, diced

1 small red bell pepper, diced

1 large carrot, peeled and grated

4 cloves garlic, minced

1 tablespoon dried parsley

½ teaspoon dried ground fennel

1 teaspoon dried basil

1 bay leaf

Pinch dried red pepper flakes

¼ teaspoon salt

1 14½-ounce can diced tomatoes in sauce

½ cup Vegetable Stock (page 29)

1. Add the oil to the pressure cooker and bring to temperature over medium-high heat. Add the onion, bell pepper, and carrots; sauté for 3 minutes. Stir in the garlic and sauté an additional 30 seconds. Stir in the remaining ingredients.

2. Lock the lid into place. Bring the pressure cooker to low pressure; maintain for 10 minutes. Quick-release the pressure. Remove the lid. Stir the sauce. Remove and discard the bay leaf. If desired, use an immersion blender to purée the sauce.

PER SERVING
Calories: 120 | Fat: 7g | Protein: 2g | Sodium: 280mg | Carbohydrates: 14g | Fiber: 3g

Fresh Tomato Sauce

You can use this sauce immediately, refrigerate it in a covered container for up to a week, or freeze it for 6 months.

INGREDIENTS | YIELDS 4 CUPS

2 tablespoons olive oil

2 cloves garlic, peeled and minced

2½ pounds fresh, vine-ripened tomatoes

1 teaspoon dried parsley

1 teaspoon dried basil

1 tablespoon balsamic vinegar

½ teaspoon granulated cane sugar

Salt, to taste

Freshly ground black pepper, to taste

Balancing the Acidity

When tasting your tomato sauce and thinking "what else do I need to add?" many cooks reach for additional salt, but that might not be the ingredient you need. To balance out the acidity, the taste you may be trying to omit, try adding sugar or even grated carrot to the sauce.

1. Add the oil to the pressure cooker and bring to temperature over medium heat. Add the garlic; sauté for 30 seconds.

2. Peel and dice the tomatoes. Add them to the pressure cooker along with any juice from the tomatoes. Add the remaining ingredients.

3. Lock the lid in place and bring to low pressure; maintain for 10 minutes. Remove from the heat and allow pressure to release naturally.

4. Remove the lid and stir the sauce. If you prefer a thicker sauce, return to the heat and simmer uncovered for 10 minutes or until it reaches the desired thickness.

PER CUP
Calories: 140 | Fat: 8g | Protein: 2g | Sodium: 10mg | Carbohydrates: 16g | Fiber: 2g

Basic Marinara Sauce

For a "meaty" marinara, add cooked Boca Ground Crumbles.

INGREDIENTS | SERVES 4–6

2 tablespoons olive oil

½ onion, diced

2 cloves garlic, minced

2 14-ounce cans diced tomatoes

½ teaspoons sugar

1 tablespoon tomato paste

⅓ cup water

1 tablespoon fresh lemon juice

2 tablespoons fresh basil, chopped

Salt and pepper, to taste

1. Add the oil to the pressure cooker and sauté the onion until golden brown. Add the garlic and sauté for an additional 30 seconds. Add the tomatoes, sugar, tomato paste, and water.

2. Lock the lid into place and bring to high pressure. Once the pressure is achieved, turn the heat to low and cook for about 5 minutes. Remove from the heat and allow pressure to release naturally. Stir in the lemon juice and basil, and add salt and pepper to taste.

PER SERVING
Calories: 120 | Fat: 7g | Protein: 2g | Sodium: 110mg | Carbohydrates: 13g | Fiber: 4g

Roasted Red Pepper Sauce

*Save time by using canned or jarred roasted red peppers
instead of roasting them yourself.*

INGREDIENTS | SERVES 4

2 cups roasted red peppers

2 cups Vegetable Stock (page 29)

2 tablespoons red wine vinegar

2 tablespoons extra-virgin olive oil

1 teaspoon garlic powder

½ cup fresh basil

Salt and pepper, to taste

1. Purée the red peppers, stock, vinegar, and oil in a food processor or blender. Pour the mixture into the pressure cooker and add the garlic powder.

2. Lock the lid into place and bring to high pressure. Once the pressure is achieved, turn the heat to low and cook for about 5 minutes. Remove from the heat and allow pressure to release naturally.

3. Add the basil and season with salt and pepper, to taste, before serving.

PER SERVING
Calories: 140 | Fat: 7g | Protein: 2g | Sodium: 760mg | Carbohydrates: 12g | Fiber: 0g

Vodka Sauce

Cooking with alcohol helps bring out flavors in some foods, including tomatoes.

INGREDIENTS | SERVES 4–6

2 tablespoons olive oil

½ onion, diced

2 cloves garlic, minced

1 teaspoon dried red pepper flakes

1 cup vodka

2 14-ounce cans diced tomatoes

2 tablespoons tomato paste

⅓ cup water

1 cup heavy cream, or unsweetened soymilk or unsweetened vegan cream, such as MimicCreme

2 tablespoons fresh parsley, chopped

2 tablespoons fresh basil, chopped

Salt and pepper, to taste

Does Alcohol Burn Off?

It's a common food myth that while cooking with alcohol, the alcohol will burn off. In fact, many cooking methods will retain a large portion of the alcohol in your dish. If you want keep as little alcohol as possible, you will have to cook it for an extended period of time, at least 2 hours.

1. Add the olive oil to the pressure cooker; sauté the onions until golden brown. Add the garlic and red pepper flakes, and sauté an additional minute. Add the vodka and simmer for about 10 minutes. Add the diced tomatoes, tomato paste, and water.

2. Lock the lid into place and bring to high pressure. Once the pressure is achieved, turn the heat to low and cook for about 5 minutes. Remove from the heat and allow pressure to release naturally.

3. Stir in the heavy cream and simmer for 2 minutes. Add the parsley and basil. Taste for seasoning, and add salt and pepper if needed.

PER SERVING
Calories: 450 | Fat: 29g | Protein: 4g | Sodium: 110mg | Carbohydrates: 15g | Fiber: 4g

White Bean Alfredo Sauce

Using white beans as the base of a creamy sauce reduces the amount of dairy and fat in the recipe, and makes for a much healthier alternative.

INGREDIENTS | **SERVES 4**

1 cup dried cannellini beans

8 cups water

¼ cup butter, or vegan margarine, such as Earth Balance

2 cloves garlic, minced

1 cup milk, or unsweetened soymilk

1 teaspoon lemon juice

1½ teaspoons salt

½ teaspoon black pepper

Flavor Variations

This recipe is for a basic sauce that can be added to. Try sprinkling in a blend of earthy herbs, such as thyme, sage, and oregano, or fresh diced tomatoes.

1. Add the beans and 4 cups of water to the pressure cooker. Lock the lid into place; bring to high pressure for 1 minute. Remove from the heat and quick-release the pressure. Drain beans and set aside.

2. Clean pressure cooker and add butter. Sauté the garlic for 2 minutes, stirring continuously. Add the drained beans and remaining 4 cups of water.

3. Lock the lid into place; bring to high pressure and maintain for 15 minutes. Quick-release the pressure.

4. Pour the beans into a blender or food processor in batches and purée. The mixture will be thick.

5. Return to the pressure cooker over low heat and slowly stir in the milk until desired consistency is reached. Add lemon juice, salt, and pepper, and heat until warm. Serve with fresh herbs, such as parsley, if desired.

PER SERVING
Calories: 290 | Fat: 12g | Protein: 14g | Sodium: 910mg | Carbohydrates: 34g | Fiber: 8g

Spicy Peanut Sauce

Use as a dipping sauce for broccoli or spring rolls.

INGREDIENTS | YIELDS 1½ CUPS

½ cup smooth peanut butter

2 tablespoons maple syrup

2 cloves garlic, peeled

1" piece ginger, peeled and chopped

¼ cup rice vinegar

¼ cup sesame oil

1 teaspoon cayenne pepper

1 teaspoon cumin

2 teaspoons dried red chili flakes

1 cup water

Salt and pepper, to taste

1. In a large blender, combine all the ingredients except salt and pepper, adding the water a little at a time to control the consistency.

2. Lock the lid into place and bring to high pressure. Once the pressure is achieved, turn the heat to low and cook for about 3 minutes. Remove from the heat and allow pressure to release naturally.

3. Taste for seasoning, and add salt and pepper if needed.

PER ¼ CUP SERVING
Calories: 230 | Fat: 20g | Protein: 6g | Sodium: 100mg | Carbohydrates: 10g | Fiber: 2g

Yellow Pepper Coulis

A coulis is a thick sauce often made from puréed fruit or vegetables.

INGREDIENTS | YIELDS 1½ CUPS

2 tablespoons olive oil

4 yellow peppers, seeded and diced

4 shallots, minced

1 cup white wine

1 cup Vegetable Stock (page 29)

1 teaspoon salt

½ teaspoon black pepper

1. Add the olive oil to the pressure cooker and sauté the yellow pepper and shallots until they start to turn golden brown. Add the white wine and reduce by half. Add the Vegetable Stock.

2. Lock the lid into place and bring to high pressure. Once the pressure is achieved, turn the heat to low and cook for 5 minutes. Remove from the heat and quick-release the pressure.

3. Season with salt and pepper.

PER CUP
Calories: 530 | Fat: 20g | Protein: 9g | Sodium: 1980mg | Carbohydrates: 62g | Fiber: 5g

Cashew Cream Sauce

To make an alcohol-free sauce, double the amount of Vegetable Stock
or water instead of including 1 cup wine.

INGREDIENTS | YIELDS 2½ CUPS

1 cup of cashews

1 cup white wine

1 cup milk, or unsweetened soymilk

1 cup Vegetable Stock (page 29) or water

2 cups Béchamel Sauce (page 48), or vegan version of Béchamel Sauce

Salt and pepper, to taste

Uses for Cashew Cream

In many recipes, cashew cream can be used in place of dairy. This savory version would be best suited to replace heavy cream or cheeses, but there are also plain versions of cashew cream that can be used in desserts.

1. Grind the cashews in a food processor or a coffee grinder. Set aside.

2. Add the white wine to the pressure cooker over medium heat and bring to a simmer. Allow the wine to reduce by half. Stir in the ground cashews, milk, stock, and Béchamel Sauce.

3. Lock the lid into place and bring to low pressure. Maintain pressure for 5 minutes then allow pressure to release naturally. Remove lid and continue to cook over low heat, until reduced by half.

4. Taste for seasoning, and add salt and pepper if needed.

PER CUP
Calories: 790 | Fat: 50g | Protein: 23g | Sodium: 1020mg | Carbohydrates: 52g | Fiber: 2g

Country Barbecue Sauce

*You can use this barbecue sauce as a sauce served on the side,
a dipping sauce, or a grilling wet-mop sauce.*

INGREDIENTS | YIELDS APPROXIMATELY
5 CUPS

4 cups ketchup

½ cup apple cider vinegar

½ cup vegetarian Worcestershire sauce

½ cup light brown sugar, firmly packed

¼ cup molasses

¼ cup prepared mustard

2 tablespoons barbecue seasoning

1 teaspoon freshly ground black pepper

Optional: 1 tablespoon liquid smoke

Optional: 2 tablespoons hot sauce, or to taste

Optional: Salt, to taste

Add all ingredients except optional seasonings to the pressure cooker. Stir to mix. Lock the lid into place. Bring to low pressure; maintain for 20 minutes. Remove from heat and quick-release the pressure. Taste for seasoning and add the desired amount of optional seasoning. Ladle into sterilized glass jars; cover and store in the refrigerator for up to 3 months.

PER CUP
Calories: 410 | Fat: 2g | Protein: 4g | Sodium: 2730mg | Carbohydrates: 103g | Fiber: 2g

Barbecue Seasoning

Barbecue seasoning is a blend of herbs and spices that can be found in the spice aisle of your local grocery store. To make your own, mix equal parts brown sugar, ground red pepper, salt, garlic powder, onion powder, paprika, and dried oregano.

Plum Sauce

Plum sauce is often served with egg rolls,
but you can also use it as a glaze on tofu or vegetables.

INGREDIENTS | YIELDS 4 CUPS

8 cups (about 3 pounds) plums, pitted and cut in half

1 small sweet onion, diced

1 cup water

1 teaspoon fresh ginger, peeled and minced

1 clove garlic, minced

¾ cup granulated sugar

½ cup rice vinegar or cider vinegar

1 teaspoon ground coriander

½ teaspoon salt

½ teaspoon cinnamon

¼ teaspoon cayenne pepper

¼ teaspoon ground cloves

1. Add the plums, onion, water, ginger, and garlic to the pressure cooker. Lock the lid into place and bring to low pressure; maintain for 5 minutes. Remove from the heat and quick-release the pressure.

2. Use an immersion blender to pulverize the contents of the pressure cooker before straining it, or press the cooked plum mixture through a sieve.

3. Return the liquefied and strained plum mixture to the pressure cooker and stir in sugar, vinegar, coriander, salt, cinnamon, cayenne pepper, and cloves. Lock the lid into place and bring to low pressure; maintain for 5 minutes. Remove from heat and quick-release the pressure. Remove the lid and check the sauce; it should have the consistency of applesauce. If it isn't yet thick enough, place the uncovered pressure cooker over medium heat and simmer until desired consistency is achieved.

PER CUP
Calories: 360 | Fat: 2.5g | Protein: 3g | Sodium: 290mg | Carbohydrates: 89g | Fiber: 6g

CHAPTER 5

Vegetables

Corn on the Cob

*"Shuck" means to peel off the husk and silk
from the corn prior to cooking.*

INGREDIENTS | SERVES 4

4 ears fresh sweet corn, shucked

½ cup water

1 tablespoon butter, or vegan margarine, such as Earth Balance

Salt and black pepper, to taste

Corn's Peak Season

Corn is at its best during the peak season summer month of July. Whenever possible, use fresh fruits and vegetables for the biggest nutritional punch, but if fresh is not an option, frozen fruits and vegetables are a good alternative.

1. Place the rack in the pressure cooker and place the corn on the rack. Pour in the water.

2. Lock the lid into place and bring to low pressure; maintain pressure for 3 minutes. Remove the pressure cooker from heat, quick-release the pressure, and remove the lid.

3. Spread ¼ of the butter over each ear of corn and season with salt and pepper, to taste.

PER SERVING
Calories: 150 | Fat: 4.5g | Protein: 5g | Sodium: 20mg | Carbohydrates: 27g | Fiber: 4g

Cilantro-Lime Corn on the Cob

*Dress up plain corn on the cob with seasoned butter.
To add a little more kick, increase the amount of cayenne pepper.*

INGREDIENTS | SERVES 4

4 ears fresh sweet corn, shucked

½ cup water

2 tablespoons butter, or vegan margarine, such as Earth Balance

2 tablespoons cilantro, chopped

2 teaspoons fresh lime juice

½ teaspoon salt

½ teaspoon cayenne pepper

1. Place the rack in the pressure cooker and place the corn on the rack. Pour in the water.

2. Lock the lid into place and bring to low pressure; maintain pressure for 3 minutes. Remove the pressure cooker from heat, quick-release the pressure, and remove the lid.

3. In a small bowl, combine the butter, cilantro, lime juice, salt, and cayenne pepper until well blended.

4. When the corn is cool enough to handle, spread ¼ of the mixture on each ear of corn.

PER SERVING
Calories: 170 | Fat: 7g | Protein: 5g | Sodium: 310mg | Carbohydrates: 28g | Fiber: 4g

Creamed Corn

Creamed corn is an almost soupy vegetable side dish
that is popular in the Midwest and South.

INGREDIENTS | SERVES 8

8 ears sweet corn, shucked

½ cup water

2 teaspoons butter, or vegan margarine, such as Earth Balance

2 teaspoons flour

1 cup milk, or unsweetened soymilk

2 teaspoons salt

1 teaspoon sugar

Creamed Corn Variations

Many creamed corn recipes don't call for cream or dairy at all. When scraping kernels from a cob of corn and pressing against the cob, you release a milky substance that can help make the corn "creamy."

1. Place the rack in the pressure cooker and place the corn on the rack. Pour in the water.

2. Lock the lid into place and bring to low pressure; maintain pressure for 3 minutes. Remove the pressure cooker from heat, quick-release the pressure, and remove the lid.

3. When the corn is cool enough to handle, place each ear of corn over a large mixing bowl and remove the kernels from the corn with a knife, using long downward strokes and rotating the cob as you go.

4. Take half of the kernels and pulse in a food processor until just smooth.

5. In a small pan, melt the butter, then stir in the flour, being careful not to brown. Slowly stir the milk into the roux, and stir until smooth.

6. Add all of the corn to the saucepan, bring to a boil, reduce heat, and simmer for 10 minutes. Add salt and sugar before removing from heat.

PER SERVING
Calories: 150 | Fat: 2.5g | Protein: 6g | Sodium: 620mg | Carbohydrates: 30g | Fiber: 4g

Okra with Corn and Tomato

The "goo" that comes out of okra while cooking helps to thicken liquids.

INGREDIENTS | SERVES 8

4 ears fresh sweet corn, shucked

½ cup water

1 teaspoon olive oil

¼ cup red onion, diced

1 pound okra, tops removed and cut into ½" rounds

2 cups tomatoes, chopped

1 cup Vegetable Stock (page 29)

2 teaspoons salt

1 teaspoon cayenne pepper

1. Place the rack in the pressure cooker and place the corn on the rack. Pour in the water.

2. Lock the lid into place and bring to low pressure; maintain pressure for 3 minutes. Remove the pressure cooker from heat, quick-release the pressure, and remove the lid.

3. When the corn is cool enough to handle, place each ear of corn over a large mixing bowl and remove the kernels from the corn with a knife, using long downward strokes and rotating the cob as you go.

4. After cleaning the pressure cooker, add the olive oil over medium heat, then sauté the onions until just soft.

5. Add the okra, tomatoes, Vegetable Stock, salt, and cayenne, then stir.

6. Lock the lid into place and bring to high pressure; maintain pressure for 3 minutes. Remove the pressure cooker from heat, quick-release the pressure, and remove the lid. Stir in the corn before serving.

PER SERVING
Calories: 100 | Fat: 1.5g | Protein: 4g | Sodium: 670mg | Carbohydrates: 21g | Fiber: 4g

Succotash

Succotash can be made with a variety of beans,
but the staple ingredients are lima beans and corn.

INGREDIENTS | SERVES 4

2 tablespoons butter, or vegan
margarine, such as Earth Balance
½ cup bell pepper, chopped
1 cup fresh lima beans
1 cup whole kernel corn
1 cup tomatoes, chopped
1 cup water
1 teaspoon salt

1. Bring the pressure cooker to medium heat; add the butter and bell pepper. Sauté for 3 minutes, or until the bell pepper begins to soften.

2. Add the lima beans, corn, tomatoes, water, and salt. Stir well.

3. Lock the lid into place and bring to high pressure; maintain pressure for 10 minutes. Remove from heat and quick-release the pressure.

Origin of Succotash

The word *succotash* derives from the Native American word *msickquatash*, which, according to Epicurious.com, means "boiled whole kernels of corn."

PER SERVING
Calories: 160 | Fat: 6g | Protein: 5g | Sodium: 610mg | Carbohydrates: 23g | Fiber: 4g

Fresh Green Beans with Toasted Sesame

If fresh green beans are unavailable, you can use frozen beans instead.

INGREDIENTS | SERVES 4

2 cups water
1 pound fresh green beans
1 tablespoon olive oil
2 tablespoons toasted sesame seeds
Salt and pepper, to taste

1. Fill the bottom of the pressure cooker with water. Place the steamer basket in the pressure cooker.

2. Trim the ends off the green beans and place in the basket. Secure the lid; cook on high until pressure-indicator rises. Lower heat and cook for 5 minutes.

3. Remove the green beans from the pressure cooker and toss in the olive oil. Sprinkle sesame seeds over green beans and season with salt and pepper.

PER SERVING
Calories: 90 | Fat: 6g | Protein: 2g | Sodium: 0mg | Carbohydrates: 8g | Fiber: 5g

Corn Maque Choux

*You can use drained canned corn, fresh corn cut from the cob,
or thawed frozen corn in this recipe.*

INGREDIENTS | SERVES 4

3 tablespoons butter, or vegan margarine, such as Earth Balance

2 small onions, diced

1 small green bell pepper, diced

½ cup celery, diced

2 cloves garlic, minced

4 cups whole kernel corn

2 Roma tomatoes, peeled, seeded, and diced

½ cup cilantro leaves, chopped, plus additional for garnish

⅛ teaspoon cayenne pepper

½ cup tomato juice

Salt, to taste

Freshly ground black pepper, to taste

Cajun Cuisine

Maque choux is a Cajun dish, popular in Southern Louisiana. Cajun food is known for being full flavored—heavy on seasoning and spice. It is similar to, and often confused with, Creole cuisine.

1. Melt the butter in the pressure cooker over medium heat. Add the onion, bell pepper, and celery; sauté for 3 minutes or until the vegetables are soft. Add the minced garlic and sauté an additional 30 seconds.

2. Stir in the corn, tomatoes, chopped cilantro, cayenne pepper, tomato juice, salt, and pepper. Lock the lid into place and bring to low pressure; maintain pressure for 5 minutes.

3. Remove from heat and quick-release the pressure. Use a slotted spoon to immediately transfer the corn and vegetables to a serving bowl. Taste for seasoning and add additional salt and pepper if needed. Garnish with cilantro and serve.

PER SERVING
Calories: 270 | Fat: 10g | Protein: 7g | Sodium: 105mg | Carbohydrates: 46g | Fiber: 6g

Ratatouille

Ratatouille is sometimes served over potatoes. This version adds the potatoes to the dish.
You can serve this ratatouille over whole grain pasta or topped with toasted garlic croutons.

INGREDIENTS | SERVES 4

2 tablespoons extra-virgin olive oil

2 zucchini, sliced

1 Japanese eggplant, peeled and sliced

1 small onion, thinly sliced

1 green bell pepper, diced

2 medium potatoes, peeled and diced

8 ounces fresh mushrooms, sliced

1 28-ounce can diced tomatoes

3 tablespoons tomato paste

3 tablespoons water

2 garlic cloves, minced

1 teaspoon oregano

1 teaspoon basil

1/8 teaspoon dried red pepper flakes

Salt and fresh black pepper, to taste

Parmigiano-Reggiano cheese, grated, or vegan mozzarella, such as Daiya Mozzarella Style Shreds

1. Coat the bottom and sides of the pressure cooker with oil. Add the remaining ingredients except cheese in layers in the order given. Lock the lid into place and bring to low pressure; maintain pressure for 6 minutes.

2. Remove from heat and quick-release the pressure. Remove the lid, stir, and taste for seasoning, adjusting if necessary. Serve topped with the grated cheese.

PER SERVING
Calories: 240 | Fat: 8g | Protein: 9g | Sodium: 190mg | Carbohydrates: 41g | Fiber: 12g

Eggplant Caponata

This versatile dish can be served hot, at room temperature, or cold.

INGREDIENTS | SERVES 8

¼ cup extra-virgin olive oil

¼ cup white wine

2 tablespoons red wine vinegar

1 teaspoon ground cinnamon

1 large eggplant, peeled and diced

1 medium onion, diced

1 medium green bell pepper, diced

1 medium red bell pepper, diced

2 cloves garlic, minced

1 14½-ounce can diced tomatoes

3 stalks celery, diced

½ cup oil-cured olives, pitted and chopped

½ cup golden raisins

2 tablespoons capers, rinsed and drained

Salt and freshly ground black pepper, to taste

1. Add all ingredients except salt and pepper to the pressure cooker. Stir well to mix. Lock the lid into place and bring to low pressure; maintain pressure for 8 minutes.

2. Remove from heat and quick-release the pressure. Remove the lid and stir the contents of the pressure cooker. Taste for seasoning and add salt and pepper, to taste.

PER SERVING
Calories: 150 | Fat: 8g | Protein: 2g | Sodium: 180mg | Carbohydrates: 19g | Fiber: 5g

Serving Suggestions

Caponata is often served as a salad but it has other uses as well. Try it as a sandwich spread on Italian bread, a dipping sauce for toasted baguette rounds, or relish.

Buttered Beets

This down-on-the-farm comfort food side dish goes well with just about any entrée.

INGREDIENTS | SERVES 8

4 large golden or red beets

1 cup water

Butter, to taste, or vegan margarine, such as Earth Balance

Salt and black pepper, to taste

Beet Peak Season

During the spring months, beets are in bloom. Look for this root vegetable in your grocery store or farmers' market in April.

1. Scrub the beets and trim both ends. Place the beets on the rack in the pressure cooker. Pour in the water.

2. Lock the lid into place and bring to high pressure; maintain pressure for 25 minutes.

3. Remove the pressure cooker from the heat, quick-release the pressure, and remove the lid. Transfer the beets to a cutting board. Test for doneness. If beets aren't cooked, simmer on the stovetop, or cook, covered, in the microwave for a few extra minutes.

4. When the beets are cool enough to handle, use a paring knife to remove the peel. Slice the beets. Reheat the beets and melt butter to taste over the heated beets. Season with salt and pepper to taste.

PER SERVING
Calories: 20 | Fat: 0g | Protein: 1g | Sodium: 30mg | Carbohydrates: 4g | Fiber: 1g

Carrots and Ginger

Boost the flavor in this dish by adding a dash of cinnamon or allspice after cooking.

INGREDIENTS | SERVES 4

1 pound carrots, peeled and sliced diagonally

¼ cup butter, or vegan margarine, such as Earth Balance

1 teaspoon fresh ginger, minced

1 cup water

Salt and black pepper, to taste

Fresh versus Ground Ginger

Ground ginger is more pungent than fresh and has a slightly different taste, so it is recommended that you don't substitute one for the other in all recipes. In this recipe, however, either will work well. If using ground ginger, use ⅛ teaspoon or less.

1. Add the carrots, butter, ginger, and water to the pressure cooker. Stir to mix. Lock the lid into place and bring to high pressure; maintain pressure for 1 minute.

2. Remove from heat and quick-release the pressure. Remove the lid and stir the contents of the pressure cooker. Add salt and pepper, to taste.

PER SERVING
Calories: 150 | Fat: 11g | Protein: 2g | Sodium: 60mg | Carbohydrates: 12g | Fiber: 3g

Sautéed Broccoli Rabe

Broccoli rabe, also known as rapini, can be prepared in the same way as broccoli.

INGREDIENTS | SERVES 6

1 pound broccoli rabe, trimmed

1 teaspoon salt

1 cup water

2 tablespoons olive oil

2 cloves garlic, sliced

2 shallots, sliced

Pepper, to taste

1. Put the broccoli, salt, and water in the pressure cooker. Lock the lid and bring to low pressure; maintain pressure for 2 minutes. Remove from heat, quick-release the pressure, remove the lid. Drain and transfer to a bowl.

2. In the cleaned pressure cooker or in a sauté pan, bring the olive oil to medium heat. Add the garlic and shallots; sauté for 1 minute, stirring often. Add the broccoli rabe and sauté for an additional minute, until heated through and coated with the olive oil mixture. Season with pepper, to taste.

PER SERVING
Calories: 80 | Fat: 4.5g | Protein: 3g | Sodium: 410mg | Carbohydrates: 8g | Fiber: 0g

Broccoli in Lemon-Butter Sauce

Serve as a side dish or toss with pasta for a complete meal.

INGREDIENTS | SERVES 6

4 cups broccoli florets

¼ teaspoon salt

1 cup water

4 tablespoons butter, melted, or vegan margarine, such as Earth Balance

1 tablespoon fresh lemon juice

¼ teaspoon Dijon mustard

Dijon Mustard

Dijon mustard is often made from mustard seeds, white wine, and grape juice, and has a stronger flavor than yellow mustard.

1. Put the broccoli, salt, and water in the pressure cooker. Lock the lid into place and bring to low pressure; maintain pressure for 2 minutes.

2. Remove the pressure cooker from the heat, quick-release the pressure, and remove the lid. Drain and transfer the broccoli to a serving bowl.

3. While the broccoli cooks, whisk together the butter, lemon juice, and mustard. Pour over the cooked broccoli and toss to coat.

PER SERVING
Calories: 80 | Fat: 8g | Protein: 2g | Sodium: 115mg | Carbohydrates: 3g | Fiber: 1g

Fennel Cooked in White Wine

To make a fennel purée, use a slotted spoon to transfer it to a food processor after completing step 2. Pulse until smooth, adding some of the cooking liquid if necessary.

INGREDIENTS | SERVES 4

4 fennel bulbs

1 tablespoon butter, or vegan margarine, such as Earth Balance

1 tablespoon olive oil

1 small onion, diced

1 cup white wine

Salt and pepper, to taste

Fennel Facts

Fennel is in season during the fall, when you'll find this celery-like food in grocery stores. Like celery, you can enjoy fennel raw and in a salad, or gently cooked.

1. Cut off the tops and bottoms of the fennel bulbs and remove the two outer leaves. Thoroughly rinse under cold running water. Dice the bulbs. Set aside.

2. Bring the butter and oil to temperature in the pressure cooker over medium heat. Add the onion; sauté for 3 minutes. Stir in the diced fennel; sauté for 3 minutes. Stir in the wine. Lock the lid into place and bring to low pressure; maintain for 8 minutes. Quick-release the pressure and remove the lid. Simmer until fennel is soft. Add salt and pepper, to taste.

PER SERVING
Calories: 170 | Fat: 7g | Protein: 3g | Sodium: 125mg | Carbohydrates: 19g | Fiber: 7g

Asparagus with Vegan Hollandaise Sauce

*By making this recipe with tofu instead of eggs, you'll eliminate
the cholesterol typically found in hollandaise sauce.*

INGREDIENTS | SERVES 4

1½ pounds fresh asparagus

½ cup water

½ cup silken tofu

1 tablespoon lemon juice

1 teaspoon Dijon mustard

⅛ teaspoon cayenne pepper

⅛ teaspoon turmeric

1 tablespoon vegetable oil

Salt, to taste

1. Trim the end off each asparagus spear. Lay flat in the pressure cooker and add water. Lock lid into place and bring to high pressure; maintain for 3 minutes. Remove from heat and allow pressure to release naturally for 2 minutes.

2. Add the silken tofu to a food processor and purée until smooth. Add the lemon juice, mustard, cayenne, and turmeric. Blend until well combined. With the food processor still running, slowly add the oil and blend until combined. Season with salt, to taste, to complete the vegan hollandaise.

3. Pour the hollandaise into a small sauce pan over low heat and cook until the sauce is warm.

4. Spoon the sauce over the asparagus spears to serve.

PER SERVING
Calories: 100 | Fat: 4.5g | Protein: 6g | Sodium: 45mg |
Carbohydrates: 9g | Fiber: 4g

Kale with Red Pepper Flakes and Cumin

Kale can be enjoyed while still tough and chewy, or completely softened.
Adjust cooking times to reach the consistency you enjoy.

INGREDIENTS | SERVES 4

2 cups water

½ teaspoon salt, plus more to taste

8 cups kale, washed, drained, and chopped

1 tablespoon olive oil

1 clove garlic, minced

1 teaspoon dried red pepper flakes

½ cup Vegetable Stock (page 29)

½ teaspoon cumin

1. Bring water to a boil in the pressure cooker. Stir in ½ teaspoon salt. Blanch kale for 1 minute, drain, and set aside.

2. Add the olive oil to the pressure cooker over medium heat. Add the garlic and red pepper flakes; cook for 30 seconds. Add the stock, cumin, and kale, then stir.

3. Lock the lid into place and bring to high pressure; maintain pressure for 6 minutes. Remove from the heat and allow pressure to release naturally. Serve.

PER SERVING
Calories: 100 | Fat: 4.5g | Protein: 5g | Sodium: 420mg | Carbohydrates: 15g | Fiber: 3g

Mashed Turnips

Serve this low-carb dish in place of mashed potatoes.

INGREDIENTS | SERVES 4

4 medium turnips, peeled and diced

1 small onion, diced

½ cup Vegetable Stock (page 29)

¼ cup sour cream, or vegan sour cream, such as Tofutti Sour Supreme

Salt and pepper, to taste

Flavor Variations

Some of the ingredients one would typically use in mashed potatoes also work well in mashed turnips. A couple of unique ingredients to try are nutmeg or horseradish, but not both in the same dish.

1. Add the turnips, onion, and stock to the pressure cooker. Lock the lid into place and bring to high pressure; maintain for 5 minutes. Remove from the heat and allow pressure to release naturally for 10 minutes.

2. Use a slotted spoon to transfer turnips to a serving bowl, reserving the broth in the pressure cooker. Use a hand-held mixer or immersion blender to purée the turnips, adding some of the broth from the pressure cooker if necessary. Stir in the sour cream. Taste for seasoning, and add salt and pepper if necessary.

PER SERVING
Calories: 80 | Fat: 3g | Protein: 2g | Sodium: 160mg | Carbohydrates: 11g | Fiber: 2g

Braised Beet Greens

Young, fresh greens will cook quicker than older, tougher ones.
Adjust the cooking time accordingly.

INGREDIENTS | SERVES 4

1 tablespoon olive oil

1 large shallot or small red onion, minced

1 pound beet greens

Salt and pepper, to taste

¼ cup Vegetable Stock (page 29)

1 tablespoon white wine

1. Bring the oil to temperature in the pressure cooker over medium heat. Add the shallot or onion; sauté for 3 minutes. Add the beet greens. Sprinkle with salt and pepper. Stir the greens to coat them in the oil. Once they're slightly wilted, add the stock, making sure not to exceed the fill line in your pressure cooker.

2. Lock the lid into place and bring to low pressure; maintain pressure for 1–3 minutes. Quick-release the pressure and remove the lid. Simmer and stir for 1 minute or until the remaining moisture in the pan evaporates.

3. Taste for seasoning, and add more salt and pepper if needed. Add white wine, stir, and serve warm.

PER SERVING
Calories: 70 | Fat: 3.5g | Protein: 3g | Sodium: 290mg | Carbohydrates: 7g | Fiber: 4g

Turnip and Carrot Purée

The nutmeg in this recipe makes it a great side dish on a crisp fall evening or for Thanksgiving dinner.

INGREDIENTS | SERVES 6

2 cups turnips, peeled and quartered

2 cups carrots, peeled and cut into 2" pieces

2 cups water

1 teaspoon salt

2 tablespoons extra-virgin olive oil

½ teaspoon nutmeg, freshly grated

2 tablespoons sour cream, or vegan sour cream, such as Tofutti Sour Supreme

1. Put the turnips, carrots, water, and salt in the pressure cooker. Lock the lid into place and bring to high pressure; maintain pressure for 8 minutes. Remove the pressure cooker from the heat, quick-release the pressure, and remove the lid.

2. Drain the vegetables. Return them to the pressure cooker and put it over low heat for 1–2 minutes to evaporate any residual moisture. Mash the vegetables together with the oil, nutmeg, and sour cream. Taste for seasoning, and add salt if needed. Serve.

PER SERVING
Calories: 80 | Fat: 6g | Protein: 1g | Sodium: 450mg | Carbohydrates: 7g | Fiber: 2g

Savory Turnip Greens

Use fresh or frozen turnip greens for best flavor and optimal nutrition.

INGREDIENTS | SERVES 4

1 pound turnip greens

1 tablespoon olive oil

½ onion, diced

1 garlic clove, minced

1 teaspoon dried red pepper flakes

2 cups Vegetable Stock (page 29)

1 teaspoon Dijon mustard

Salt and pepper, to taste

1. To prepare the greens, cut away the tough stalks and stems. Wash greens, chop into large pieces, set aside.

2. Bring the pressure cooker to medium heat. Add the olive oil, onion, garlic, and red pepper flakes. Cook until the onions begin to soften, about 5 minutes. Add the stock, mustard, and chopped greens; stir well.

3. Lock the lid into place and bring to high pressure; maintain for 5 minutes. Remove from the heat and release pressure naturally. Add salt and pepper, to taste.

PER SERVING
Calories: 90 | Fat: 4g | Protein: 2g | Sodium: 370mg | Carbohydrates: 13g | Fiber: 4g

Butternut Squash

Winter is the peak season for this squash, which is loaded with vitamin A.

INGREDIENTS | SERVES 4–6

2 pounds butternut squash, peeled and cubed into 1" pieces

Water, as needed

2 tablespoons butter or vegan margarine such as Earth Balance

1 tablespoon brown sugar

1 teaspoon salt

Butternut Squash Peak Season

Butternut squash is a type of winter squash. It is similar in flavor to pumpkin and can be steamed, baked, or puréed into a creamy soup.

1. Add the butternut squash, and enough water to cover the squash, to the pressure cooker. Lock the lid into place and bring to high pressure; maintain pressure for 4 minutes. Remove from the heat and quick-release pressure.

2. Drain the liquid, then place the squash in a medium-sized mixing bowl. Stir in the butter, brown sugar, and salt.

PER SERVING
Calories: 170 | Fat: 6g | Protein: 2g | Sodium: 590mg | Carbohydrates: 30g | Fiber: 5g

Spaghetti Squash

Spaghetti squash looks like (and can be used like) strands of pasta.
Top with marinara sauce or olive oil for a low-carb dish.

INGREDIENTS | SERVES 4

2 pound spaghetti squash, halved lengthwise

½ cup water

1 tablespoon olive oil

1 teaspoon salt

1. Scoop out the center of the squash, including the seeds, and discard. Place the squash face down in the steamer basket, then add water.

2. Lock the lid into place and bring to high pressure; maintain pressure for 10 minutes. Remove from the heat and quick-release pressure.

3. When squash is cool enough to handle, use a fork to scoop the strands of "spaghetti" from the squash and place in a medium bowl. Drizzle the olive oil and sprinkle salt on top before serving.

PER SERVING
Calories: 100 | Fat: 4.5g | Protein: 1g | Sodium: 620mg | Carbohydrates: 16g | Fiber: 0g

Southern-Style Collards

Collard greens are a Southern staple typically flavored with animal fat,
but a tasty vegetarian version can be made by adding liquid smoke and soy sauce to the broth.

INGREDIENTS | SERVES 4–6

1 pound collard greens
1 tablespoon olive oil
½ onion, diced
1 garlic clove, minced
1 chipotle chili pepper
4 cups Vegetable Stock (page 29)
1 teaspoon liquid smoke
1 tablespoon soy sauce
1 teaspoon white vinegar
Salt and pepper, to taste

1. To prepare the greens, cut away the tough stalks and stems and discard any leaves that are bruised or yellow. Wash the collards two or three times thoroughly to remove the grit, chop into large pieces, and set aside.

2. Bring the pressure cooker to medium heat. Add the olive oil, onion, garlic, and chipotle pepper. Cook until the onions begin to soften, about 5 minutes. Add all remaining ingredients, except salt and pepper, and the chopped collards; stir well.

3. Lock the lid into place and bring to high pressure; maintain pressure for 10 minutes. Remove from the heat and allow pressure to release naturally.

4. Remove the chipotle before serving. Season with salt and pepper, to taste.

PER SERVING
Calories: 110 | Fat: 4g | Protein: 4g | Sodium: 870mg |
Carbohydrates: 17g | Fiber: 5g

Parsnip Purée

The techniques in this recipe are inspired by Julia Child's famous preparation of this dish.

INGREDIENTS | SERVES 4

1 pound parsnips, peeled and diced

Water, as needed

3 tablespoons butter, or vegan margarine, such as Earth Balance

½ teaspoon salt

½ teaspoon pepper

Parsnips

Parsnips are a mildly flavored root vegetable that look like off-white carrots. Because of the mild flavor, they can be used in a variety of ways, such as baking with other herbed root vegetables or whipping into a purée to serve like mashed potatoes. Look for parsnips during the peak seasons of fall and winter.

1. Place the parsnips in the pressure cooker and add enough water to just cover.

2. Lock on the lid. Bring to high pressure; maintain pressure for 3 minutes. Remove the pan from the heat, quick-release the pressure, and remove the lid. Remove the parsnips but reserve the cooking water.

3. Add the drained parsnips and ¼ cup cooking water to a food processor. Blend until smooth, adding more water if necessary.

4. Return the purée to the cleaned pressure cooker or a saucepan. Add the butter, salt, and pepper, and cook over low heat for 10 minutes, stirring often, before serving.

PER SERVING
Calories: 160 | Fat: 9g | Protein: 1g | Sodium: 300mg | Carbohydrates: 21g | Fiber: 6g

Kimchi-Style Cabbage

*If you can't find Korean chili powder, substitute plain chili powder,
which is also made from crushed red peppers.*

INGREDIENTS | YIELDS 1 QUART

1 clove garlic, minced

1 teaspoon ginger, minced

1 bunch scallions, sliced

½ cup water

¼ cup soy sauce

1 tablespoon Korean chili powder

4 cups Napa cabbage, cut into 2" pieces

1 cup carrots, julienned

Add the garlic, ginger, scallions, water, soy sauce, and chili powder to the pressure cooker and stir well. Add the cabbage and carrots. Lock on the lid. Bring to high pressure; maintain pressure for 2 minutes. Remove the pan from the heat, quick-release the pressure, and remove the lid.

PER ½ CUP SERVING
Calories: 30 | Fat: 0g | Protein: 2g | Sodium: 560mg | Carbohydrates: 5g | Fiber: 2g

Kimchi

Kimchi is a popular Korean condiment that is often used as the base for other recipes. Traditional recipes call for fermenting the mixture until pickled, but you can make "kimchi-style" cabbage by pressure cooking the ingredients instead of fermenting.

Winter Vegetable Medley

*Any earthy herbs, such as rosemary, thyme, or sage,
will work well in this delicious recipe.*

INGREDIENTS | SERVES 4–6

2 tablespoons olive oil

1 sprig rosemary

3 carrots, peeled and sliced

1 large sweet potato, diced and peeled

6 red potatoes, quartered

2½ cups butternut squash, peeled and cubed

1 cup water

Salt and pepper, to taste

1. Bring the olive oil and rosemary to medium heat in the pressure cooker. Add all of the vegetables, stirring until well coated, and cook for 5 minutes.

2. Add the water, then lock on the lid. Bring to high pressure; maintain pressure for 6 minutes. Remove the pan from the heat, slowly release the pressure, and remove the lid. Drain the water. Season with salt and pepper, to taste, and remove the rosemary sprig before serving.

PER SERVING
Calories: 400 | Fat: 7g | Protein: 8g | Sodium: 65mg | Carbohydrates: 79g | Fiber: 11g

Mashed Eggplant and Tomato Salad

Serve this dish as a salad or as a dip with pita bread.
It can be enjoyed hot or cold.

INGREDIENTS | SERVES 4–6

1 large eggplant, peeled and diced

½ cup water

3 tablespoons olive oil

3 cloves garlic, minced

2 cups tomatoes, chopped

2 teaspoons lemon juice

1 teaspoon paprika

1 teaspoon salt

2 tablespoons parsley

Preparing Eggplant

Many cooks swear by salting eggplant before cooking with it to remove the bitter flavor. However, it's not necessary, and is up to the taste preferences of the cook.

1. Add the eggplant and water to the pressure cooker. Lock on the lid. Bring to high pressure; maintain pressure for 4 minutes. Remove the pan from the heat, quick-release the pressure, and remove the lid. Drain and set aside.

2. Add the olive oil to the pressure cooker over medium heat. Add the garlic and sauté for 30 seconds. Add the cooked eggplant, tomatoes, lemon juice, paprika, and salt.

3. Lock on the lid. Bring to high pressure; maintain pressure for 2 minutes. Remove the pan from the heat, quick-release the pressure, and remove the lid.

4. Stir in the parsley, then serve.

PER SERVING
Calories: 140 | Fat: 11g | Protein: 2g | Sodium: 590mg | Carbohydrates: 11g | Fiber: 5g

Pan-Seared Brussels Sprouts

*Pan searing Brussels sprouts brings out a buttery sweetness
that is otherwise missing from the vegetable.*

INGREDIENTS | SERVES 4

1 pound Brussels sprouts

2 tablespoons olive oil

¼ cup water

Salt and pepper, to taste

1. Trim the stems of the Brussels sprouts and remove the discolored outer leaves. Cut in half, from the stem to the top, and place into a medium bowl. Add 1 tablespoon of the oil and gently toss until coated.

2. Add the remaining tablespoon of oil to the pressure cooker and bring to medium-high heat. Place the Brussels sprouts in the pressure cooker and cook for about 5 minutes, stirring often, or until the sides begin to brown. Add the water.

3. Lock on the lid. Bring to high pressure; maintain pressure for 1 minute. Remove the pan from the heat, quick-release the pressure, and remove the lid. Season with salt and pepper, to taste.

PER SERVING
Calories: 110 | Fat: 7g | Protein: 4g | Sodium: 30mg | Carbohydrates: 10g | Fiber: 4g

Aloo Gobi

Aloo gobi is a vegetarian Indian dish made from potatoes and cauliflower.

INGREDIENTS | SERVES 4–6

2 cups potatoes, peeled and cubed

Water, as needed, plus 2 tablespoons

2 cups cauliflower, chopped

2 tablespoons vegetable oil

1 teaspoon cumin seeds

1 clove garlic, minced

1 teaspoon ginger, minced

1 teaspoon turmeric

1 teaspoon garam masala

1 teaspoon salt

1. Add the potatoes to the pressure cooker and enough water to cover. Lock on the lid. Bring to high pressure; maintain pressure for 4 minutes. Remove the pan from the heat, quick-release the pressure, and remove the lid.

2. Add the cauliflower and reattach the lid. Bring to high pressure; maintain pressure for 2 minutes. Remove the pan from the heat, quick-release the pressure, and remove the lid. Drain all ingredients.

3. Place the vegetable oil in the cleaned pressure cooker over low heat. Add the cumin seeds, garlic, and ginger; cook for 1 minute. Add the turmeric, garam masala, and salt; cook for an additional minute.

4. Stir in 2 tablespoons water, then add the cooked potatoes and cauliflower. Simmer over low heat, stirring occasionally, for 10 minutes.

PER SERVING
Calories: 130 | Fat: 7g | Protein: 2g | Sodium: 660mg | Carbohydrates: 17g | Fiber: 2g

Soy-Glazed Bok Choy

Any type of bok choy—such as Chinese cabbage or baby bok choy—works well in this recipe.

INGREDIENTS | SERVES 4

1 pound bok choy

½ cup water, plus 2 teaspoons warm water

¼ cup soy sauce

1 teaspoon rice wine vinegar

1 teaspoon peanut oil

1 teaspoon ginger, minced

1 teaspoon cornstarch

1. Trim the ends off the bok choy and slice in half lengthwise. Add to the steamer basket, then pour in ½ cup water.

2. Lock on the lid. Bring to high pressure; maintain pressure for 1 minute. Remove the pan from the heat, quick-release the pressure, and remove the lid. Remove the steamer basket and drain water.

3. Add the soy sauce, rice wine vinegar, peanut oil, and ginger to the pressure cooker and bring to medium heat. Combine the cornstarch with remaining 2 teaspoons of water then slowly add to the pressure cooker, stirring constantly. Add the bok choy and stir until it's completely coated.

4. Lock on the lid. Bring to high pressure; maintain pressure for 1 minute. Remove the pan from the heat, quick-release the pressure, and remove the lid.

PER SERVING
Calories: 40 | Fat: 1.5g | Protein: 4g | Sodium: 1080mg | Carbohydrates: 4g | Fiber: 1g

CHAPTER 6

Potatoes

Garlic Parsley Mashed Potatoes

Russet potatoes are also commonly called Idaho potatoes.

INGREDIENTS | SERVES 6-8

1 cup water

8 cups russet potatoes, quartered

8 tablespoons butter, or vegan margarine, such as Earth Balance

½ onion, diced

4 cloves garlic, minced

½ cup milk, or unsweetened soymilk

½ cup parsley

2 teaspoons salt

½ teaspoon black pepper

1. Pour the water into the pressure cooker and add the potatoes. Lock the lid into place and bring to high pressure. Once the pressure is achieved, turn the heat to low and cook for 5 minutes. Remove from the heat and allow pressure to release naturally.

2. Drain the potatoes into a colander. Add the butter to the pressure cooker and sauté the onion and garlic for 3 minutes. Add the milk and potatoes, and remove from the heat. Mash the potatoes using a potato masher. Mix in the parsley, salt, pepper, and serve.

PER SERVING
Calories: 320 | Fat: 15g | Protein: 6g | Sodium: 800mg | Carbohydrates: 40g | Fiber: 4g

Rosemary Mashed Potatoes

These basic flavors can be used in other potato dishes if you're not in the mood for mashed potatoes. Instead, try roasting quartered red potatoes or whole fingerlings with rosemary.

INGREDIENTS | SERVES 6-8

1 cup water

8 cups russet potatoes, quartered

¼ cup extra-virgin olive oil

4 cloves garlic, minced

1 tablespoon rosemary

½ cup milk, or unsweetened soymilk

2 teaspoons salt

½ teaspoon black pepper

1. Pour the water into the pressure cooker and add the potatoes. Lock the lid into place and bring to high pressure. Once the pressure is achieved, turn the heat to low and cook for 5 minutes. Remove from the heat and allow pressure to release naturally.

2. Drain the potatoes into a colander. Add the olive oil to the pressure cooker and sauté the garlic and rosemary until golden brown. Add the milk and potatoes and remove from the heat. Mash the potatoes using a potato masher. Season with salt and pepper.

Growing Rosemary

Rosemary is one of the easiest herbs to grow—in many areas it can grow year round, and does not need constant sunlight.

PER SERVING
Calories: 260 | Fat: 10g | Protein: 5g | Sodium: 800mg | Carbohydrates: 39g | Fiber: 4g

Mediterranean Sweet Potato Salad

Serve this salad at room temperature or chilled after refrigerating for a few hours.

INGREDIENTS | SERVES 4

¼ cup olive oil

1 onion, diced

2 cloves garlic, minced

1 teaspoon cumin

1 teaspoon paprika

¼ cup fresh lemon juice

1 cup water

3 cups sweet potatoes, peeled and cubed

¼ cup green olives

3 tablespoons parsley, chopped

Salt and pepper, to taste

1. Add olive oil to pressure cooker; sauté the onion until golden brown. Add the garlic, cumin, paprika, and lemon juice; cook for 2 minutes. Pour into a bowl. Set aside.

2. Add the water and the sweet potatoes to the pressure cooker. Lock the lid into place and bring to high pressure. Once achieved, turn the heat to low and cook for 5 minutes. Remove from heat; release pressure naturally.

3. Drain the sweet potatoes in a colander. In a large bowl, toss the onion mixture with the potatoes. Add the olives and parsley. Season with salt and pepper.

PER SERVING
Calories: 220 | Fat: 15g | Protein: 2g | Sodium: 160mg | Carbohydrates: 22g | Fiber: 3g

Chipotle and Thyme Mashed Sweet Potatoes

To substitute fresh thyme for dried thyme, use ½ tablespoon of the fresh herb.

INGREDIENTS | SERVES 4–6

2 cups water

6 cups sweet potatoes, cubed

4 tablespoons butter, or vegan margarine, such as Earth Balance

3 cloves garlic, minced

½ teaspoon dried chipotle pepper

½ teaspoon dried thyme

Salt and pepper, to taste

1. Pour water into the pressure cooker and add potatoes. Lock the lid into place and bring to high pressure. Once achieved, turn the heat to low and cook for 5 minutes. Remove from the heat and release pressure naturally.

2. Drain the potatoes into a colander. Add the butter to the pressure cooker and sauté the garlic for about 2 minutes. Remove the pressure cooker from the heat. Add the sweet potatoes, chipotle pepper, and thyme. Mash the potatoes using a potato masher or electric mixer. Season with salt and pepper, to taste.

PER SERVING
Calories: 240 | Fat: 11g | Protein: 2g | Sodium: 45mg | Carbohydrates: 34g | Fiber: 4g

Mashed Sweet Potatoes

*Turn this into a sweet potato casserole by covering with vegetarian marshmallows, such as Sweet and Sara brand, and baking in an uncovered dish.
Traditional marshmallows contain gelatin, which is made from animal skin and bones.*

INGREDIENTS | SERVES 3–5

1 cup water

5 cups sweet potatoes, cubed

4 tablespoons butter, or vegan margarine, such as Earth Balance

¼ cup Vegetable Stock (page 29)

⅛ cup orange juice

2 tablespoons maple syrup

Salt and pepper, to taste

1. Add water and potatoes to the pressure cooker. Lock the lid into place and bring to high pressure. Once achieved, turn heat to low and cook 5 minutes. Remove from heat and allow pressure to release naturally for 20 minutes.

2. Drain the sweet potatoes in a colander. Add the butter, stock, orange juice, and maple syrup to the pressure cooker, and heat until the butter has melted. Remove from the heat and add the sweet potatoes. Mash with a potato masher. Season with salt and pepper, to taste.

Recipe Substitutions

It's alright to use inexpensive pancake syrup instead. It won't be as flavorful as pure maple syrup but it will do the job.

PER SERVING
Calories: 310 | Fat: 15g | Protein: 2g | Sodium: 100mg | Carbohydrates: 44g | Fiber: 4g

Maple-Glazed Sweet Potatoes

*You can remove the sugar from this recipe by
replacing it with a sweetener, such as Splenda.*

INGREDIENTS | SERVES 2–4

1 cup water

4 cups sweet potatoes, diced

1 tablespoon butter, or vegan
margarine, such as Earth Balance

¼ cup maple syrup

1 tablespoon brown sugar

⅓ cup chopped pecans

1. Add water and potatoes to the pressure cooker. Lock the lid and bring to high pressure. Once achieved, turn the heat to low and cook for 5 minutes. Remove from the heat and allow pressure to release naturally.

2. Drain potatoes in a colander. Preheat the oven to 375°F. Place the butter, syrup, and sugar in a small bowl and microwave for 30 seconds, or until the butter is melted. In a bowl, toss potatoes, butter mixture, and pecans, then pour into the casserole dish. Bake for 10 minutes.

PER SERVING
Calories: 450 | Fat: 20g | Protein: 4g | Sodium: 50mg | Carbohydrates: 69g | Fiber: 6g

Herbed Potatoes

*Any combination of herbs will work in this potato side dish.
Rosemary, thyme, dill, and coriander are great alternatives.*

INGREDIENTS | SERVES 8

2 tablespoons olive oil

1 medium onion, diced

8 cups red potatoes, scrubbed and
quartered

¼ cup water

1 teaspoon dried oregano

1 teaspoon dried basil

Salt and pepper, to taste

1. Bring the oil to temperature over medium heat in the pressure cooker. Add the onion; sauté for 3 minutes or until the onion is softened. Add the potatoes, cut-side down. Fry uncovered for 5 minutes, or until the potatoes begin to brown. Pour in the water. Sprinkle the herbs over the potatoes. Season with salt and pepper.

2. Lock the lid into place and bring to high pressure; maintain pressure for 5 minutes. Remove from the heat and allow pressure to release naturally.

PER SERVING
Calories: 190 | Fat: 3.5g | Protein: 4g | Sodium: 15mg | Carbohydrates: 36g | Fiber: 4g

Potato Piccata

Piccata typically means a dish that contains butter, lemon, and herbs.

INGREDIENTS | SERVES 4

2 cups water

4 russet potatoes, sliced

2 tablespoons butter, or vegan margarine, such as Earth Balance

1 onion, julienned

1 red pepper, sliced

¼ cup Vegetable Stock (page 29)

2 tablespoons fresh lemon juice

¼ cup parsley

Salt and pepper, to taste

Julienne

Julienne is a type of cut that turns food into long, thin, matchstick-like pieces. Each julienned piece is typically ⅛" to ¼" thick.

1. Pour the water into the pressure cooker and add the potatoes. Lock the lid into place and bring to high pressure. Once the pressure is achieved, turn the heat to low and cook for 5 minutes. Remove from the heat and allow pressure to release naturally.

2. Drain the potatoes in a colander. Add the butter to the pressure cooker and sauté the onion and red pepper until the onion begins to turn golden brown. Add the potatoes, stock, and lemon juice. Cook for an additional 3–5 minutes.

3. Remove from the heat and add the parsley. Add salt and pepper to taste.

PER SERVING
Calories: 250 | Fat: 6g | Protein: 6g | Sodium: 55mg | Carbohydrates: 44g | Fiber: 5g

Potato Risotto

Risotto is typically made with Arborio rice, but the same technique can be applied to a finely diced potato for a unique twist.

INGREDIENTS | SERVES 6

2 leeks (white part only)

¼ cup plus 1 tablespoon olive oil

3 sprigs fresh thyme

3 pounds russet potatoes

2 cups dry white wine

2 quarts Mushroom Broth (page 29)

4 cups fresh spinach leaves

Salt and pepper, to taste

1. Thinly slice leeks crosswise into semicircles and rinse. Add ¼ cup olive oil to the pressure cooker and sauté the leeks until translucent. Add the thyme and cook for 10 minutes.

2. Peel the potatoes. Cut into ⅛" slices and then into ⅛" dice. In a small bowl, toss the potatoes with 1 tablespoon olive oil to thinly coat.

3. Add the potatoes to the pressure cooker and cook for 3 minutes. Deglaze with the wine and reduce until the potatoes are dry. Add the leek mixture and the broth to the potatoes. Lock the lid into place and bring to high pressure. Once the pressure is achieved, turn the heat to low and cook for 5 minutes. Allow pressure to release naturally and remove the lid.

4. Continue to cook and stir the potato risotto without the lid on until all the liquid has been absorbed. Julienne the spinach leaves and add to the risotto once the potatoes are cooked.

5. Season with salt and pepper, to taste.

PER SERVING
Calories: 370 | Fat: 12g | Protein: 6g | Sodium: 560mg | Carbohydrates: 49g | Fiber: 4g

Scalloped Potatoes

*Many recipes that are traditionally baked in an oven
can be steamed in a pressure cooker instead.*

INGREDIENTS | SERVES 4

2 tablespoons butter, or vegan margarine, such as Earth Balance

½ cup onion, julienned

2 cloves garlic, minced

3 cups Béchamel Sauce (page 48), or vegan version of Béchamel Sauce

1 teaspoon salt

¼ teaspoon black pepper

4 potatoes, thinly sliced

2 cups water

Scalloped

Scalloped traditionally means a dish that is covered in sauce and breadcrumbs. You can skip the breadcrumbs to make a crust out of a well-cooked sauce instead.

1. Add the butter to the pressure cooker and sauté the onion until it begins to turn golden brown. Add the garlic and sauté for 1 minute more. Add the Béchamel Sauce, salt, and pepper, and cook until the sauce has thickened. Pour the sauce into a bowl and set aside.

2. Thinly slice the potatoes. Grease a small pressure cooker–safe casserole dish with nonstick spray or butter. Place half of the potatoes on the bottom of the casserole dish. Cover the potatoes with half of the Béchamel Sauce. Make another layer of potatoes and sauce, and then cover the dish in aluminum foil.

3. Place the steamer rack into the pressure cooker. Add the water and place the casserole dish in the pressure cooker.

4. Lock the lid into place and bring to high pressure. Once the pressure is achieved, turn the heat to low and cook for about 15 minutes. Remove from the heat and allow pressure to release naturally.

5. Remove the casserole dish from the pressure cooker and serve.

PER SERVING
Calories: 500 | Fat: 29g | Protein: 14g | Sodium: 1270mg | Carbohydrates: 52g | Fiber: 4g

Braised Fingerling Potatoes

*Braising is a technique that involves browning food first
and then slowly cooking in liquid until softened.*

INGREDIENTS | SERVES 3–4

2 tablespoons extra-virgin olive oil

1 pound fingerling potatoes, halved
(root to stem)

1 cup Vegetable Stock (page 29)

4 whole garlic cloves

1 tablespoon rosemary, chopped

1 tablespoon thyme, chopped

Salt and pepper, to taste

1. Add 2 tablespoons olive oil to the pressure cooker and cook the potatoes over medium-high heat 3 minutes on each side. Add the Vegetable Stock and whole garlic cloves to the pressure cooker.

2. Lock the lid into place and bring to high pressure. Once the pressure is achieved, turn the heat to low and cook for 5 minutes. Remove from the heat and allow pressure to release naturally.

3. Drain the potatoes and garlic in a colander. Put the potatoes in a mixing bowl and mince the cooked garlic.

4. Add the garlic, rosemary, and thyme to the potatoes, then season with salt and pepper to taste.

PER SERVING
Calories: 220 | Fat: 9g | Protein: 4g | Sodium: 210mg |
Carbohydrates: 30g | Fiber: 2g

Dill Potato Salad

*Instead of—or in addition to—fresh dill,
you can use minced dill pickles in this potato salad recipe.*

INGREDIENTS | SERVES 6–8

1 cup water

2 pounds red potatoes, quartered

½ cup mayonnaise, or vegan mayonnaise, such as Vegenaise

1 teaspoon yellow mustard

1 teaspoon cider vinegar

1 tablespoon fresh dill, chopped

Salt and pepper, to taste

½ cup red onion, chopped

½ cup celery, chopped

Using Warm Potatoes

Making potato salad with warm potatoes will lead to a mushier product that has fewer large chunks. Rinsing the cooked potatoes with cold water will help cool them off, or you can refrigerate, or let stand at room temperature, for an hour before mixing with additional ingredients.

1. Add the water and the potatoes to the pressure cooker. Lock the lid into place and bring to high pressure. Once the pressure is achieved, turn the heat to low and cook for 3–4 minutes. Remove from the heat and allow pressure to release naturally. Drain the potatoes and rinse with cold water.

2. Whisk together the mayonnaise, yellow mustard, cider vinegar, dill, salt, and pepper.

3. Combine the potatoes with the chopped onion and celery and then add the mayonnaise mixture.

4. Season with more salt and pepper, if necessary.

PER SERVING
Calories: 250 | Fat: 15g | Protein: 3g | Sodium: 130mg | Carbohydrates: 26g | Fiber: 3g

German Potato Salad

Be careful not to overcook the potatoes.
Overcooking can lead to a mushy potato salad.

INGREDIENTS | SERVES 6–8

1 cup water

2 pounds red potatoes, quartered

½ cup olive oil

2 tablespoons Dijon mustard

2 tablespoons white wine vinegar

2 tablespoons mayonnaise, or vegan mayonnaise, such as Vegenaise

1 teaspoon garlic powder

1½ teaspoons salt

½ cup red pepper, chopped

½ cup celery, chopped

⅓ cup red onion, chopped

1. Add the water and the potatoes to the pressure cooker. Lock the lid into place and bring to high pressure. Once the pressure is achieved, turn the heat to low and cook for 3–4 minutes. Remove from the heat and allow pressure to release naturally. Drain the potatoes and rinse with cold water.

2. To make the dressing, whisk together the olive oil, mustard, vinegar, mayonnaise, garlic powder, and salt in a small bowl.

3. In a large bowl, combine the pepper, celery, onion, cooked potatoes, and the dressing. Toss to coat.

PER SERVING
Calories: 320 | Fat: 22g | Protein: 4g | Sodium: 750mg |
Carbohydrates: 27g | Fiber: 3g

Potatoes Au Gratin

Panko bread crumbs are made from bread without crusts and are almost always vegan.

INGREDIENTS | SERVES 4

1 cup water

8 cups potatoes, peeled and diced

2 cups Béchamel Sauce (page 48), or vegan version of Béchamel Sauce

1 cup Cheddar cheese, shredded, or vegan Cheddar, such as Daiya Cheddar Style Shreds

Salt and pepper, to taste

1 cup bread crumbs

Au Gratin

Similar to scalloped, *au gratin* means a dish topped with a sauce or breadcrumbs and baked until a crust forms on top.

1. Pour the water into the pressure cooker and add the potatoes. Lock the lid into place and bring to high pressure. Once the pressure is achieved, turn the heat to low and cook for 5 minutes. Remove from the heat and allow pressure to release naturally. Drain the potatoes into a colander.

2. In a saucepan, heat the Béchamel Sauce, mix in the cheese, and cook until the cheese is melted. Add salt and pepper to taste.

3. Put the potatoes into a casserole dish and pour the Béchamel mixture over the potatoes, mixing gently. Sprinkle the bread crumbs over the top of the potatoes and bake at 400°F for 15 minutes, or until the bread crumbs are golden brown.

PER SERVING
Calories: 550 | Fat: 26g | Protein: 21g | Sodium: 830mg | Carbohydrates: 62g | Fiber: 5g

Twice-Cooked Potatoes

Cooking the potatoes for the first time in a pressure cooker will shorten the cooking time and help lock in nutrients.

INGREDIENTS | SERVES 4

2 cups water

4 russet potatoes

1 cup sour cream, or vegan sour cream, such as Tofutti Sour Supreme

½ cup milk, or unsweetened soymilk

¼ cup butter, or vegan margarine

1 teaspoon salt

½ teaspoon black pepper

1 cup shredded Cheddar cheese, or vegan Cheddar, such as Daiya Cheddar Style Shreds

4 green onions, sliced

1. Pour the water into the pressure cooker and add the potatoes. Lock the lid into place and bring to high pressure. Maintain for 20 minutes, then remove from the heat and allow pressure to release naturally.

2. Drain the potatoes in a colander. Cut the potatoes in half lengthwise and scoop the flesh of the potatoes into a bowl. Set potato skins aside.

3. Add the sour cream, milk, butter, salt, and pepper to the potato filling in the bowl. Mash the filling with a potato masher or electric mixer.

4. Spoon the blended mixture back into the potato skins and top with Cheddar cheese.

5. Preheat the oven to 350°F. Place the potatoes on a baking sheet, and cook for 15 minutes. Garnish with green onions before serving.

PER SERVING
Calories: 520 | Fat: 33g | Protein: 15g | Sodium: 820mg | Carbohydrates: 43g | Fiber: 4g

Rice and Grains

Brown Rice

For short- or medium-grain brown rice, you will need to allow for additional cooking time.

INGREDIENTS | SERVES 4

1 cup long-grain brown rice

2 cups water

Nutritional Benefits

Brown rice is partially milled rice and has only the outer husk removed. Removing only the inedible outer part of the rice helps retain key nutrients, such as fiber and iron.

1. Add the rice and water to the pressure cooker.

2. Lock the lid into place; bring to high pressure and maintain for 15 minutes. Remove from the heat and allow pressure to release naturally.

3. Fluff with a fork before serving or using in a recipe.

PER SERVING
Calories: 170 | Fat: 1.5g | Protein: 4g | Sodium: 0mg | Carbohydrates: 36g | Fiber: 2g

White Rice

As with brown rice, the shorter the grain, the longer the cooking time.

INGREDIENTS | SERVES 4

1 cup long-grain white rice

1½ cups water

1. Add the rice and water to the pressure cooker.

2. Lock the lid into place; bring to high pressure and maintain for 5 minutes. Remove from the heat and allow pressure to release naturally.

3. Fluff with a fork before serving or using in a recipe.

PER SERVING
Calories: 170 | Fat: 0g | Protein: 3g | Sodium: 0mg | Carbohydrates: 37g | Fiber: <1g

Wild Rice

Try a blend of cooked wild rice and cooked white or brown rice for a more subtle flavor.

INGREDIENTS | SERVES 4

1 cup wild rice
4 cups water

Wild Rice

Wild rice is actually a type of grass, not rice, that grows in marshlands. Most wild rice has a nutty flavor, but it varies slightly depending on the type.

1. Add the wild rice and water to the pressure cooker.

2. Lock the lid into place; bring to high pressure and maintain for 22 minutes. Remove from the heat and allow pressure to release naturally.

3. Fluff with a fork before serving or using in a recipe.

PER SERVING
Calories: 140 | Fat: 0g | Protein: 6g | Sodium: 0mg | Carbohydrates: 30g | Fiber: 2g

Quinoa

Quinoa is an excellent source of protein for vegans and vegetarians.

INGREDIENTS | SERVES 4

1 cup quinoa
2 cups water

1. Add the quinoa and water to the pressure cooker.

2. Lock the lid into place; bring to high pressure and maintain for 6 minutes. Remove from the heat and allow pressure to release naturally.

3. Fluff with a fork before serving or using in a recipe.

PER SERVING
Calories: 160 | Fat: 2.5g | Protein: 6g | Sodium: 10mg | Carbohydrates: 29g | Fiber: 3g

Couscous

Couscous is really a type of pasta cut into tiny balls, but it is often served as a grain, with vegetables as a topping or on the side.

INGREDIENTS | SERVES 4

1 cup couscous
2 cups water

1. Add the couscous and water to the pressure cooker. Lock the lid into place; bring to high pressure and maintain for 2 minutes. Remove from the heat and allow pressure to release naturally.

2. Fluff with a fork before serving or using in a recipe.

PER SERVING
Calories: 160 | Fat: 0g | Protein: 6g | Sodium: 0mg | Carbohydrates: 33g | Fiber: 2g

Wild Mushroom Risotto

Exotic mushrooms such as shiitakes, hen of the woods, and oysters add earthy flavor and diverse textures. For a budget-friendly mushroom, choose portobello.

INGREDIENTS | SERVES 6

1 tablespoon olive oil
½ onion, diced
1 clove garlic, minced
2 cups Arborio rice
6 cups Vegetable Stock (page 29)
2 cups assorted exotic mushrooms, chopped
1 tablespoon butter, or vegan margarine, such as Earth Balance
Salt and pepper, to taste

1. Heat the olive oil in the pressure cooker over medium heat. Add the onions and sauté until just soft, about 3 minutes. Add the garlic and sauté for an additional 30 seconds. Add the rice and sauté for 4 minutes or until the rice becomes opaque.

2. Add 5 cups of the Vegetable Stock. Lock the lid into place; bring to high pressure and maintain for 6 minutes. Quick-release the pressure and remove the lid.

3. Stir in the remaining stock and mushrooms and let simmer over medium heat until the liquid is absorbed.

4. Add the butter to the risotto and season with salt and pepper just before serving.

PER SERVING
Calories: 180 | Fat: 4g | Protein: 3g | Sodium: 590mg | Carbohydrates: 32g | Fiber: <1g

Risotto Technique

The technique used to make risotto results in a creamy consistency without the use of milk or soymilk. Instead, the creaminess is achieved by gradually adding stock to rice while stirring.

Barley Risotto

If you're not a fan of Parmigiano-Reggiano cheese, you can substitute crumbled blue cheese or grated Cheddar cheese to taste.

INGREDIENTS | SERVES 4

1 tablespoon butter, or vegan margarine, such as Earth Balance

1 tablespoon olive oil

1 large onion, diced

1 clove garlic, minced

1 stalk celery, finely minced

1½ cups pearl barley, well rinsed

⅓ cup dried mushrooms

4 cups Vegetable Stock (page 29)

2¼ cups water

1 cup Parmigiano-Reggiano cheese, grated, or vegan cheese, such as Daiya Mozzarella Style Shreds

2 tablespoons fresh parsley, minced

Salt, to taste

Flavor Variations

To further enhance the earthy flavor of the mushrooms and barley, add ½ teaspoon of dried thyme and ½ teaspoon of dried sage instead of fresh parsley.

1. Bring the butter and oil to temperature in the pressure cooker over medium heat. Add the onion; sauté for 3 minutes or until the onion is soft. Add the garlic; sauté for 30 seconds. Stir in the celery and barley until the barley is coated with the fat. Add the mushrooms, stock, and water. Lock the lid into place and bring to high pressure; maintain pressure for 18 minutes. Quick-release the pressure and remove the lid.

2. Drain off any excess liquid not absorbed by the barley, leaving just enough to leave the risotto slightly soupy. Reduce heat to low and stir in the cheese and parsley. Taste for seasoning, and add salt if needed.

PER SERVING
Calories: 520 | Fat: 16g | Protein: 21g | Sodium: 1090mg | Carbohydrates: 70g | Fiber: 13g

Peppery Brown Rice Risotto

If you avoid alcohol, replace the wine in this recipe with ¼ cup Vegetable Stock (page 29).

INGREDIENTS | SERVES 8

2 medium leeks

1 small fennel bulb

3 tablespoons butter, or vegan margarine, such as Earth Balance

2 cups short-grain brown rice, rinsed and drained

½ teaspoon salt

2½ cups water

¼ cup white wine

¾ cup Fontina cheese, grated, or vegan cheese, such as Daiya Mozzarella Style Shreds

1½ teaspoons freshly ground or cracked black pepper

Italian Cheese

Fontina is an Italian cheese with a mild flavor that is creamy and melts easily. Mozzarella is a more common alternative to fontina in this recipe.

1. Cut the leeks into quarters lengthwise, and then slice into ½" slices; wash thoroughly, drain, and dry.

2. Clean the fennel. Trim the fronds from the fennel, chop, and set aside. Dice the bulb.

3. Melt the butter in the pressure cooker over medium heat. Add the leeks and fennel bulb; sauté for 1 minute or until the leeks begin to wilt.

4. Add the rice and stir-fry into the leeks until the rice begins to turn golden brown. Stir in the salt, water, and white wine.

5. Lock the lid into place and bring to high pressure; maintain pressure for 20 minutes. Remove from the heat and allow pressure to release naturally for 10 minutes. Quick-release any remaining pressure. Remove the lid.

6. Fluff the rice with a fork. Stir in the cheese, fennel fronds, and pepper. Taste for seasoning and add additional salt if needed.

PER SERVING
Calories: 280 | Fat: 9g | Protein: 7g | Sodium: 250mg | Carbohydrates: 46g | Fiber: 4g

Pumpkin Risotto

This seasonal risotto will make for a unique entrée on any Thanksgiving table.

INGREDIENTS | SERVES 6–8

1 tablespoon olive oil

1 cup diced sweet yellow onion

2 cups Arborio rice

1 cup white wine

2 cups Vegetable Stock (page 29)

2 cups water

1 cup canned pumpkin purée

1 teaspoon grated ginger

1 teaspoon grated nutmeg

Salt and pepper, to taste

1. Bring the oil to medium heat in the pressure cooker. Sauté the onion until translucent. Add the rice and sauté until opaque, about 4 minutes. Add the wine and stir until the liquid is absorbed. Add stock and 1 cup water.

2. Lock the lid into place; bring to high pressure and maintain for 6 minutes. Quick-release the pressure and remove the lid.

3. Add the remaining cup of water, pumpkin purée, ginger, and nutmeg. Simmer over medium heat until the liquid is absorbed. Season with salt and pepper, to taste.

PER SERVING
Calories: 190 | Fat: 2.5g | Protein: 3g | Sodium: 200mg | Carbohydrates: 33g | Fiber: 2g

Tomato, Garlic, and Parsley Quinoa Salad

The combination of tomato, garlic, and parsley goes well with just about any grain, so if you don't like quinoa, substitute couscous or rice instead.

INGREDIENTS | SERVES 4

1 cup quinoa

2 cups water

2 tablespoons olive oil

2 cloves garlic, minced

1 cup diced tomatoes

¼ cup chopped parsley

1 tablespoon lemon juice

1 teaspoon salt

1. Add the quinoa and water to the pressure cooker. Lock the lid into place; bring to high pressure and maintain for 6 minutes. Remove from the heat and allow pressure to release naturally. Fluff with a fork.

2. In a small sauté pan, add the olive oil over medium heat. Sauté the garlic for 30 seconds, then add the tomatoes, parsley, and lemon juice. Sauté for 1 minute. Stir the tomato mixture and salt into the cooked quinoa. Season with additional salt, to taste.

PER SERVING
Calories: 230 | Fat: 9g | Protein: 6g | Sodium: 600mg | Carbohydrates: 32g | Fiber: 3g

Wheat Berry Salad

For an elegant presentation, place a teaspoon of Wheat Berry Salad on individual sections of baby romaine hearts.

INGREDIENTS | SERVES 12

1½ tablespoons vegetable oil
6¾ cups water
1½ cups wheat berries
1½ teaspoons Dijon mustard
1 teaspoon sugar
1 teaspoon sea salt
½ teaspoon freshly ground black pepper
¼ cup white wine vinegar
½ cup extra-virgin olive oil
½ small red onion, peeled and diced
1⅓ cups frozen corn or peas, thawed
1 medium zucchini, peeled, grated, and drained
2 stalks celery, finely diced
1 red bell pepper, seeded and diced
4 green onions, diced
¼ cup sun-dried tomatoes, diced
¼ cup fresh parsley, chopped

Tasty Substitutions

You can add a bit more flavor to this salad by substituting tomato juice or Vegetable Stock (page 29) for some of the wheat berry cooking liquid.

1. Add the oil, water, and wheat berries to the pressure cooker. Lock the lid into place and bring to high pressure; maintain pressure for 50 minutes. Remove from the heat and quick-release the pressure. Fluff with a fork. If the grains aren't yet as tender as you'd like, simmer and stir the mixture for a few minutes, adding more water if necessary. When done to your liking, drain and transfer to a large bowl.

2. Make the dressing by puréeing the mustard, sugar, salt, pepper, vinegar, olive oil, and red onion in a food processor or blender. Start by stirring ½ cup dressing into the cooled wheat berries. Toss the seasoned wheat berries with remaining ingredients. Taste for seasoning; add additional salt, pepper, or dressing if needed. Cover and refrigerate any leftover dressing for up to 3 days.

PER SERVING
Calories: 210 | Fat: 14g | Protein: 4g | Sodium: 250mg |
Carbohydrates: 24g | Fiber: 4g

Quinoa Artichoke Hearts Salad

The amount of dressing called for in this recipe is a suggestion. You may wish to use more or less dressing, depending on how strongly the dressing you're using is seasoned.

INGREDIENTS | SERVES 4

1 cup pecans

1 cup quinoa

2½ cups water

2 cups frozen artichoke hearts

2 cups cherry or grape tomatoes, halved

½ small red onion, thinly sliced

¼ cup Italian salad dressing

2 heads Belgian endive

Tasty Substitutions

Customize this dish to your liking by choosing your favorite dressing in place of Italian. A creamy dressing, such as a vegetarian Caesar or creamy dill, is a delicious option.

1. Roughly chop the pecans and add them to the pressure cooker over medium heat. Dry roast for several minutes, stirring continuously to prevent the nuts from burning. The pecans are sufficiently toasted when they're fragrant and slightly brown. Transfer to a bowl and set aside to cool.

2. Add the quinoa and water to the pressure cooker. Lock the lid into place and bring to high pressure; maintain pressure for 2 minutes. Remove from the heat and allow pressure to release naturally for 10 minutes. Quick-release any remaining pressure. Transfer to a colander; drain and rinse under cold water. Drain well and transfer to a large bowl.

3. While the quinoa is cooking, prepare the artichoke hearts according to package directions and then plunge into cold water to cool and stop the cooking process. When cooled, cut into quarters.

4. Stir the artichoke hearts into the quinoa along with the tomatoes and red onion. Toss with the salad dressing. At this point, the quinoa mixture can be covered and refrigerated until ready to serve. This allows the flavors to blend. However, if you'll be refrigerating the quinoa mixture for more than 1 hour, leave the cherry or grape tomatoes whole rather than halving them.

5. To prepare the salad, separate the endive leaves. Rinse, drain, and divide them between 4 plates. Top each with one-fourth of the quinoa mixture. Sprinkle ¼ cup of the toasted pecans over the top of each salad.

PER SERVING
Calories: 510 | Fat: 29g | Protein: 15g | Sodium: 360mg | Carbohydrates: 56g | Fiber: 21g

Couscous-Stuffed Red Peppers

Pine nuts are also known as pinoli or pignol, and are most commonly known for being a key ingredient in pesto.

INGREDIENTS | SERVES 4

1 cup couscous

2 cups water

2 tablespoons pine nuts

4 ounces crumbled feta cheese, or vegan feta, such as Sunergia Soy Feta Cheese

1 teaspoon dried oregano

1 teaspoon salt

4 large red bell peppers, stemmed and seeded

Pepper Peak Season

Peppers are available in most grocery stores year round, but red peppers are at their best during the summer months.

1. Preheat the oven to 350°F. Add the couscous and water to the pressure cooker.

2. Lock the lid into place; bring to high pressure and maintain for 2 minutes. Remove from the heat and allow pressure to release naturally.

3. While the couscous is cooking, toast the pine nuts in a small sauté pan over low heat, stirring often to avoid burning. Once they begin to turn golden brown, remove from heat.

4. When the couscous is done, remove the lid of the pressure cooker. Fluff the couscous, and add the cooked pine nuts, feta, oregano, and salt. Stir well to combine.

5. Stuff one-fourth of the couscous mixture into each of the red bell peppers and place in an ungreased baking dish. Bake for 15 minutes, or until the pepper begins to soften.

PER SERVING
Calories: 310 | Fat: 10g | Protein: 12g | Sodium: 910mg | Carbohydrates: 45g | Fiber: 6g

Bulgur Stuffing

Bulgur is a healthier alternative to white bread in stuffing.

INGREDIENTS | SERVES 4–5

1 cup bulgur

3 cups Vegetable Stock (page 29)

2 tablespoons butter, or vegan margarine, such as Earth Balance

½ onion, diced

½ cup celery rib, diced

½ cup chopped mushrooms

½ teaspoon dried thyme

½ teaspoon dried sage

½ teaspoon salt

¾ teaspoon black pepper

Tasty Substitutions

Turn this dish into a cranberry stuffing by adding dried cranberries and chopped pecan pieces instead of the mushrooms and celery.

1. Add the bulgur and Vegetable Stock to the pressure cooker.

2. Lock the lid into place; bring to high pressure and maintain for 9 minutes. Remove from the heat and allow pressure to release naturally.

3. In a large sauté pan over medium heat, melt the butter and sauté the onion and celery until soft, about 7 minutes. Add the mushrooms, thyme, sage, salt, and pepper, and sauté for an additional 2 minutes.

4. Pour the vegetable mixture into the cooked bulgur and stir until well combined.

PER SERVING
Calories: 200 | Fat: 6g | Protein: 5g | Sodium: 750mg | Carbohydrates: 34g | Fiber: 7g

Olive and Pepper Couscous Salad

Kalamata olives are a type of black olive that will add a "meaty" flavor to this dish and are a recommend variety for your mixed olives.

INGREDIENTS | SERVES 4

1 cup couscous
2 cups water
½ cup mixed olives, pitted and chopped
1 red bell pepper, diced
1 clove garlic, minced
1 teaspoon olive oil
1 teaspoon red wine vinegar
1 teaspoon salt

1. Add the couscous and water to the pressure cooker.

2. Lock the lid into place; bring to high pressure and maintain for 2 minutes. Remove from the heat and allow pressure to release naturally.

3. Fluff the couscous with a fork. Add all remaining ingredients and stir until combined. Add additional salt, to taste.

4. Refrigerate for 2 hours before serving.

PER SERVING
Calories: 200 | Fat: 3.5g | Protein: 6g | Sodium: 730mg | Carbohydrates: 37g | Fiber: 4g

Three Grain Pilaf

Millet is a good source of protein and B vitamins.

INGREDIENTS | SERVES 4

2 tablespoons extra-virgin olive oil
½ cup scallions, sliced
1 cup jasmine rice
½ cup millet
½ cup quinoa
2½ cups Vegetable Stock (page 29) or water
Salt and pepper, to taste

1. Add the olive oil to the pressure cooker and sauté the scallions for 2–3 minutes. Add the grains and sauté for 2–3 minutes. Add the stock and bring to a boil.

2. Lock the lid into place and bring to high pressure; maintain for 4 minutes. Remove from heat and release pressure naturally for 5 minutes.

3. Quick-release any remaining pressure and remove the lid. Fluff the pilaf with a fork. Taste for seasoning and add salt and pepper if necessary.

PER SERVING
Calories: 320 | Fat: 9g | Protein: 7g | Sodium: 10mg | Carbohydrates: 52g | Fiber: 4g

Rice Pilaf

A pilaf is a rice dish seasoned with spices, vegetables, and/or meat.

INGREDIENTS | SERVES 6–8

1½ tablespoons unsalted butter, or vegan margarine, such as Earth Balance

1 medium carrot, peeled and grated

1 stalk celery, finely diced

1 medium onion, diced

2 cups long-grain white rice

¼ teaspoon salt

½ teaspoon black pepper

3 cups Vegetable Stock (page 29)

White Rice

Rice is a culinary staple around the world and has been used as food for thousands of years. It provides some nutritional benefits, as it is a source of protein, iron, and vitamins, but white rice is less healthy than brown rice.

1. Melt the butter in the pressure cooker over medium heat. Add the carrot and celery; sauté for 3 minutes.

2. Add the onion; sauté for 3 minutes or until the onion is tender. Add the rice and stir into the vegetables. Add the salt, pepper, and stock; stir.

3. Lock the lid into place and bring to high pressure; maintain pressure for 3 minutes. Remove from the heat and allow pressure to release naturally for 5 minutes.

4. Quick-release any remaining pressure and remove the lid. Fluff the rice with a fork. Serve.

PER SERVING
Calories: 280 | Fat: 3.5g | Protein: 5g | Sodium: 410mg | Carbohydrates: 57g | Fiber: 2g

Vegetable Rice Pilaf

Instant pilaf that comes in cardboard boxes at the supermarket is no match for this dish.

INGREDIENTS | SERVES 4

1 tablespoon butter, or vegan margarine, such as Earth Balance

1 tablespoon vegetable oil

½ small yellow onion, thinly sliced

2 cloves garlic, minced

1½" piece fresh ginger, peeled and grated

1 serrano pepper, seeded and minced

1½ cups cauliflower florets, quartered

1 cup green beans, cleaned, and cut into 1" pieces

½ cup carrot, peeled and sliced diagonally

1 teaspoon ground cumin

½ teaspoon ground turmeric

¼ teaspoon cardamom seeds

1 teaspoon chili powder

⅛ teaspoon ground cloves

⅛ teaspoon hot paprika

½ teaspoon salt

1 cup long-grain white rice

1½ cups water

¼ cup slivered almonds, toasted

1. Melt the butter in the pressure cooker over medium heat. Add the oil and bring to temperature.

2. Add the onion, garlic, ginger, and serrano pepper; sauté for 2 minutes. Stir in the cauliflower, green beans, carrot, cumin, turmeric, cardamom seeds, chili powder, ground cloves, paprika, salt, rice, and water.

3. Lock the lid into place and bring to high pressure; maintain pressure for 6 minutes. Remove from the heat and allow pressure to release naturally for 15 minutes. Quick-release any remaining pressure and remove the lid.

4. Fluff rice with a fork. Transfer to a serving bowl. Top with toasted almonds.

PER SERVING
Calories: 300 | Fat: 10g | Protein: 7g | Sodium: 330mg | Carbohydrates: 46g | Fiber: 5g

Cranberry-Pecan Pilaf

To make this a complete meal, add vegan beef,
such as Gardein Beefless Tips.

INGREDIENTS | SERVES 4

1 cup long-grain white rice
2 cups Vegetable Stock (page 29)
⅔ cup dried cranberries
1 teaspoon dried thyme
1 bay leaf
1 cup pecan pieces
2 tablespoons butter, or vegan
margarine, such as Earth Balance
Salt and pepper, to taste

Serving Suggestions

Turn this pilaf into a holiday dinner center-
piece by serving it in a cooked acorn
squash or small pumpkin.

1. Add the rice, Vegetable Stock, cranberries, thyme, and bay leaf to the pressure cooker.

2. Lock the lid into place and bring to high pressure; maintain pressure for 5 minutes. Remove from the heat and allow pressure to release naturally.

3. Stir in the pecans and butter, then season with salt and pepper.

PER SERVING
Calories: 500 | Fat: 27g | Protein: 6g | Sodium: 300mg |
Carbohydrates: 61g | Fiber: 5g

Pan-Fried Polenta with Marinara

Similar to grits, polenta is made from boiled cornmeal, and can be enjoyed firm or creamy in dishes such as Creamy Thyme Polenta (page 110).

INGREDIENTS | SERVES 4–5

2 tablespoons butter, or vegan margarine, such as Earth Balance

½ onion, diced

2 cloves garlic, minced

4 cups Vegetable Stock (page 29), or water

1 teaspoon salt

½ teaspoon thyme

½ cup cornmeal

½ cup coarse polenta

1 cup corn kernels, canned or fresh

¼ cup olive oil

2 cups Basic Marinara Sauce (page 51)

Flavor Variations

Jazz up this dish by adding cooked vegetables to the polenta before you allow it to cool. Chopped and sautéed leeks are a nice addition, as well as fresh sautéed bell pepper.

1. Add the butter to the pressure cooker and sauté the onion until it begins to turn golden brown. Add the garlic and sauté for 1 minute more. Add the stock or water, salt, and thyme, and bring to a boil. Slowly add the cornmeal, coarse polenta, and corn, stirring so they will not clump.

2. Lock the lid into place and bring to high pressure; maintain pressure for 10 minutes. Remove from the heat and quick-release the pressure. Allow the polenta to cool and firm for at least 30 minutes.

3. When the polenta is firm, cut into 2½" squares, and remove from the pressure cooker. Add the olive oil to a sauté pan and fry the polenta squares until brown on both sides. Serve with Marinara Sauce.

PER SERVING
Calories: 620 | Fat: 41g | Protein: 8g | Sodium: 2090mg | Carbohydrates: 56g | Fiber: 8g

Creamy Thyme Polenta

To substitute fresh herbs in this recipe, increase the amount of thyme to 1 tablespoon.

INGREDIENTS | SERVES 4–5

3½ cups water
½ cup coarse polenta
½ cup fine cornmeal
1 cup corn kernels
1 teaspoon dried thyme
1 teaspoon salt

1. Add all of the ingredients to the pressure cooker and stir.

2. Lock the lid into place and bring to high pressure; maintain pressure for 10 minutes. Remove from the heat and quick-release the pressure. Season with additional salt, if necessary.

PER SERVING
Calories: 190 | Fat: 2.5g | Protein: 6g | Sodium: 770mg | Carbohydrates: 39g | Fiber: 4g

Paella

Turmeric is a budget-friendly alternative to saffron in any recipe.

INGREDIENTS | SERVES 4–6

3 tablespoons olive oil
1 medium onion, chopped
1 cup grated carrot
1 red bell pepper, seeded and chopped
1 cup green peas, fresh or frozen
1 clove garlic, minced
1 cup basmati rice
1½ teaspoons turmeric
2 cups Vegetable Stock (page 29)
¼ cup chopped parsley
Salt and pepper, to taste

1. Add the olive oil to the pressure cooker over medium heat and sauté the onion, carrot, bell pepper, and peas until they begin to soften, about 5 minutes. Add the garlic, rice, and turmeric, and stir until well coated.

2. Add the Vegetable Stock and parsley. Lock the lid into place; bring to high pressure and maintain for 7 minutes. Remove from the heat and allow pressure to release naturally.

3. Season with salt and pepper, to taste, before serving.

PER SERVING
Calories: 250 | Fat: 10g | Protein: 5g | Sodium: 350mg | Carbohydrates: 34g | Fiber: 4g

Paella Staples

There aren't many right or wrong ingredients for paella because it comes in many varieties. The two ingredients that are consistently used are rice and saffron (or turmeric).

Vegan Chorizo Paella

Trader Joe's grocery store chain carries a delicious kind of vegan chorizo sausage.

INGREDIENTS | SERVES 4

¼ cup olive oil

14 ounces vegan chorizo, cut into 1" slices

1 cup onion, diced

4 garlic cloves, minced

½ cup fresh parsley, chopped

1 14-ounce can diced tomatoes, drained

1 cup grated carrot

1 red bell pepper, seeded and chopped

1 cup green peas, fresh or frozen

1½ teaspoons turmeric

1 cup basmati rice

2 cups Vegetable Stock (page 29)

Salt and pepper, to taste

1. Add the oil to the pressure cooker and sauté the sausage until it is browned. Remove the sausage and add the onion, garlic, half the parsley, tomatoes, carrot, red bell pepper, peas, and turmeric. Sauté for 3–5 minutes. Add the rice and stock and return the sausage to the pressure cooker. Bring to a boil.

2. Lock the lid; bring to high pressure and maintain for 7 minutes. Remove from the heat and allow pressure to release naturally. Garnish with the rest of the parsley. Season with salt and pepper, to taste, before serving.

PER SERVING
Calories: 520 | Fat: 30g | Protein: 18g | Sodium: 1160mg | Carbohydrates: 50g | Fiber: 11g

Chinese Black Rice

Chinese black rice can be used in savory or sweet dishes.
For a sweet approach, try adding coconut milk and sugar.

INGREDIENTS | SERVES 4

1 cup Chinese black rice

2 cups Vegetable Stock (page 29)

1 teaspoon rice wine vinegar

1 teaspoon Chinese five-spice powder

½ teaspoon salt

1. Add the rice and stock to the pressure cooker.

2. Lock the lid into place; bring to high pressure and maintain for 15 minutes. Remove from the heat and allow pressure to release naturally.

3. Once the pressure has released, open the lid and stir in the rice wine vinegar, Chinese five-spice powder, and salt.

PER SERVING
Calories: 190 | Fat: 2g | Protein: 5g | Sodium: 590mg | Carbohydrates: 41g | Fiber: 3g

Creole Jambalaya

Try Morningstar Farms Meal Starter Chik'n Strips and Tofurky sausage as an alternative to real meat in this recipe.

INGREDIENTS | SERVES 8

½ cup butter, or vegan margarine, such as Earth Balance

1 cup onion, chopped

1 medium bell pepper, chopped

2 stalks celery, chopped

3 cloves garlic, minced

3 cups Vegetable Stock (page 29)

1 cup water

8 ounces tomato sauce

2 cups white rice

2 bay leaves

2 teaspoons thyme

2 teaspoons cayenne

2 teaspoons Cajun seasoning

2 cups cooked vegetarian chicken and sausage, optional

Salt, to taste

1. Melt the butter in the pressure cooker over medium-low heat, then add the onion, bell pepper, celery, and garlic. Cook for about 15 minutes, until soft.

2. Add the stock, water, tomato sauce, rice, bay leaves, thyme, cayenne, and Cajun seasoning, then stir.

3. Lock the lid into place; bring to high pressure and maintain for 6 minutes. Remove from the heat and allow pressure to release naturally.

4. Stir in prepared chopped vegetarian chicken and sausage, if using, and let stand for 5 minutes. Season with salt, to taste.

PER SERVING
Calories: 310 | Fat: 12g | Protein: 4g | Sodium: 520mg | Carbohydrates: 46g | Fiber: 2g

Creole Cuisine

Creole cuisine is similar to, but more refined than, Cajun cooking, and both use the Holy Trinity of onion, bell pepper, and celery as the base of many dishes. It hails from southern Louisiana, but is influenced by Spanish, French, and African cuisines.

CHAPTER 8

Pasta

Macaroni and Cheese

You can speed up the process by cooking the milk, cream, and cheeses and stirring the mixture into the macaroni over very low heat until it's melted. Then follow the directions in Step 2, eliminating the need to preheat the broiler and brown the breadcrumbs under the broiler.

INGREDIENTS | SERVES 6

1 tablespoon olive or vegetable oil

1 medium sweet onion, peeled and diced

1 clove garlic, peeled and minced

2 cups elbow macaroni

3 cups Vegetable Stock (page 29)

1 teaspoon salt

⅛ teaspoon freshly ground white pepper

½ cup whole milk, or unsweetened soymilk

½ cup heavy cream, or unsweetened soymilk

4 ounces Cheddar cheese, grated, or vegan Cheddar, such as Daiya Cheddar Style Shreds

4 ounces mozzarella cheese, grated, or vegan mozzarella (use vegan Cheddar if unavailable)

4 ounces Colby cheese, grated, or vegan Colby (use vegan Cheddar if unavailable)

¼ cup dried breadcrumbs

2 tablespoons butter, melted or vegan margarine, such as Earth Balance

1. Bring the oil to temperature in the pressure cooker over medium heat. Add the onion; sauté for 3 minutes or until the onion is soft. Add the garlic; sauté for 30 seconds. Add the macaroni and stir to coat it in the oil. Stir in the stock, salt, and pepper. Lock the lid into place and bring to high pressure; maintain pressure for 6 minutes. Quick-release the pressure and remove the lid.

2. Preheat the oven to 350°F. Drain the macaroni. Transfer to a 9" × 13" ovenproof baking dish. Stir in the milk, cream, and cheeses. Mix the breadcrumbs together with the melted butter and sprinkle over the top of the macaroni and cheese. Bake for 30 minutes or until the cheeses are melted and the breadcrumbs are golden brown. Remove from the oven and let rest for 5 minutes. Serve.

PER SERVING
Calories: 520 | Fat: 32g | Protein: 20g | Sodium: 1040mg | Carbohydrates: 38g | Fiber: 2g

Pasta Primavera with Vegetables

This light pasta dish is perfect for a mild spring day.

INGREDIENTS | SERVES 6–8

Water, as needed

1 pound dry bowtie pasta

1 tablespoon extra-virgin olive oil

1½ cups squash, chopped

1½ cups zucchini, chopped

1 head broccoli, chopped

½ cup sun-dried tomatoes

2 cloves garlic

1 cup white wine

¾ cup cold butter or vegan margarine, such as Earth Balance

¼ cup basil, chopped

Salt and pepper, to taste

1. Fill the pressure cooker with enough water to cover the pasta. Bring the water to a boil. Add the pasta. Lock the lid into place and bring to high pressure; maintain pressure for 5 minutes. Use the natural-release method to release the pressure and then remove the lid. Drain and set the pasta aside.

2. While the pasta is cooking, add the olive oil to a pan over medium-low heat and sauté the squash, zucchini, broccoli, and sun-dried tomatoes until they begin to turn golden brown. Add the garlic and the white wine. Allow the white wine to reduce for about 2–3 minutes.

3. Add the butter to the pan, stirring constantly into the wine to create an emulsion.

4. Once the butter has melted, pour the sauce and veggies over the pasta and stir to coat. Garnish with the basil. Taste for seasoning, and add salt and pepper if necessary.

PER SERVING
Calories: 580 | Fat: 27g | Protein: 15g | Sodium: 140mg | Carbohydrates: 69g | Fiber: 7g

Pasta Salad with Tomato, Arugula, and Feta

*Serve this pasta salad at room temperature or
after chilling in the refrigerator for at least 2 hours.*

INGREDIENTS | SERVES 6–8

1 pound dry rotini pasta

Water, as needed

2 Roma tomatoes, diced

2 garlic cloves, minced

1 red bell pepper, diced

2 tablespoons white wine vinegar

⅓ cup extra-virgin olive oil

2 cups arugula or spinach, chopped

1 cup feta cheese or vegan feta cheese

Salt and pepper, to taste

Vegan Feta Cheese

Sunergia makes three flavors of prepackaged soy feta cheese that you can order
from TheVeganStore.com, or try making
your own. Mix crumbled firm tofu with olive
oil, vinegar, salt, and herbs, such as basil
and oregano.

1. Fill the pressure cooker with enough water to cover
   the pasta. Bring the water to a boil. Add the pasta.
   Lock the lid into place and bring to high pressure;
   maintain pressure for 7 minutes. Use the natural-
   release method to release the pressure and then
   remove the lid. Drain the pasta, then run cold water
   over the pasta until cooled. Set aside.

2. In a large bowl, mix the tomatoes, garlic, red bell pepper, vinegar, olive oil, arugula or spinach, and feta.
   Mix in the pasta and add salt and pepper to taste.

PER SERVING
Calories: 480 | Fat: 19g | Protein: 16g | Sodium: 330mg |
Carbohydrates: 62g | Fiber: 4g

Gnocchi and Mushrooms in Rosemary Alfredo Sauce

Gnocchi can be made from flour or potato but is typically treated like pasta in cooking, regardless of the main ingredient. Some stores carry vegetarian prepackaged gnocchi, such as Delallo brand, or you can try making your own.

INGREDIENTS | SERVES 2–3

Water, as needed

16 ounces uncooked gnocchi

1 tablespoon extra-virgin olive oil

½ cup mushrooms, sliced

1 teaspoon fresh lemon juice

2 cups Béchamel Sauce (page 48), or vegan version of Béchamel Sauce

½ cup Parmesan cheese, or vegan Parmesan or mozzarella

½ cup tomatoes, diced

1 teaspoon rosemary, chopped

Salt and pepper, to taste

1. Fill the pressure cooker with enough water to cover the gnocchi. Bring the water to a boil. Add the gnocchi. Lock the lid into place and bring to high pressure; maintain pressure for 1 minute. Use the natural-release method to release the pressure and then remove the lid. Drain the gnocchi and set aside.

2. Add the olive oil to a pan over medium heat and sauté the mushrooms for about 1 minute. Add the gnocchi and sauté for 1 minute more.

3. Deglaze the pan with the lemon juice, then add the Béchamel Sauce and Parmesan cheese, and allow it to reduce until desired consistency is reached.

4. Stir in the tomatoes and rosemary. Taste for seasoning, and add salt and pepper, if necessary.

PER SERVING
Calories: 710 | Fat: 44g | Protein: 21g | Sodium: 970mg | Carbohydrates: 60g | Fiber: 3g

Vegetable Linguine in White Bean Alfredo Sauce

*Vegan white bean alfredo mimics the taste of the dairy-based version
but only contains a fraction of the fat!*

INGREDIENTS | SERVES 6–8

Water, as needed

1 pound dry linguine

1 tablespoon olive oil

1 cup red bell pepper, diced

1 cup tomato, diced

3–4 cups White Bean Alfredo Sauce (page 53) or vegan version of White Bean Alfredo Sauce

¼ cup basil, chopped

Salt and pepper, to taste

1. Fill the pressure cooker with enough water to cover the pasta. Bring the water to a boil. Add the pasta. Lock the lid into place and bring to high pressure; maintain pressure for 6 minutes. Use the natural-release method to release the pressure and then remove the lid. Drain the pasta, then set aside.

2. While the pasta is cooking, heat the olive oil in a pan over medium heat. Sauté the red bell pepper until it just begins to soften, about 3 minutes, then remove from heat.

3. In a large bowl, combine cooked pasta with the sautéed red pepper, fresh tomatoes, Alfredo Sauce, and basil.

4. Stir gently, and add salt and pepper to taste.

PER SERVING
Calories: 500 | Fat: 11g | Protein: 20g | Sodium: 610mg | Carbohydrates: 82g | Fiber: 8g

Rotini with Red Wine Marinara

When cooking pasta in a pressure cooker you only need to add the amount of water the pasta will absorb, which should be enough to just cover the dried pasta.

INGREDIENTS | SERVES 6–8

Water, as needed

1 pound dry rotini pasta

1 tablespoon extra-virgin olive oil

½ yellow onion, diced

3 cloves garlic, minced

1 16-ounce can crushed tomatoes

½ cup red wine

1 teaspoon sugar

⅛ cup basil, chopped

Salt and pepper, to taste

1. Fill the pressure cooker with enough water to cover the pasta. Bring to a boil. Add the pasta. Lock the lid into place and bring to high pressure; maintain pressure for 7 minutes. Use the natural-release method and then remove the lid. Drain and set aside.

2. Add the olive oil to a pan over medium heat and sauté the onion until it begins to caramelize. Add the garlic and sauté for an additional 30 seconds. Add the crushed tomatoes, red wine, and sugar and simmer for about 10 minutes. Add the basil. Taste, and add salt and pepper.

PER SERVING
Calories: 340 | Fat: 3.5g | Protein: 12g | Sodium: 105mg | Carbohydrates: 65g | Fiber: 4g

Pasta Fagiole

This Italian dish is often served as a soup, but this less brothy version can be served as a main course pasta dish, too.

INGREDIENTS | SERVES 6–8

Water, as needed

1 pound spaghetti pasta

4 cups cooked pinto beans

4 cups Basic Marinara Sauce (page 51)

1 cup mozzarella cheese, or vegan mozzarella, such as Daiya Mozzarella Style Shreds

⅛ cup basil, chopped

1. Fill the pressure cooker with enough water to cover the pasta. Bring to a boil. Add the pasta. Lock the lid and bring to high; maintain pressure for 6 minutes. Use the natural-release method and then remove the lid. Set the pasta aside.

2. Preheat the oven to the broiler setting. Place one serving of pasta in a small bowl. Cover with the beans and sauce. Sprinkle cheese on top. Repeat with remaining servings. Place under the broiler until the cheese melts. Garnish with basil and serve.

PER SERVING
Calories: 580 | Fat: 10g | Protein: 26g | Sodium: 180mg | Carbohydrates: 96g | Fiber: 15g

Orzo-Stuffed Poblano Peppers

Kick up the heat on these stuffed peppers by stirring cayenne pepper
or minced pickled jalapeños into the orzo mixture.

INGREDIENTS | SERVES 4

Water, as needed
½ cup orzo pasta
¼ cup onions, diced
¼ cup tomatoes, diced
1 clove garlic, minced
2 tablespoons cilantro, chopped
1 tablespoon extra-virgin olive oil
Salt and pepper, to taste
4 large poblano peppers

Orzo Pasta

Orzo is a small rice-shaped pasta that is often used similarly to rice in cooking. It's a great alternative for chilled pasta salads, stuffing peppers or tomatoes, or tossed in a light sauce. Serving it with a heavy marinara or cream-based sauce is not recommended.

1. Preheat the oven to 350°F. Fill the pressure cooker with enough water to cover the pasta. Bring the water to a boil. Add the pasta. Lock the lid into place and bring to high pressure; maintain pressure for 3 minutes. Use the natural-release method to release the pressure and then remove the lid. Set the pasta aside.

2. In a medium bowl, combine the orzo, onions, tomatoes, garlic, cilantro, olive oil, salt, and pepper. Stir until combined.

3. Place the poblano peppers on a flat surface and cut out a long triangular portion from the top (stem to tip) to make room for the filling. Remove the seeds.

4. Fill each pepper with the orzo mixture and put the triangular piece of pepper back in place, covering the hole. Place on a baking sheet.

5. Bake for 45–50 minutes, or until tender.

PER SERVING
Calories: 160 | Fat: 4g | Protein: 5g | Sodium: 5mg | Carbohydrates: 27g | Fiber: 4g

Orzo-Stuffed Tomatoes

Any type of larger tomato will work for this recipe.
Use what is in season and available at a store near you.

INGREDIENTS | SERVES 4

Water, as needed

½ cup orzo pasta

4 beefsteak or large vine-ripe tomatoes

1 cup fresh mozzarella, chopped, or vegan mozzarella, such as Daiya Mozzarella Style Shreds

2 cloves garlic, minced

2 tablespoons fresh basil, minced

2 tablespoons fresh parsley, minced

Salt and pepper, to taste

2 tablespoons extra-virgin olive oil

1. Fill the pressure cooker with enough water to cover the pasta. Bring the water to a boil. Add the pasta. Lock the lid into place and bring to high pressure; maintain pressure for 3 minutes. Use the natural-release method to release the pressure and then remove the lid. Set the pasta aside.

2. Preheat the oven to 350°F. Cut the tops off the tomatoes and scoop out the pulp. Roughly chop the pulp with a knife and place it in a medium bowl. Add the orzo, mozzarella, garlic, basil, and parsley, and salt and pepper to taste.

3. Stuff the tomatoes with orzo mixture and place them on a baking sheet. Drizzle the olive oil over the tomatoes and bake them in the oven for 15–20 minutes.

PER SERVING
Calories: 230 | Fat: 9g | Protein: 13g | Sodium: 230mg | Carbohydrates: 26g | Fiber: 3g

Pasta Puttanesca

Rumor has it that this popular dish was invented by prostitutes,
but depending on who is telling the story, the creator varies.

INGREDIENTS | SERVES 6–8

Water, as needed
1 pound linguine
2 teaspoons olive oil
2 garlic cloves, slivered
1 tablespoon fresh basil, chopped
2 tablespoons capers
¼ cup kalamata olives, pitted and halved
1 teaspoon dried red pepper flakes
1 tablespoon brine (juice from the olives)
1 14-ounce can crushed tomatoes, drained
Salt and pepper, to taste

1. Fill the pressure cooker with enough water to cover the pasta. Bring the water to a boil. Add the pasta. Lock the lid into place and bring to high pressure; maintain pressure for 6 minutes. Use the natural-release method to release the pressure and then remove the lid. Drain with a colander and set the pasta aside.

2. In a sauté pan over medium heat, warm the oil. Add the garlic and cook for 2–3 minutes. Stir in the basil, capers, olives, and red pepper flakes and cook for 2 more minutes.

3. Stir in the brine and crushed tomatoes and simmer over low heat for 10–15 minutes. Season with salt and pepper to taste.

4. Combine the sauce with the linguine and serve.

PER SERVING
Calories: 320 | Fat: 3.5g | Protein: 12g | Sodium: 230mg | Carbohydrates: 62g | Fiber: 4g

Whole Wheat Fettuccine with Mushroom Cream Sauce

Whole wheat pasta has a slightly different flavor and texture than regular pasta, and it pairs well with the earthy flavor of mushrooms.

INGREDIENTS | SERVES 6–8

Water, as needed

1 pound whole wheat fettuccine

2 tablespoons butter, or vegan margarine, such as Earth Balance

1 cup mushrooms, sliced (try button, shiitake, oyster, or portobello)

2 cloves garlic, minced

1 tablespoon all-purpose flour

1¼ cups milk, or unsweetened soymilk

1 tablespoon fresh parsley, chopped

1 tablespoon fresh lemon juice

Salt and pepper, to taste

1. Fill the pressure cooker with enough water to cover the pasta. Bring the water to a boil. Add the pasta. Lock the lid into place and bring to high pressure; maintain pressure for 7 minutes. Use the natural-release method to release the pressure and then remove the lid. Set the pasta aside.

2. Melt 1 tablespoon of the butter in a sauté pan, then add the mushrooms and garlic. Sauté until the mushrooms are soft, about 4 minutes. Remove from the pan and set aside.

3. Melt the second tablespoon of butter, then stir in the flour and cook for about 1 minute to make a roux. Gradually stir in the milk, stirring continuously until smooth.

4. Add the cooked mushrooms, parsley, lemon juice, salt, and pepper and cook for 1–2 minutes.

5. Pour the sauce over warm pasta and serve immediately.

PER SERVING
Calories: 420 | Fat: 6g | Protein: 27g | Sodium: 45mg | Carbohydrates: 76g | Fiber: 15g

Broccoli–Pine Nut Pasta Salad

Broccoli contains over 5 grams of protein per cup, making it a good staple ingredient in anyone's diet.

INGREDIENTS | SERVES 6–8

Water, as needed

1 pound rotini

⅓ cup pine nuts, toasted

1 head broccoli, blanched and chopped

1 red bell pepper, chopped

½ onion, diced

2 cloves garlic, minced

2 tablespoons red wine vinegar

⅓ cup extra-virgin olive oil

Salt and pepper, to taste

Blanching

Boiling a vegetable for a very short period of time, then draining and plunging it into an ice-water bath is known as blanching. Cooks use this technique to soften vegetables or reduce cooking times so that a recipe will cook evenly.

1. Fill the pressure cooker with enough water to cover the pasta. Bring the water to a boil. Add the pasta. Lock the lid into place and bring to high pressure; maintain pressure for 7 minutes. Use the natural-release method to release the pressure and then remove the lid. Pour the pasta and run cold water over it until cooled. Set the pasta aside.

2. In a sauté pan over low heat, toast the pine nuts until they are golden brown. Be careful not to burn them.

3. In a large bowl, combine the pine nuts, broccoli, red pepper, onion, garlic, vinegar, olive oil, and pasta. Taste for seasoning and add salt and pepper if needed.

PER SERVING
Calories: 480 | Fat: 19g | Protein: 15g | Sodium: 40mg | Carbohydrates: 67g | Fiber: 6g

Fresh Spinach–White Wine Angel Hair Pasta

This light pasta dish can be made alcohol-free by substituting Vegetable Stock and 1 teaspoon of vinegar for the white wine.

INGREDIENTS | SERVES 6–8

Water, as needed

1 pound angel hair pasta

1 tablespoon olive oil

¼ yellow onion, diced

2 cloves garlic, minced

½ cup white wine

¼ cup water, or as needed

1 tablespoon butter, or vegan margarine, such as Earth Balance

1 tablespoon flour

Salt and pepper, to taste

1 cup steamed spinach

1. Fill the pressure cooker with enough water to cover the pasta. Bring the water to a boil. Add the pasta. Lock the lid into place and bring to high pressure; maintain pressure for 4 minutes. Use the natural-release method to release the pressure and then remove the lid. Set the pasta aside.

2. In a medium saucepan over low heat, add the olive oil, onion, and garlic. Cook until the onions are soft, about 5 minutes. Add the white wine and water, then bring to a low simmer. Continue simmering for about 10 minutes.

3. Add the butter and flour, stirring until completely combined and the sauce begins to thicken. If the sauce becomes too thick, add more water until you reach the desired consistency, then season with salt and pepper.

4. In a large mixing bowl, combine the spinach, pasta, and white-wine sauce, then toss until the pasta is completely coated.

PER SERVING
Calories: 340 | Fat: 6g | Protein: 11g | Sodium: 30mg | Carbohydrates: 58g | Fiber: 4g

Portobello Stroganoff

Beef is commonly used in stroganoff recipes, but you can make a vegetarian or vegan version by using the "meaty" flavor of portobello mushrooms instead.

INGREDIENTS | SERVES 6–8

Water, as needed

1 pound linguine

1 tablespoon extra-virgin olive oil

1 yellow onion, diced

3 cups portobello mushrooms, roughly chopped

1 tablespoon all-purpose flour

4 cups Espagnole (page 47), or vegan version of Espagnole

½ cup sour cream, or vegan sour cream, such as Tofutti Sour Supreme

1 tablespoon ground mustard

Salt and pepper, to taste

¼ cup chopped parsley

1. Fill the pressure cooker with enough water to cover the pasta. Bring the water to a boil. Add the pasta. Lock the lid into place and bring to high pressure; maintain pressure for 6 minutes. Use the natural-release method to release the pressure and then remove the lid. Set the pasta aside.

2. Heat the oil and sauté the onion and mushrooms. Sprinkle in the flour and cook to a paste. Add the Espagnole sauce and cook at a slow simmer for 20 minutes. Mix the sour cream and mustard together. Pour into the sauce and heat thoroughly. Taste for seasoning, and add salt and pepper if necessary.

3. Serve over the linguine and garnish with the parsley.

PER SERVING
Calories: 530 | Fat: 18g | Protein: 14g | Sodium: 570mg | Carbohydrates: 79g | Fiber: 5g

Bowtie Pasta in a Sage Beurre Blanc Sauce

Sage is an herb with an earthy and slightly minty flavor.

INGREDIENTS | SERVES 6–8

Water, as needed

1 pound bowtie pasta

1 tablespoon extra-virgin olive oil

1 cup white mushrooms, sliced

1 small red onion, julienned

2 cloves garlic, minced

1 cup white wine

2 tablespoons white wine vinegar

¾ cup cold butter, or vegan margarine, such as Earth Balance

1 cup tomatoes, diced

1 teaspoon dried sage

Salt and pepper, to taste

1. Fill the pressure cooker with enough water to cover the pasta. Bring the water to a boil. Add the pasta. Lock the lid into place and bring to high pressure; maintain pressure for 5 minutes. Use the natural-release method to release the pressure and then remove the lid. Set the pasta aside.

2. Add the olive oil to a pan and sauté the mushrooms and onion until golden brown. Add the garlic and sauté for an additional 30 seconds. Add the wine and vinegar, and let reduce for about 3 minutes. Add the cold butter to the pan, 1 tablespoon at a time, stirring the butter constantly into the wine to create an emulsion.

3. Once the butter has emulsified, add the tomatoes, sage, and salt and pepper, to taste. Toss with the pasta before serving.

PER SERVING
Calories: 540 | Fat: 26g | Protein: 11g | Sodium: 10mg | Carbohydrates: 60g | Fiber: 3g

CHAPTER 9

Beans

Pinto Beans

Most beans must be soaked for 4 hours before cooking.
You can also try a "quick soak," which is described in this recipe.

INGREDIENTS | SERVES 4

1 cup dried pinto beans
8 cups water
1 tablespoon vegetable oil
1 teaspoon salt

1. Add the beans and 4 cups water to the pressure cooker. Lock the lid into place; bring to high pressure for 1 minute. Remove from the heat and quick-release the pressure.

2. Drain the water, rinse the beans, and add to the pressure cooker again with the remaining 4 cups of water. Soak for 1 hour.

3. Add the vegetable oil and salt. Lock the lid into place; bring to high pressure and maintain for 11 minutes. Remove from the heat and allow pressure to release naturally.

PER SERVING
Calories: 180 | Fat: 4g | Protein: 10g | Sodium: 580mg | Carbohydrates: 27g | Fiber: 8g

Adzuki Beans

Adzuki beans are an Asian bean that is typically enjoyed
sweetened, but they can be served savory, too.

INGREDIENTS | SERVES 4

1 cup dried adzuki beans
4 cups water
1 tablespoon vegetable oil
1 teaspoon salt

1. Add the beans, water, oil, and salt to the pressure cooker.

2. Lock the lid into place; bring to high pressure and maintain for 8 minutes. Remove from the heat and allow pressure to release naturally.

PER SERVING
Calories: 190 | Fat: 4g | Protein: 11g | Sodium: 580mg | Carbohydrates: 29g | Fiber: 6g

Lima Beans

All beans should be finished using the natural-release method.

INGREDIENTS | SERVES 4

1 cup dried lima beans

4 cups water

4 cups Vegetable Stock (page 29)

1 tablespoon vegetable oil

1. Add the beans and water to the pressure cooker. Lock the lid into place; bring to high pressure for 1 minute. Remove from the heat and quick-release the pressure. Drain the water, rinse the beans, and add to the pressure cooker again with the stock. Let soak for 1 hour.

2. Add the vegetable oil and salt. Lock the lid into place; bring to high pressure and maintain for 6 minutes. Remove from the heat and allow pressure to release naturally.

PER SERVING
Calories: 210 | Fat: 4g | Protein: 10g | Sodium: 600mg | Carbohydrates: 34g | Fiber: 8g

Black Beans

Adding fat—such as vegetable oil—to the water while cooking beans will reduce the foaming.

INGREDIENTS | SERVES 4

1 cup dried black beans

8 cups water

1 tablespoon vegetable oil

1 teaspoon salt

1. Add the beans and 4 cups water to the pressure cooker. Lock the lid into place; bring to high pressure for 1 minute. Remove from the heat and quick-release the pressure. Drain the water, rinse the beans, and add to the pressure cooker again with the remaining 4 cups water. Soak for 1 hour.

2. Add the vegetable oil and salt. Lock the lid into place; bring to high pressure for 12 minutes. Remove from the heat and allow pressure to release naturally.

PER SERVING
Calories: 190 | Fat: 3.5g | Protein: 9g | Sodium: 580mg | Carbohydrates: 29g | Fiber: 4g

White Beans

*Adding a pinch of salt while cooking will help
bring out the flavor of the beans.*

INGREDIENTS | SERVES 4

1 cup dried cannellini beans

8 cups water

1 tablespoon vegetable oil

1 teaspoon salt

1. Add the beans and 4 cups water to the pressure cooker. Lock the lid into place; bring to high pressure for 1 minute. Remove from the heat and quick-release the pressure.

2. Drain the water, rinse the beans, and add to the pressure cooker again with the remaining 4 cups water. Let soak for 1 hour.

3. Add the vegetable oil and salt. Lock the lid into place; bring to high pressure and maintain for 12 minutes. Remove from the heat and allow pressure to release naturally.

PER SERVING
Calories: 200 | Fat: 4g | Protein: 12g | Sodium: 590mg |
Carbohydrates: 30g | Fiber: 8g

Lentils

*Lentils, which are commonly used in Indian cuisine,
do not require soaking before cooking.*

INGREDIENTS | SERVES 4

1 cup dried lentils

4 cups water

1 tablespoon vegetable oil

1 teaspoon salt

1. Add the beans, water, oil, and salt to the pressure cooker.

2. Lock the lid into place; bring to high pressure and maintain for 7 minutes. Remove from the heat and allow pressure to release naturally.

PER SERVING
Calories: 210 | Fat: 3.5g | Protein: 14g | Sodium: 580mg |
Carbohydrates: 32g | Fiber: 6g

Refried Beans

Refried beans can be made with black beans or the more commonly used pinto beans. It's typically served as a side dish with Mexican meals.

INGREDIENTS | SERVES 8

2 cups dried pinto beans

8 cups water

8 cups Vegetable Stock (page 29)

1 tablespoon olive oil

½ onion, diced

½ small jalapeño pepper, seeded and minced

1 clove garlic, minced

½ teaspoon chipotle powder

½ teaspoon cumin

1 teaspoon salt

8 ounces shredded Monterey jack cheese, or vegan Monterey jack cheese, such as Follow Your Heart

Minus the Meat

Traditional refried beans are often made with lard, which is not suitable for vegetarians and vegans. To make a vegetarian version, oil and Vegetable Stock are used instead.

1. Add the beans and water to the pressure cooker. Lock the lid into place; bring to high pressure for 1 minute. Remove from the heat and quick-release the pressure.

2. Drain the water, rinse the beans, and add to the pressure cooker again with the stock. Soak for 1 hour.

3. Lock the lid into place; bring to high pressure and maintain for 11 minutes. Remove from the heat and allow pressure to release naturally.

4. In a small sauté pan, heat the oil and sauté the onion, jalapeno, and garlic until just softened, about 5 minutes. Add the chipotle, cumin, and salt, then add the vegetable mixture to the cooked beans and stir.

5. Use a masher or immersion blender to mash the pinto beans, adding more stock if necessary to achieve a creamy consistency.

PER SERVING
Calories: 300 | Fat: 11g | Protein: 17g | Sodium: 1030mg | Carbohydrates: 34g | Fiber: 8g

Chipotle-Thyme Black Beans

There are actually 5 different varieties of black beans,
but when you purchase black beans, they are often just labeled as "black beans."

INGREDIENTS | SERVES 8

2 cups dried black beans

16 cups water

1 tablespoon vegetable oil

1 teaspoon chipotle powder

2 teaspoons fresh thyme, minced

1 teaspoon salt

1. Add the beans and 8 cups water to the pressure cooker. Lock the lid into place; bring to high pressure for 1 minute. Remove from the heat and quick-release the pressure.

2. Drain the water, rinse the beans, and add to the pressure cooker again with the remaining 8 cups water. Let soak for 1 hour.

3. Add the vegetable oil, chipotle, thyme, and salt. Lock the lid into place; bring to high pressure and maintain for 12 minutes. Remove from the heat and allow pressure to release naturally.

PER SERVING
Calories: 180 | Fat: 2g | Protein: 9g | Sodium: 290mg | Carbohydrates: 30g | Fiber: 4g

Cuban Black Beans and Rice

Cuban food is the combination of African, Caribbean, and Spanish cuisines.

INGREDIENTS | SERVES 6

1 cup dried black beans

4 cups water

3 tablespoons olive or vegetable oil

1 medium green bell pepper, seeded and diced

½ stalk celery, finely diced

½ cup carrots, peeled and grated

1 medium onion, diced

2 cloves garlic, minced

¾ cup medium- or long-grain white rice

2 cups Vegetable Stock (page 29)

2 teaspoons paprika

½ teaspoon cumin

¼ teaspoon chili powder

1 bay leaf

Salt and freshly ground black pepper, to taste

Bay Leaf

Bay leaf comes from the bay laurel plant and is most commonly used to season soups and stews. When used whole, they should be removed from a dish before serving.

1. Rinse the beans and add them to a covered container. Pour in the water, cover, and let the beans soak overnight. Drain.

2. Bring the oil to temperature in the pressure cooker over medium-high heat. Add the green bell pepper, celery, and carrots; sauté for 2 minutes. Add the onion; sauté for 3 minutes or until the onions are soft. Stir in the garlic and sauté for 30 seconds.

3. Stir in the rice and stir-fry until the rice begins to brown. Add the drained beans, stock, paprika, cumin, chili powder, and bay leaf.

4. Lock the lid into place and bring to low pressure; maintain pressure for 18 minutes. Remove from the heat and allow pressure to release naturally. Stir, taste for seasoning, and add salt and pepper to taste. Remove bay leaf and serve.

PER SERVING
Calories: 290 | Fat: 7g | Protein: 9g | Sodium: 170mg | Carbohydrates: 46g | Fiber: 5g

Beer-Lime Black Beans

Try a Mexican beer, such as Negra Modelo, Tecate, or Corona to complement the beans in this recipe.

INGREDIENTS | SERVES 8

2 cups dried black beans

14 cups water

1 tablespoon vegetable oil

½ red onion, diced

1 clove garlic, minced

2 teaspoons salt

2 12-ounce bottles light-colored beer, such as an ale

¼ cup cilantro, chopped

1 tablespoon lime juice

1. Add the beans and 8 cups water to the pressure cooker. Lock the lid into place; bring to high pressure for 1 minute. Remove from the heat and quick-release the pressure.

2. Drain the water, rinse the beans, and add to the pressure cooker again with the remaining 6 cups water. Soak for 1 hour.

3. Lock the lid into place; bring to high pressure and maintain for 10 minutes. Remove from the heat and quick-release the pressure.

4. Remove the lid and add the oil, onion, garlic, salt, and beer to the pressure cooker, then stir. Lock the lid into place; bring to high pressure and maintain for 2 minutes. Remove from the heat and allow pressure to release naturally.

5. Stir in the chopped cilantro and lime juice before serving.

PER SERVING
Calories: 220 | Fat: 2g | Protein: 10g | Sodium: 590mg | Carbohydrates: 34g | Fiber: 4g

Black Bean–Cilantro Fritters

For an extra-crunchy exterior, try rolling the fritters in panko bread crumbs before frying.

INGREDIENTS | SERVES 8–10

1 cup black beans

8 cups water

1 tablespoon vegetable oil

1 teaspoon salt

1 red bell pepper, diced

1 jalapeño, minced

½ cup onion, diced

¼ cup cilantro

1 cup flour

1 cup cornmeal

1 tablespoon baking powder

½ cup heavy cream, or unsweetened soymilk

2 eggs, beaten, or 2 teaspoons cornstarch mixed with 2 tablespoons water

2 quarts canola oil, for frying

Salt and pepper, to taste

Egg Replacements

Other options for replacing eggs in fritters are using mixes such as Ener-G Egg Replacer, or tofu. If using tofu, use half a cup of soft tofu to replace two eggs.

1. Add the beans and 4 cups water to the pressure cooker. Lock the lid into place; bring to high pressure for 1 minute. Remove from the heat and quick-release the pressure.

2. Drain the water, rinse the beans, and add to the pressure cooker again with the remaining 4 cups water. Soak for 1 hour.

3. Add the vegetable oil and salt. Lock the lid into place; bring to high pressure and maintain for 12 minutes. Remove from the heat and allow pressure to release naturally. Drain and set aside.

4. In a bowl, combine the red bell pepper, jalapeño, onion, cilantro, and black beans.

5. In another bowl combine the flour, cornmeal, baking powder, heavy cream, and 2 eggs. Add the vegetable and bean mixture to the flour mixture and stir until well combined. Form the batter into 1" fritters.

6. In a large pot, heat the oil to 350°F and fry the fritters until golden brown, about 3–4 minutes.

PER SERVING
Calories: 540 | Fat: 37g | Protein: 10g | Sodium: 500mg | Carbohydrates: 43g | Fiber: 4g

Three Bean Salad

Cover and refrigerate this salad for at least 2 hours before serving.
It can even be made a day in advance and left in the refrigerator overnight.

INGREDIENTS | SERVES 8–10

⅓ cup apple cider vinegar

¼ cup sugar

2½ teaspoons salt, plus more to taste

½ teaspoon pepper, plus more to taste

¼ cup olive oil

½ cup dried chickpeas

½ cup dried kidney beans

8 cups water

1 tablespoon vegetable oil

1 cup fresh or frozen green beans, cut into 1" pieces

1 cup flat leaf parsley, chopped

½ cup onion, diced

½ cup cucumber, diced

Bean Variations

Almost any combination of beans can be used to make a bean salad. Try black beans, pinto beans, and navy beans mixed with Mexican flavors, or adzuki beans, soybeans, and green beans with Japanese flavors.

1. In a small bowl, whisk together the vinegar, sugar, 1½ teaspoons salt, and ½ teaspoon pepper. While whisking continuously, slowly add the olive oil. Once well combined, cover and refrigerate.

2. Add the chickpeas, kidney beans, and 4 cups water to the pressure cooker. Lock the lid into place; bring to high pressure for 1 minute. Remove from the heat and quick-release the pressure.

3. Drain the water, rinse the beans, and add to the pressure cooker again with the remaining 4 cups water. Soak for 1 hour.

4. Add the vegetable oil and 1 teaspoon salt. Lock the lid into place; bring to high pressure and maintain for 20 minutes. Quick-release the pressure and open the lid. Add the green beans, lock the lid, and bring to high pressure for an additional 3 minutes. Remove from heat and allow the pressure to release naturally.

5. Drain the cooked beans and add to a large mixing bowl. Stir in all remaining ingredients and dressing. Cover and refrigerate for 2 hours before serving.

PER SERVING
Calories: 190 | Fat: 9g | Protein: 6g | Sodium: 740mg | Carbohydrates: 24g | Fiber: 5g

Boston-Style Baked Beans

If you're missing the bacon in these baked beans,
add pieces of Lightlife Fakin' Bacon.

INGREDIENTS | SERVES 8

2 cups dried navy beans

16 cups water

2 tablespoons vegetable oil

1 teaspoon salt

1 teaspoon liquid smoke

¼ cup onion, diced

1 tablespoon yellow mustard

1 tablespoon brown sugar

1 teaspoon molasses

1. Add the beans and 8 cups water to the pressure cooker. Lock the lid into place; bring to high pressure for 1 minute. Remove from the heat and quick-release the pressure.

2. Drain the water, rinse the beans, and add to the pressure cooker again with the remaining 8 cups water. Soak for 1 hour.

3. Add 1 tablespoon vegetable oil, salt, and liquid smoke. Lock the lid into place; bring to high pressure and maintain for 10 minutes. Quick-release the pressure.

4. Add all remaining ingredients; stir and lock the lid into place. Bring to high pressure and maintain for 5 minutes. Remove from heat and allow pressure to release naturally.

PER SERVING
Calories: 220 | Fat: 4.5g | Protein: 12g | Sodium: 320mg | Carbohydrates: 34g | Fiber: 13g

New Orleans Red Beans and Rice

*Red beans and rice is a New Orleans staple
that is traditionally served on Mondays.*

INGREDIENTS | SERVES 8

2¼ cups dried red kidney beans

16 cups water

3 tablespoons butter, or vegan margarine, such as Earth Balance

1 cup onion, diced

1 cup bell pepper, diced

1 cup celery, diced

2 cloves garlic, minced

6 cups Vegetable Stock (page 29)

1 teaspoon liquid smoke

½ teaspoon vegan Worcestershire sauce

1 teaspoon hot sauce (or more if desired)

½ teaspoon dried thyme

1 teaspoon cayenne pepper

2 bay leaves

2 teaspoons salt

8 cups cooked long-grain white rice

Make It "Meaty"

Sausage and ham hocks are the most common meats used in red beans and rice. To make a vegetarian "meaty" version, add cooked, sliced vegetarian sausage and chunks of cooked vegetarian bacon right before serving.

1. Add the beans and 8 cups water to the pressure cooker. Lock the lid into place; bring to high pressure for 1 minute. Remove from the heat and quick-release the pressure.

2. Drain the water, rinse the beans, and add to the pressure cooker again with the remaining 8 cups water. Soak for 1 hour.

3. Drain the beans and clean the pressure cooker. Add the butter to the pressure cooker over medium heat. Add the onion, bell pepper, and celery. Sauté until very soft, about 15 minutes. Add the garlic and sauté an additional 30 seconds.

4. Add the Vegetable Stock, liquid smoke, vegan Worcestershire, hot sauce, thyme, cayenne, bay leaves, and salt.

5. Lock the lid into place; bring to high pressure and maintain for 11 minutes. Remove from the heat and allow pressure to release naturally.

6. Remove the bay leaves before serving and season with additional salt and hot sauce to taste. Serve over cooked white rice.

PER SERVING
Calories: 920 | Fat: 6g | Protein: 26g | Sodium: 1090mg | Carbohydrates: 185g | Fiber: 16g

Red Beans with Plantains

*Beans served with plantains is a common dish
in the West African country of Ghana.*

INGREDIENTS | SERVES 8

2 cups red beans

16 cups water

4 tablespoons olive oil

2 teaspoons salt, plus more to taste

1 cup onion, diced

4 cloves garlic, minced

1 teaspoon fresh ginger, peeled and minced

½ teaspoon cayenne pepper

1 cup tomatoes, diced

3 ripened plantains, peeled and sliced diagonally

1 cup canola oil

Pepper, to taste

1. Add the beans and 8 cups water to the pressure cooker. Lock the lid into place; bring to high pressure for 1 minute. Remove from the heat and quick-release the pressure.

2. Drain the water, rinse the beans, and add to the pressure cooker again with the remaining 8 cups water. Soak for 1 hour.

3. Add 2 tablespoons olive oil and 2 teaspoons salt. Lock the lid into place; bring to high pressure and maintain for 11 minutes. Remove from the heat and allow pressure to release naturally.

4. While cooking the beans, add the remaining olive oil in a pan and sauté the onion until caramelized. Add the garlic, ginger, and cayenne and sauté 1 minute more. Add the tomatoes and bring to a simmer for 3–5 minutes. Add the mixture to the beans.

5. For the plantains, simply fry in the canola oil. Season with salt and pepper and serve with the red beans.

PER SERVING
Calories: 550 | Fat: 35g | Protein: 12g | Sodium: 15mg |
Carbohydrates: 49g | Fiber: 13g

Red Bean Fritters

*Serve these fritters with a side of sour cream
or vegan sour cream, for dipping.*

INGREDIENTS | SERVES 6–8

1 cup red beans

8 cups water

1 tablespoon olive oil

1 teaspoon salt

1 jalapeño, minced

½ onion, diced

4 cloves garlic, minced

¼ cup cilantro

1 cup flour

1 cup cornmeal

1 tablespoon baking powder

½ cup heavy cream, or unsweetened soymilk

2 eggs, beaten, or 2 teaspoons cornstarch mixed with 2 tablespoons water

2 quarts canola oil, for frying

Salt and pepper, to taste

Alternate Methods of Preparation

To reduce the amount of oil used in this recipe, pan-fry the fritters instead of deep frying. After the fritters are formed, heat 1 tablespoon of oil in a sauté pan over medium heat and cook the fritters for 3 minutes on each side.

1. Add the beans and 4 cups water to the pressure cooker. Lock the lid into place; bring to high pressure for 1 minute. Remove from the heat and quick-release the pressure.

2. Drain the water, rinse the beans, and add to the pressure cooker again with the remaining 4 cups water. Soak for 1 hour.

3. Add the olive oil and salt. Lock the lid into place; bring to high pressure and maintain for 11 minutes. Remove from the heat and allow pressure to release naturally. Drain and set aside.

4. In a bowl, combine the jalapeño, onion, garlic, cilantro, and red beans.

5. In another bowl combine the flour, cornmeal, baking powder, heavy cream, and 2 eggs. Add the bean mixture to the flour mixture and stir until well combined. Form the batter into 1" fritters.

6. In a large pot, heat the canola oil to 350°F and fry the fritters until golden brown, about 3–4 minutes.

PER SERVING
Calories: 710 | Fat: 49g | Protein: 14g | Sodium: 670mg | Carbohydrates: 54g | Fiber: 10g

White Beans with Garlic and Fresh Tomato

Cherry or Roma tomatoes work best for this recipe,
but in a pinch, any variety will do.

INGREDIENTS | SERVES 4–6

1 cup dried cannellini beans

4 cups water

4 cups Vegetable Stock (page 29)

1 tablespoon vegetable oil

1 teaspoon salt

2 cloves garlic, minced

½ cup tomato, diced

½ teaspoon dried sage

½ teaspoon black pepper

1. Add the beans and water to the pressure cooker. Lock the lid into place; bring to high pressure for 1 minute. Remove from the heat and quick-release the pressure.

2. Drain the water, rinse the beans, and add to the pressure cooker again with the stock. Soak for 1 hour.

3. Add the vegetable oil and salt. Lock the lid into place; bring to high pressure and maintain for 10 minutes. Quick-release the pressure.

4. Add all remaining ingredients to the pressure cooker and lock the lid. Bring to high pressure and maintain for 4 minutes. Remove from heat and allow the pressure to release naturally.

PER SERVING
Calories: 230 | Fat: 4g | Protein: 12g | Sodium: 1180mg | Carbohydrates: 38g | Fiber: 8g

White Beans and Rice

It may sound like an odd condiment, but a touch of yellow mustard finishes off this dish surprisingly well.

INGREDIENTS | SERVES 8

2 cups dried white beans

16 cups water

3 tablespoons canola oil

1 cup onion, diced

1 green bell pepper, chopped

1 stalk celery, chopped

3 cloves garlic, minced

2 bay leaves

¼ teaspoon cayenne pepper

Salt and pepper, to taste

4 cups cooked white rice

Flavor Variations

Give this dish Italian flair by adding chopped tomatoes, fresh basil, and chopped and pitted kalamata olives.

1. Add the beans and 8 cups water to the pressure cooker. Lock the lid into place; bring to high pressure for 1 minute. Remove from the heat and quick-release the pressure. Drain the water, rinse the beans, and add to the pressure cooker again with the remaining 8 cups water. Soak for 1 hour. Lock the lid into place; bring to high pressure and maintain for 12 minutes. Remove from the heat and allow pressure to release naturally.

2. Add the oil to a pan and sauté the onion, green pepper, celery, and garlic until they are fragrant and browned. Add the mixture to the pressure cooker along with the bay leaves and cayenne pepper.

3. Lock the lid into place; bring to high pressure and maintain for 10–15 minutes. Remove from the heat and allow pressure to release naturally.

4. Season with salt and pepper and serve over the white rice.

PER SERVING
Calories: 330 | Fat: 6g | Protein: 14g | Sodium: 15mg | Carbohydrates: 56g | Fiber: 9g

White Bean–Leek Purée

Tarragon is a pungent herb that isn't enjoyed by all.
If you don't care for tarragon, replace it with sage in this recipe.

INGREDIENTS | SERVES 4

1 cup dried cannellini beans

4 cups water

4 cups Vegetable Stock (page 29)

1 tablespoon vegetable oil

1 cup thinly sliced leeks

1 teaspoon lemon juice

2 cloves garlic, minced

¼ teaspoon dried tarragon

½ teaspoon salt

1. Add the beans and water to the pressure cooker. Lock the lid into place; bring to high pressure for 1 minute. Remove from the heat and quick-release the pressure.

2. Drain the water, rinse the beans, and add to the pressure cooker again with the stock. Soak for 1 hour.

3. Add the vegetable oil and salt. Lock the lid into place; bring to high pressure and maintain for 10 minutes. Quick-release the pressure.

4. Add all remaining ingredients to the pressure cooker and lock the lid. Bring to high pressure and maintain for 4 minutes. Remove from heat and allow the pressure to release naturally.

5. Pour the beans and remaining liquid into a large food processor or blender and blend until creamy. Season with additional salt, if desired.

PER SERVING
Calories: 240 | Fat: 4g | Protein: 12g | Sodium: 890mg | Carbohydrates: 40g | Fiber: 8g

Wasabi-Barbecue Chickpeas

Most bottled barbecue sauces in your local grocery store are vegetarian, but to be sure, read the label before purchasing.

INGREDIENTS | SERVES 4

1 cup dried chickpeas

8 cups water, plus 1 tablespoon

2 tablespoons vegetable oil

½ cup onion, diced

1 tablespoon wasabi powder

1 cup barbecue sauce

Wasabi

Wasabi is a condiment also known as Japanese horseradish. It has a spicy and pungent flavor that is known to clear nasal passages if enough is consumed.

1. Add the chickpeas and 4 cups water to the pressure cooker. Lock the lid into place; bring to high pressure for 1 minute. Remove from the heat and quick-release the pressure.

2. Drain the water, rinse the chickpeas, and add to the pressure cooker again with the remaining 4 cups water. Soak for 1 hour.

3. Add 1 tablespoon vegetable oil. Lock the lid into place; bring to high pressure and maintain for 20 minutes. Remove from the heat and allow pressure to release naturally. Drain chickpeas and water. Set chickpeas aside.

4. Add the remaining tablespoon of oil to the pressure cooker over medium heat. Sauté the onions until just soft, about 5 minutes.

5. Reconstitute the wasabi powder by combining with 1 tablespoon water, then add to the sautéd onions. Stir in the barbecue sauce and cooked chickpeas.

6. Lock the lid into place; bring to high pressure and maintain for 3 minutes. Remove from the heat and allow pressure to release naturally.

PER SERVING
Calories: 290 | Fat: 10g | Protein: 11g | Sodium: 520mg | Carbohydrates: 39g | Fiber: 7g

Chickpea "Tuna" Salad Sandwich

Chickpeas are also commonly known as garbanzo beans.

INGREDIENTS | SERVES 4

1 cup dried chickpeas

8 cups water

6" piece dried kombu

1 tablespoon vegetable oil

2 tablespoons sweet relish

½ celery stalk, minced

¼ red onion, minced

4 tablespoons mayonnaise, vegan mayonnaise, such as Vegenaise

1 teaspoon lemon juice

½ teaspoon dried dill

1 teaspoon salt

4 sandwich buns

4 lettuce leaves and 4 slices tomato, optional

Kombu

Kombu is a type of edible seaweed that is often sold in sheets. It is often used to flavor soups and other savory dishes because it adds the umami flavor.

1. Add the chickpeas and 4 cups water to the pressure cooker. Lock the lid into place; bring to high pressure for 1 minute. Remove from the heat and quick-release the pressure.

2. Drain the water, rinse the chickpeas, and add to the pressure cooker again with the remaining 4 cups water. Soak for 1 hour.

3. Add the kombu and vegetable oil. Lock the lid into place; bring to high pressure and maintain for 20 minutes. Remove from the heat and allow pressure to release naturally.

4. Once the pressure is released, remove the lid, remove the kombu, and drain the chickpeas.

5. Transfer the drained chickpeas to a large bowl and mash.

6. Add the relish, celery, red onion, mayonnaise, lemon juice, dill, and salt, and stir until well combined. Scoop into a small dish, cover, and refrigerate for 1–2 hours.

7. Divide the mixture evenly over the 4 sandwich buns, top with lettuce and tomato, if desired, and serve.

PER SERVING
Calories: 390 | Fat: 18g | Protein: 12g | Sodium: 880mg | Carbohydrates: 47g | Fiber: 7g

Warm Chickpea Salad

In the summer, you can put the salad in an aluminum baking pan and cook it over indirect heat on a covered grill. Or skip the baking part entirely, chill the salad, and serve it cold.

INGREDIENTS | SERVES 12

1 pound dried chickpeas

10 cups water

1½ tablespoons vegetable oil

2 teaspoons salt

4 green onions, sliced

1 cup red onion, diced

1 small green bell pepper, diced

1 small red bell pepper, diced

½ cup fresh parsley, minced

1 large carrot, peeled and grated

¼ cup extra-virgin olive oil

2 teaspoons fresh lemon juice

2 teaspoons white wine vinegar

1 tablespoon mayonnaise, or vegan mayonnaise, such as Vegenaise

1 clove garlic, minced

⅛ teaspoon freshly ground white pepper

½ teaspoon dried oregano

¼ cup Parmigiano-Reggiano and Romano cheese, grated, or vegan cheese, such as Daiya Mozzarella Style Shreds

1. Rinse and drain the chickpeas. Soak them in 6 cups of water for at least 4 hours or overnight. Drain. Add chickpeas to the pressure cooker along with 4 cups of water and the vegetable oil. Lock the lid in place and bring to high pressure; maintain pressure for 20 minutes. Remove from heat and allow pressure to release naturally. Drain the beans and transfer them to an ovenproof 9" × 13" casserole dish.

2. Add the salt, green onion, red onion, green and red bell peppers, parsley, and carrot to the casserole dish and toss with the beans.

3. Preheat the oven to 375°F.

4. To prepare the dressing, add the oil, lemon juice, vinegar, mayonnaise, garlic, pepper, and oregano to a small bowl or measuring cup. Whisk to mix. Pour the dressing over the bean mixture; stir to combine. Sprinkle the cheese over the dressed beans. Bake for 6 minutes. Stir before serving.

PER SERVING
Calories: 220 | Fat: 9g | Protein: 9g | Sodium: 50mg | Carbohydrates: 26g | Fiber: 6g

Hoppin' John

Hoppin' John is a New Year's Day tradition in the southern United States.

INGREDIENTS | SERVES 4

1 tablespoon olive oil
½ cup onion, diced
1 clove garlic, minced
1 cup dried black-eyed peas
4¾ cups Vegetable Stock (page 29)
1 bay leaf
1 teaspoon chipotle powder
1 teaspoon salt
½ cup dried white rice

1. Pour the olive oil into the pressure cooker and bring to medium heat. Add the onion and sauté for 5 minutes. Add the garlic and sauté 30 seconds.

2. Add the black-eyed peas, stock, bay leaf, chipotle powder, and salt to the pressure cooker. Lock the lid into place; bring to high pressure and maintain for 5 minutes. Quick-release the pressure. Open the lid and pour in the rice. Lock the lid into place; bring to high pressure and maintain for 6 minutes. Allow the pressure to release naturally. Remove the bay leaf before serving.

PER SERVING
Calories: 210 | Fat: 4g | Protein: 10g | Sodium: 1190mg | Carbohydrates: 33g | Fiber: 5g

Lentil-Spinach Curry

*Once-exotic curry powder can now be found in almost any grocery store.
There are several varieties, and any will work in this recipe.*

INGREDIENTS | SERVES 4

1 cup yellow lentils
4 cups water
1 tablespoon olive oil
½ cup onion, diced
1 clove garlic, minced
½ teaspoon coriander
½ teaspoon turmeric
½ teaspoon curry powder
½ cup tomato, diced
2 cups fresh spinach

1. Add the lentils and water to the pressure cooker. Lock the lid into place; bring to high pressure and maintain for 6 minutes. Quick-release the pressure, then drain the beans. Clean the pressure cooker.

2. Add the oil to the pressure cooker over medium heat. Sauté the onion for 3 minutes; add the garlic, coriander, turmeric, and curry powder and sauté for an additional 30 seconds. Stir in the tomato, fresh spinach, and cooked lentils. Simmer for 10 minutes before serving.

PER SERVING
Calories: 220 | Fat: 3.5g | Protein: 15g | Sodium: 15mg | Carbohydrates: 36g | Fiber: 8g

Lentil Pâté

Paté is typically made from ground meat,
but for a vegetarian version try ground beans or mushrooms.

INGREDIENTS | SERVES 8–10

2 cups dried lentils

8 cups water

2 tablespoons olive oil

1 teaspoon salt, plus more to taste

3 tablespoons butter, or vegan margarine, such as Earth Balance

1 cup onion, diced

3 cloves garlic, minced

1 teaspoon red wine vinegar

Pepper, to taste

Serving Suggestions

For an eye-pleasing presentation, pour the pâté into a lightly oiled ramekin and pack tightly. Flip the ramekin over onto a serving dish and gently the remove the ramekin. Serve with a variety of crackers and baguette slices.

1. Add the beans, water, 1 tablespoon olive oil, and 1 teaspoon salt to the pressure cooker.

2. Lock the lid into place; bring to high pressure and maintain for 7 minutes. Remove from the heat and allow pressure to release naturally.

3. Add the butter to a pan and sauté the onion until it begins to turn golden brown. Add the garlic and vinegar, and sauté 1 minute more. Add the mixture to the lentils. Pour the mixture into a food processor and blend until smooth. Taste and season with salt and pepper, if desired.

PER SERVING
Calories: 250 | Fat: 8g | Protein: 15g | Sodium: 290mg | Carbohydrates: 34g | Fiber: 7g

Red Lentil Curry

You can simplify the seasoning in this dish by omitting the turmeric and ginger.

INGREDIENTS | SERVES 8

2 cups dried lentils

8 cups water

3 tablespoons olive oil

1 teaspoon salt, plus more to taste

1 cup onion, diced

1 teaspoon garlic, minced

1 teaspoon ginger, peeled and minced

3 tablespoons curry powder

1 teaspoon turmeric

1 teaspoon cumin

1 teaspoon chili powder

1 teaspoon sugar

1 6-ounce can tomato paste

Pepper, to taste

1. Add the beans, water, 1 tablespoon oil, and 1 teaspoon salt to the pressure cooker.

2. Lock the lid into place; bring to high pressure and maintain for 7 minutes. Remove from the heat and allow pressure to release naturally.

3. In a pan, add the remaining oil and sauté the onion until it is caramelized. Add the garilc and ginger and sauté for 1 minute more. Add the curry powder, turmeric, cumin, chili powder, sugar, and tomato paste, and bring the mixture to a simmer for 2–3 minutes, stirring constantly.

4. Drain the lentils and add to the curry mixture. Taste for seasoning and add salt and pepper if needed.

PER SERVING
Calories: 250 | Fat: 5g | Protein: 15g | Sodium: 380mg | Carbohydrates: 38g | Fiber: 8g

Chana Masala

The main ingredient in the popular Indian dish chana masala is chickpeas.

INGREDIENTS | SERVES 4–6

1 cup dried chickpeas

8 cups water

1 tablespoon vegetable oil

1 tablespoon butter, or vegan margarine, such as Earth Balance

½ onion, diced

1 garlic clove, minced

1 teaspoon ground cumin

¼ teaspoon ground cayenne pepper

½ teaspoon ground turmeric

¼ cup tomatoes, diced

½ cup water

1 teaspoon paprika

½ teaspoon garam masala

1 teaspoon salt

1 tablespoon lemon juice

1 teaspoon ginger, grated

Indian Cuisine

Indian cuisine varies by regions of the country, but they are all similar. Herbs and spices, such as coriander, curry powder, and garam masala are commonly used, as well as rice and a variety of lentils.

1. Add the chickpeas and 4 cups water to the pressure cooker. Lock the lid into place; bring to high pressure for 1 minute. Remove from the heat and quick-release the pressure.

2. Drain the water, rinse the beans, and add to the pressure cooker again with the remaining 4 cups water. Soak for 1 hour.

3. Add the vegetable oil. Lock the lid into place; bring to high pressure and maintain for 20 minutes. Remove from the heat and allow pressure to release naturally. Drain and set chickpeas aside.

4. Add the butter to the pressure cooker over medium heat and sauté the onion and garlic. Add all remaining ingredients, including the cooked chickpeas, and let simmer until the sauce has reduced, about 15–20 minutes.

PER SERVING
Calories: 240 | Fat: 9g | Protein: 11g | Sodium: 590mg | Carbohydrates: 33g | Fiber: 7g

Sea Salt Edamame

Edamame is the same vegetable as baby soybeans
and they're often enjoyed as an appetizer or in salads.

INGREDIENTS | SERVES 4

1 cup edamame, shelled

8 cups water

1 tablespoon vegetable oil

1 teaspoon coarse sea salt

1 tablespoon soy sauce

1. Add the edamame and 4 cups water to the pressure cooker. Lock the lid into place; bring to high pressure for 1 minute. Remove from the heat and quick-release the pressure.

2. Drain the water, rinse the edamame, and add to the pressure cooker again with the remaining 4 cups water. Soak for 1 hour.

3. Add the vegetable oil. Lock the lid into place; bring to high pressure and maintain for 11 minutes. Remove from the heat and allow pressure to release naturally.

4. Once the pressure has released, drain the edamame and transfer to a serving bowl. Sprinkle with coarse sea salt and serve with soy sauce on the side, for dipping.

PER SERVING
Calories: 80 | Fat: 5g | Protein: 4g | Sodium: 850mg |
Carbohydrates: 5g | Fiber: 2g

Edamame-Seaweed Salad

There are many types of edible seaweed.
The most popular varieties include aramae, hijiki, and wakame.

INGREDIENTS | SERVES 4

1 cup edamame, shelled
8 cups water, plus more as needed
1 tablespoon vegetable oil
½ cup dried arame, chopped
1 tablespoon sesame oil
1 clove garlic, minced
½ teaspoon fresh ginger, minced
1 teaspoon rice wine vinegar
1 teaspoon salt

1. Add the edamame and 4 cups water to the pressure cooker. Lock the lid into place; bring to high pressure for 1 minute. Remove from the heat and quick-release the pressure.

2. Drain the water, rinse the edamame, and add to the pressure cooker again with the remaining 4 cups water. Soak for 1 hour.

3. Add the vegetable oil. Lock the lid into place; bring to high pressure and maintain for 11 minutes. Remove from the heat and allow pressure to release naturally. Drain and set aside.

4. While the edamame is cooking, cover the arame with water in a small bowl and let sit for 7 minutes. Drain and set aside.

5. In a small sauté pan, heat the sesame oil over medium heat. Add the garlic and ginger and sauté for 30 seconds. Add the vinegar and salt, then the cooked edamame and arame.

6. Serve warm or chilled.

PER SERVING
Calories: 120 | Fat: 8g | Protein: 4g | Sodium: 600mg | Carbohydrates: 6g | Fiber: 2g

Dinner Loaf

*You won't be missing the meatloaf on your
dinner table if you try this dinner loaf instead!*

1 cup dried pinto beans

8 cups water

1 tablespoon vegetable oil

1 teaspoon salt

1 cup onion, diced

1 cup chopped walnuts

½ cup plain dried oats

1 egg, beaten, or 1 teaspoon cornstarch
combined with 1 tablespoon water

¾ cup ketchup

1 teaspoon garlic powder

1 teaspoon dried basil

1 teaspoon dried parsley

Salt and pepper, to taste

Mock Meatloaf

There are many ingredients you can use to
make mock meatloaf. For the easiest
option, use vegetarian ground beef, such
as Gimme Lean Ground Beef, instead of
real meat in your favorite recipe.

1. Add the beans and 4 cups water to the pressure
   cooker. Lock the lid into place; bring to high pressure
   for 1 minute. Remove from the heat and quick-release
   the pressure.

2. Drain the water, rinse the beans, and add to the pressure cooker again with the remaining 4 cups water.
   Soak for 1 hour.

3. Add the vegetable oil and salt. Lock the lid into place;
   bring to high pressure and maintain for 11 minutes.
   Remove from the heat and allow pressure to release
   naturally. Drain the beans and pour into a large mixing bowl.

4. Combine the rest of the ingredients with the beans.
   Spread the mixture into a loaf pan and bake at 350°F
   for 30–35 minutes.

PER SERVING
Calories: 340 | Fat: 17g | Protein: 13g | Sodium: 730mg |
Carbohydrates: 38g | Fiber: 9g

CHAPTER 10

Burgers

Spicy Black Bean Burger

Black bean burgers are one of the most commonly consumed homemade veggie burgers. Omit the spice from this recipe to use it as a base for your own veggie burger creation.

INGREDIENTS | SERVES 2

1 cup dried black beans

8 cups water

2 tablespoons vegetable oil

1 teaspoon salt, plus more to taste

1 jalapeño, seeded and minced

3 cloves garlic, minced

½ onion, diced

1 tablespoon chili powder

1 tablespoon cumin

½ cup panko bread crumbs

¼ cup parsley, chopped

Pepper, to taste

1. Add the beans and 4 cups water to the pressure cooker. Lock the lid into place; bring to high pressure for 1 minute. Remove from the heat and quick-release the pressure.

2. Drain the water, rinse the beans, and add to the pressure cooker again with the remaining 4 cups of water. Let soak for 1 hour.

3. Add 1 tablespoon of the vegetable oil and 1 teaspoon salt. Lock the lid into place; bring to high pressure and maintain for 12 minutes. Remove from the heat and allow pressure to release naturally. Drain the beans.

4. Pour the beans into a large bowl and add the rest of the ingredients except remaining oil. Mash the mixture with a potato masher. Form the bean mixture into burger patties. Add the remaining oil to a pan and cook the burgers until they are browned on both sides.

PER SERVING
Calories: 600 | Fat: 17g | Protein: 24g | Sodium: 1410mg | Carbohydrates: 88g | Fiber: 13g

Pinto Bean Burger

Making homemade burgers can be time consuming for a busy family, even with a pressure cooker. If you're pressed for time, try a frozen burger, such as Boca, instead.

INGREDIENTS | SERVES 6–8

1 cup dried pinto beans

8 cups water

2 tablespoons vegetable oil

1 teaspoon salt, plus more to taste

1 onion, diced

1 cup walnuts, chopped

½ cup oats

1 egg, beaten, or 2 teaspoons cornstarch combined with 2 tablespoons warm water

¾ cup ketchup

1 teaspoon garlic powder

1 teaspoon dried basil

1 teaspoon dried parsley

Pepper, to taste

1. Add the beans and 4 cups water to the pressure cooker. Lock the lid into place; bring to high pressure for 1 minute. Remove from the heat and quick-release the pressure.

2. Drain the water, rinse the beans, and add to the pressure cooker again with the remaining 4 cups of water. Let soak for 1 hour.

3. Add 1 tablespoon vegetable oil and 1 teaspoon salt. Lock the lid into place; bring to high pressure and maintain for 11 minutes. Remove from the heat and allow pressure to release naturally. Drain the beans.

4. Combine the rest of the ingredients except remaining oil. Mash the mixture with a potato masher. Form the bean mixture into burger patties. Add the remaining oil to a pan and cook the burgers until they are browned on both sides.

PER SERVING
Calories: 350 | Fat: 19g | Protein: 12g | Sodium: 780mg | Carbohydrates: 36g | Fiber: 8g

Roasted Vegetable Burger

Roasting veggies before mixing into the patty mixture will bring out more flavor in the bell pepper, onion, squash, and zucchini.

INGREDIENTS | SERVES 2–4

1 cup dried black beans

8 cups water

2 tablespoons vegetable oil

1 teaspoon salt, plus more to taste

½ onion, chopped

½ red bell pepper, chopped

½ cup yellow squash, chopped

½ zucchini, chopped

4 cloves garlic, minced

1 tablespoon extra-virgin olive oil

½ jalapeño, seeded and minced

½ cup panko bread crumbs

Pepper, to taste

1. Add the beans and 4 cups water to the pressure cooker. Lock the lid into place; bring to high pressure for 1 minute. Remove from the heat and quick-release the pressure.

2. Drain the water, rinse the beans, and add to the pressure cooker again with the remaining 4 cups of water. Let soak for 1 hour.

3. Add 1 tablespoon vegetable oil and 1 tablespoon salt. Lock the lid into place; bring to high pressure and maintain for 12 minutes. Remove from the heat and allow pressure to release naturally. Drain the beans and set aside.

4. Preheat the oven to 450°F. Toss the onion, bell pepper, yellow squash, zucchini, and garlic in the olive oil. Place on a baking sheet and cook for 30–35 minutes in the oven, turning once.

5. Pour the beans into a large bowl and add the rest of the ingredients except remaining 1 tablespoon vegetable oil. Mash the mixture with a potato masher. Form the bean mixture into burger patties. Add the remaining oil to a pan and cook the burgers until they are browned on both sides.

PER SERVING
Calories: 670 | Fat: 23g | Protein: 26g | Sodium: 1370mg | Carbohydrates: 92g | Fiber: 13g

Beet Red Burger

*Beets will give your burger the appearance
of rare meat but without all of the fat.*

INGREDIENTS | SERVES 4

5 beets, quartered

1½ cups water

½ cup onions, chopped

1½ cups walnuts, chopped

2 eggs, beaten, or 4 teaspoons
cornstarch combined with 4 tablespoons
warm water

2 tablespoons soy sauce

1 cup Cheddar cheese, grated, or vegan
Cheddar, such as Daiya Cheddar Style
Shreds

⅛ cup flour

2 tablespoons olive oil

Salt and pepper, to taste

1. Add the beets and the water to the pressure cooker. Lock the lid into place; bring to high pressure for 8 minutes. Remove from the heat and quick-release the pressure. Drain the beets and add to a mixing bowl.

2. Combine the rest of the ingredients with the beets. Mash the mixture with a potato masher. Form the beet mixture into burger patties.

3. Preheat the oven to 350°F. Place the patties on a greased baking sheet and bake for 25–30 minutes.

PER SERVING
Calories: 580 | Fat: 48g | Protein: 20g | Sodium: 790mg |
Carbohydrates: 22g | Fiber: 6g

Brown Rice Burger

Protein and iron are two of the vital nutrients found in brown rice.

INGREDIENTS | SERVES 4

1 cup long-grain brown rice

2 cups water

½ cup mushrooms, chopped

½ cup corn, chopped

½ cup carrot, shredded

¼ onion, diced

Salt and pepper, to taste

2 cups bread crumbs

1 tablespoon olive oil

1. Add the rice and water to the pressure cooker. Lock the lid into place; bring to high pressure and maintain for 15 minutes. Remove from the heat and allow pressure to release naturally. Fluff with a fork.

2. Combine the rice, mushrooms, corn, carrot, onion, salt, and pepper. Mash the mixture and form into patties. Dredge with bread crumbs and set aside. Add the olive oil to a pan and fry the burgers over medium heat until they are browned on each side.

PER SERVING
Calories: 440 | Fat: 8g | Protein: 12g | Sodium: 410mg |
Carbohydrates: 81g | Fiber: 5g

BBQ Tempeh Burger

It's recommended that you always marinate tempeh or cook tempeh in liquid for optimal results. If you don't, it can easily become too dry to eat.

INGREDIENTS | SERVES 4–6

1 cup lentils

1 8-ounce package tempeh, crumbled

4½ cups water

1 tablespoon vegetable oil

1 teaspoon salt, plus more to taste

½ cup flour

½ cup mustard

¼ cup sugar

⅛ cup brown sugar

¼ cup cider vinegar

1 tablespoon chili powder

⅛ teaspoon cayenne pepper

½ teaspoon soy sauce

1 tablespoon butter, melted, or vegan margarine, such as Earth Balance

½ tablespoon liquid smoke

Pepper, to taste

1. Add the lentils, tempeh, water, oil, and 1 teaspoon salt to the pressure cooker.

2. Lock the lid into place; bring to high pressure and maintain for 7 minutes. Remove from the heat and allow pressure to release naturally. Drain the lentils and tempeh and add to a large mixing bowl.

3. Combine the rest of the ingredients with the lentils and tempeh. Mash the mixture with a potato masher. Form the tempeh mixture into burger patties.

4. Preheat the oven to 350°F. Place the burgers on a greased baking sheet. Bake in the oven for 25–30 minutes, flipping after 15 minutes.

PER SERVING
Calories: 480 | Fat: 11g | Protein: 28g | Sodium: 1040mg | Carbohydrates: 73g | Fiber: 12g

Tropical Veggie Burger

To tone down this flavor-rich burger,
feel free to omit one or more of the spices.

INGREDIENTS | SERVES 2–4

1 cup red lentils

¼ cup brown rice

5 cups water

2 tablespoons vegetable oil

1 teaspoon salt

1½ tablespoons butter, or vegan margarine, such as Earth Balance

1 onion, chopped

4 teaspoons curry powder

⅓ cup carrots, shredded

2 tablespoons white wine

2 tablespoons hot sauce

½ cup panko bread crumbs

4 garlic cloves, minced

4 teaspoons fresh ginger, minced

½ teaspoon allspice

1 teaspoon cumin

1. Add the lentils, brown rice, water, 1 tablespoon of oil, and salt to the pressure cooker.

2. Lock the lid into place; bring to high pressure and maintain for 7 minutes. Remove from the heat and allow pressure to release naturally. Drain the rice and lentils and set aside.

3. Add the butter to a pan and sauté the onion until it begins to caramelize. Add the curry powder, carrots, and white wine. Sauté for 1 minute longer.

4. Pour the lentils and rice into a large bowl and add the rest of the ingredients except remaining oil. Mash the mixture with a potato masher. Form the bean mixture into burger patties. Add the remaining oil to a pan and cook the burgers until they are browned on both sides.

PER SERVING
Calories: 770 | Fat: 26g | Protein: 30g | Sodium: 620mg | Carbohydrates: 106g | Fiber: 20g

Serving Suggestions

Typical burger toppings, such as ketchup and mustard, might not be the best condiments for this burger. Try topping it with a grilled pineapple ring or mango salsa.

Bulgur-Nut Burger

Try topping this basic burger with avocado slices or traditional toppings, such as lettuce, tomato, and cheese.

INGREDIENTS | SERVES 4–6

1 cup bulgur
3 cups Vegetable Stock (page 29)
2 tablespoons olive oil
½ cup onion, diced
2 garlic cloves, minced
2 cups canned pinto beans, drained
¾ cup walnuts
½ cup cilantro, chopped
1 teaspoon cumin
¼ teaspoon cayenne pepper

1. Add the bulgur and stock to the pressure cooker.

2. Lock the lid into place; bring to high pressure and maintain for 9 minutes. Remove from the heat and allow pressure to release naturally.

3. In a pan, add 1 tablespoon of the olive oil and sauté the onion until it begins to caramelize. Add the garlic and sauté for 1 minute more. Add the pinto beans and cook until the beans are tender. Add a little water if needed.

4. In a large bowl, combine all of the ingredients except remaining oil. Put the mixture in a food processor and pulse until it is finely chopped. Form the mixture into patties.

5. Add 1 tablespoon of olive oil to a pan and fry the patties until they are browned on both sides.

PER SERVING
Calories: 440 | Fat: 21g | Protein: 13g | Sodium: 800mg | Carbohydrates: 55g | Fiber: 14g

Smoked Portobello Burger

*Portobello mushroom caps can be cooked in a pressure cooker,
on a stovetop, on a grill, or in the oven.*

INGREDIENTS | SERVES 4

4 large portobello mushroom caps
¼ cup red wine vinegar
2 tablespoons extra-virgin olive oil
1 tablespoon shallots, minced
½ tablespoon soy sauce
Salt and pepper, to taste
1 cup water
1 tablespoon liquid smoke

Liquid Smoke

Liquid smoke helps give food a true barbecue flavor without the hassle of traditional barbecue cooking. It's often sold in small bottles in the condiment aisle (near steak sauce, ketchup, and mustard), or can be ordered online. Use liquid smoke by combining with a liquid when cooking, or brush directly onto ingredients such as mushrooms or veggie burgers.

1. Place the mushrooms in a shallow dish. In a small bowl, mix the red wine vinegar, olive oil, shallots, soy sauce, salt, and pepper. Pour the mixture over the mushrooms and allow them to marinate for about 20 minutes, turning 2–3 times throughout.

2. Pour the water and liquid smoke into the pressure cooker and place the steamer tray inside. Place the mushrooms on top of the steamer tray.

3. Lock the lid into place; bring to high pressure and maintain for 5 minutes. Remove from the heat and allow pressure to release naturally.

PER SERVING
Calories: 90 | Fat: 7g | Protein: 2g | Sodium: 130mg | Carbohydrates: 5g | Fiber: 1g

"Bacon" and Avocado Burger

There are plenty of tasty vegetarian "bacon" options at your local health food store or a national grocery store chain near you. Use one of these fast-cooking options if you don't have time to make your own.

INGREDIENTS | SERVES 4

1 cup dried black beans
8 cups water
2 tablespoons vegetable oil
1 teaspoon salt
1 jalapeño, seeded and minced
3 cloves garlic, minced
½ onion, diced
1 tablespoon chili powder
1 tablespoon cumin
½ cup panko bread crumbs
¼ cup parsley
Salt and pepper, to taste
8–12 pieces of Tempeh Bacon (page 217)
1 avocado, sliced

1. Add the beans and 4 cups water to the pressure cooker. Lock the lid into place; bring to high pressure for 1 minute. Remove from the heat and quick-release the pressure.

2. Drain the water, rinse the beans, and add to the pressure cooker again with the remaining 4 cups of water. Let soak for 1 hour.

3. Add 1 tablespoon of the vegetable oil and salt. Lock the lid into place; bring to high pressure and maintain for 12 minutes. Remove from the heat and allow pressure to release naturally. Drain the beans.

4. Pour the beans into a large bowl and add the rest of the ingredients except remaining oil, tempeh bacon, and avocado. Mash the mixture with a potato masher. Form the bean mixture into burger patties. Add the remaining oil to a pan and cook the burgers until they are browned on both sides.

5. Top each of the hamburgers with 1 cooked patty, Tempeh Bacon, and avocado slices.

PER SERVING
Calories: 730 | Fat: 31g | Protein: 40g | Sodium: 3930mg | Carbohydrates: 78g | Fiber: 18g

Onion, Mushroom, and Cheese-Stuffed Burger

*To make this burger in a hurry, use canned beans instead
of dried beans and cook for 1 minute to warm through.*

INGREDIENTS | SERVES 2–4

1 cup dried black beans

8 cups water

3 tablespoons vegetable oil

1 teaspoon salt

½ onion, diced

2 cups white mushrooms, chopped

2 cloves garlic, minced

¾ cup panko bread crumbs

½ tablespoon cumin

1 teaspoon chili powder

½ teaspoon dried thyme

Salt and pepper, to taste

8 slices Swiss cheese, or vegan mozzarella, such as Daiya Mozzarella Style Shreds

1. Add the beans and 4 cups water to the pressure cooker. Lock the lid into place; bring to high pressure for 1 minute. Remove from the heat and quick-release the pressure.

2. Drain the water, rinse the beans, and add to the pressure cooker again with the remaining 4 cups of water. Let soak for 1 hour.

3. Add 1 tablespoon of the vegetable oil and salt. Lock the lid into place; bring to high pressure and maintain for 12 minutes. Remove from the heat and allow pressure to release naturally. Drain the beans.

4. Pour the beans into a large bowl and add the rest of the ingredients, except the remaining oil and the Swiss cheese. Mash the mixture with a potato masher. Fold a slice of cheese in half and form the patties around the cheese to make a stuffed burger.

5. Add the rest of the oil to the pan and cook the burgers until they are browned on both sides.

PER SERVING
Calories: 1140 | Fat: 56g | Protein: 58g | Sodium: 1700mg | Carbohydrates: 102g | Fiber: 13g

South of the Border Burger

Think "Mexican" when deciding on toppings for this festive burger.
Try avocado, pickled jalapeño slices, or even salsa.

INGREDIENTS | SERVES 2–4

1 cup dried black beans

8 cups water

2 tablespoons vegetable oil

1 teaspoon salt

½ green bell pepper, chopped

½ onion, diced

3 cloves garlic, minced

1 egg, or 2 teaspoons cornstarch combined with 2 tablespoons warm water

1 tablespoon cumin

1 teaspoon chipotle chili powder

½ cup salsa

½ cup panko bread crumbs

Salt and pepper, to taste

1. Add the beans and 4 cups water to the pressure cooker. Lock the lid into place; bring to high pressure for 1 minute. Remove from the heat and quick-release the pressure.

2. Drain the water, rinse the beans, and add to the pressure cooker again with the remaining 4 cups of water. Let soak for 1 hour.

3. Add 1 tablespoon of the vegetable oil and salt. Lock the lid into place; bring to high pressure and maintain for 12 minutes. Remove from the heat and allow pressure to release naturally. Drain the beans and pour into a large mixing bowl.

4. Add all of the ingredients except remaining oil to the bowl. Mash with a potato masher and form the mixture into patties.

5. Add remaining oil to a pan and cook the burgers until they are brown on both sides.

PER SERVING
Calories: 650 | Fat: 19g | Protein: 28g | Sodium: 1810mg | Carbohydrates: 91g | Fiber: 13g

Chili Cheeseburger

If you are short on time, try using a store-bought vegetarian chili,
such as Hormel's vegetarian canned chili.

INGREDIENTS | SERVES 6–8

1 cup dried black beans

8 cups water

2 tablespoons vegetable oil

1 teaspoon salt

1 jalapeño, seeded and minced

3 cloves garlic, minced

½ onion, diced

1 tablespoon chili powder

1 tablespoon cumin

½ cup panko bread crumbs

¼ cup parsley

Salt and pepper, to taste

6–8 hamburger buns

6–8 slices American cheese, or vegan Cheddar

2 cups Speedy Chili con "Carne" (page 176)

1. Add the beans and 4 cups water to the pressure cooker. Lock the lid into place; bring to high pressure for 1 minute. Remove from the heat and quick-release the pressure.

2. Drain the water, rinse the beans, and add to the pressure cooker again with the remaining 4 cups of water. Let soak for 1 hour.

3. Add 1 tablespoon of the vegetable oil and salt. Lock the lid into place; bring to high pressure and maintain for 12 minutes. Remove from the heat and allow pressure to release naturally. Drain the beans.

4. Pour the beans into a large bowl and add the rest of the ingredients except remaining oil, buns, cheese, and chili. Mash the mixture with a potato masher. Form the bean mixture into burger patties. Add the remaining oil to a pan and cook the burgers until they are browned on both sides.

5. Place 1 patty on each hamburger bun and top with a slice of cheese. Melt the cheese under a broiler or in the microwave for a few seconds, then top with a scoop of chili.

PER SERVING
Calories: 480 | Fat: 18g | Protein: 25g | Sodium: 1750mg | Carbohydrates: 55g | Fiber: 9g

Quinoa Burger

*Quinoa is a lesser-known grain popular with some vegetarians because
of its high protein and iron content and fast cooking time.*

INGREDIENTS | SERVES 2

½ cup quinoa

1 cup water

1 carrot, shredded

½ onion, diced

2 15-ounce cans white beans, drained

1 egg, beaten, or 2 teaspoons
cornstarch combined with 2 tablespoons
warm water

1 tablespoon cumin

1 teaspoon dried sage or basil

Salt and pepper, to taste

1 tablespoon olive oil

1. Add the quinoa and water to the pressure cooker.

2. Lock the lid into place; bring to high pressure and
   maintain for 6 minutes. Remove from the heat and
   allow pressure to release naturally. Fluff with a fork.

3. In a large bowl, combine all the ingredients except
   olive oil and mash with a potato masher. Form the
   mixture into patties.

4. Add the olive oil to a pan and cook the burgers until
   they are browned on each side.

PER SERVING
Calories: 800 | Fat: 14g | Protein: 41g | Sodium: 95mg |
Carbohydrates: 132g | Fiber: 26g

Loaded Mushroom Burger

Stuffed and topped, this burger is at maximum mushroom capacity!

INGREDIENTS | SERVES 2

1 cup dried black beans
8 cups water
3 tablespoons vegetable oil
1 teaspoon salt
½ onion, diced
2 cups white mushrooms, chopped
2 cloves garlic, minced
¾ cup panko bread crumbs
½ tablespoon cumin
1 teaspoon chili powder
½ teaspoon dried thyme
Salt and pepper, to taste
1 teaspoon olive oil
¼ onion, sliced
½ cup button mushrooms, sliced
2 hamburger buns

1. Add the beans and 4 cups water to the pressure cooker. Lock the lid into place; bring to high pressure for 1 minute. Remove from the heat and quick-release the pressure. Drain the water, rinse the beans, and add to the pressure cooker again with the remaining 4 cups of water. Let soak for 1 hour.

2. Add 1 tablespoon vegetable oil and salt. Lock the lid into place; bring to high pressure, and maintain for 12 minutes. Remove from the heat and allow pressure to release naturally. Drain the beans and pour into a large mixing bowl.

3. Add 1 tablespoon of vegetable oil to a pan and sauté the onions until they begin to caramelize. Add the mushrooms and garlic and sauté for 2–3 minutes more.

4. Add the onions, mushrooms, garlic, bread crumbs, cumin, chili powder, thyme, salt, and pepper to the bowl of beans, and mash with a potato masher. Form the mixture into patties.

5. Add 1 tablespoon vegetable oil to a pan and cook the burgers until they are browned on both sides. After the burgers are done, heat the olive oil in a clean sauté pan over medium heat. Add the sliced onions and sauté until they begin to soften, about 3 minutes. Add sliced button mushrooms and sauté for 2 additional minutes.

6. Top each of the hamburger buns with 1 cooked patty, half of the onion-mushroom mixture, and your favorite condiments.

PER SERVING
Calories: 810 | Fat: 27g | Protein: 30g | Sodium: 1610mg |
Carbohydrates: 112g | Fiber: 14g

CHAPTER 11

Chilis and Stews

Vegetable Chili

Canned beans can also be used in a pressure cooker for an even faster protein-rich meal.

INGREDIENTS | SERVES 8

2 tablespoons olive or vegetable oil

1 large sweet onion, diced

3 cloves garlic, minced

1 15-ounce can pinto beans, rinsed and drained

1 15-ounce can kidney beans, rinsed and drained

1 15-ounce can cannellini or white beans, rinsed and drained

1 large green bell pepper, seeded and diced

2 cups zucchini, diced

1½ cups corn

1 28-ounce can diced tomatoes

2 cups Vegetable Stock (page 29)

2 tablespoons chili powder

1 teaspoon cumin

1 teaspoon dried oregano

¼ teaspoon freshly ground black pepper

⅛ teaspoon cayenne pepper

Salt, to taste

8 ounces shredded Monterey jack cheese, or vegan Monterey jack cheese

1. Bring the oil to temperature in the pressure cooker over medium heat. Add the onion; sauté for 3 minutes or until it begins to soften. Stir in the garlic; sauté for 30 seconds. Stir in the canned beans, green bell pepper, zucchini, corn, tomatoes, stock, chili powder, cumin, oregano, black pepper, and cayenne pepper. Stir to mix.

2. Lock the lid into place and bring to high pressure; maintain pressure for 5 minutes. Remove from the heat and allow pressure to release naturally.

3. Remove the lid, stir, and taste for seasoning. Add salt if desired. Serve topped with grated cheese.

PER SERVING
Calories: 370 | Fat: 14g | Protein: 20g | Sodium: 690mg | Carbohydrates: 47g | Fiber: 12g

Black Bean and Lentil Chili

If you prefer hotter chili, substitute a Scotch bonnet or serrano pepper for the jalapeño.

INGREDIENTS | SERVES 6

2 tablespoons vegetable oil

1 large Spanish onion, diced

1 jalapeño, seeded and minced

1 clove garlic, minced

1 cup brown or green lentils

1 15½-ounce can black beans, drained and rinsed

1 cup pearl barley

3 tablespoons chili powder

1 tablespoon sweet paprika

1 teaspoon dried oregano

1 teaspoon ground cumin

1 28-ounce can diced tomatoes

6 cups Vegetable Stock (page 29)

Optional: 1 12-ounce can chipotle peppers in adobo sauce

Salt and pepper, to taste

Handling Peppers

Scotch bonnet peppers are some of the hottest peppers in the world and must be handled carefully if you choose to use them in this recipe. Wear gloves while handling and wash your hands thoroughly once gloves are removed.

1. Bring the oil to temperature in the pressure cooker over medium heat. Add the onion; sauté for 3 minutes. Stir in the jalapeño; sauté for 1 minute.

2. Stir in the garlic; sauté for 30 seconds. Stir in the lentils, black beans, barley, chili powder, paprika, oregano, cumin, undrained tomatoes, and stock. If using, mince 1 or more chipotle peppers and add them along with some sauce to taste.

3. Lock the lid into place and bring to high pressure; maintain for 10 minutes. Remove from the heat and allow pressure to release naturally for 10 minutes. Quick-release any remaining pressure. Remove the lid. Stir and check that the lentils and barley are tender. If not, lock the lid back into place, return to the heat, and bring to pressure for 2–3 more minutes. Remove from heat and allow pressure to release naturally.

4. Remove the lid and return the pan to the heat. Bring to a simmer. Taste for seasoning, and add salt and pepper if needed. Simmer until slightly thickened.

PER SERVING
Calories: 380 | Fat: 6g | Protein: 15g | Sodium: 1060mg | Carbohydrates: 73g | Fiber: 18g

Red Bean Chili

Use this basic chili recipe as the foundation for your own creation and add a variety of vegetables or faux meats while cooking. Or you can serve it plain over rice.

INGREDIENTS | SERVES 4–6

2 cups dried kidney beans

16 cups water

1 tablespoon olive oil

½ cup onion, diced

2 cloves garlic, minced

8 cups Vegetable Stock (page 29)

1 tablespoon chili powder

½ tablespoon chipotle powder

½ tablespoon cumin

½ tablespoon paprika

2 cups fresh tomatoes, diced

2 teaspoons salt

1. Add the beans and 8 cups water to the pressure cooker. Lock the lid into place; bring to high pressure for 1 minute. Remove from the heat and quick-release the pressure.

2. Drain the water, rinse the beans, and add to the pressure cooker again with the remaining 8 cups of water. Let soak for 1 hour and then drain.

3. Heat the oil in the empty pressure cooker over medium heat. Add the onions and sauté about 3 minutes. Add the garlic and cook for an additional 30 seconds.

4. Add all remaining ingredients. Lock the lid into place; bring to high pressure and maintain for 15 minutes. Remove from heat and allow pressure to release naturally.

5. If the desired consistency has not been reached, place the chili back on the burner over medium-low heat and simmer with the lid off.

PER SERVING
Calories: 440 | Fat: 5g | Protein: 24g | Sodium: 2380mg | Carbohydrates: 78g | Fiber: 23g

Cincinnati Chili

Cincinnati chili is native to the state of Ohio and is typically eaten over spaghetti or on hot dogs.

INGREDIENTS | SERVES 4–6

1 tablespoon olive oil

1 onion, chopped

1 12-ounce package frozen veggie burger crumbles

1 clove garlic, minced

1 cup tomato sauce

1 cup water

2 tablespoons red wine vinegar

2 tablespoons chili powder

½ teaspoon cumin

½ teaspoon ground cinnamon

½ teaspoon paprika

½ teaspoon ground allspice

1 tablespoon light brown sugar

1 tablespoon unsweetened cocoa powder

1 teaspoon hot pepper sauce

16 ounces cooked spaghetti

Optional: shredded Cheddar, or vegan Cheddar, such as Daiya Cheddar Style Shreds

Optional: diced white onion *or* beans

1. Heat the oil in the pressure cooker over medium heat. Add the onions and sauté about 3 minutes. Add the burger crumbles and garlic and cook until the crumbles are heated.

2. Add the tomato sauce, water, vinegar, chili powder, cumin, cinnamon, paprika, allspice, light brown sugar, cocoa powder, and hot sauce. Lock the lid into place; bring to high pressure and maintain for 5 minutes. Quick-release the pressure and remove the lid.

3. Continue to simmer, without the lid, until the sauce has thickened.

4. Serve over cooked pasta and topped with cheese and onions, if desired.

PER SERVING
Calories: 380 | Fat: 9g | Protein: 24g | Sodium: 740mg | Carbohydrates: 54g | Fiber: 9g

Ways to Serve

Cincinnati chili is known for being served up to five ways: "Two-way" means chili and spaghetti; "three-way" means chili, spaghetti, and cheese; "four-way" means chili, spaghetti, cheese, and onions *or* beans; and "five-way" means all of the above!

Southwest Chili

Southwest cuisine is similar to Mexican and is known for its spiciness.

INGREDIENTS | SERVES 4–6

2 cups dried kidney beans

16 cups water

1 tablespoon vegetable oil

1 large onion, diced

1 red bell pepper, diced

1 cup uncooked corn kernels

2 cups fresh tomato, diced

2 tablespoons tomato paste

1 4-ounce can chopped green chilies

8 cups Vegetable Stock (page 29)

1 tablespoon chili powder

1 teaspoon ground cumin

1 teaspoon salt

Optional: chopped cilantro

Optional: shredded Cheddar, or vegan Cheddar, such as Daiya Cheddar Style Shreds

1. Add the beans and 8 cups water to the pressure cooker. Lock the lid into place; bring to high pressure for 1 minute. Remove from the heat and quick-release the pressure.

2. Drain the water, rinse the beans, and add to the pressure cooker again with the remaining 8 cups of water. Let soak for 1 hour and then drain.

3. Heat the oil in the empty pressure cooker over medium heat. Add the onions and red bell pepper and sauté about 3 minutes. Add the corn, tomato, tomato paste, chilies, stock, chili powder, cumin, and salt. Stir to combine.

4. Lock the lid into place; bring to high pressure and maintain for 15 minutes. Remove from heat and allow pressure to release naturally.

5. If the desired consistency has not been reached, place the chili back on the burner over medium-low heat and simmer with the lid off.

6. Serve topped with cilantro and cheese, if desired.

PER SERVING
Calories: 500 | Fat: 6g | Protein: 26g | Sodium: 1970mg | Carbohydrates: 91g | Fiber: 25g

Speedy Chili con "Carne"

*Try Boca Ground Crumbles in this fast recipe
as a vegan alternative to ground beef.*

INGREDIENTS | SERVES 4–6

1 tablespoon olive oil

½ cup onion, diced

½ cup bell pepper, diced

1 12-ounce package frozen veggie burger crumbles

2 cloves garlic, minced

1 15-ounce can kidney beans, rinsed and drained

2 cups Vegetable Stock (page 29)

1 tablespoon chili powder

½ tablespoon chipotle powder

½ tablespoon cumin

1 teaspoon thyme

1 tablespoon oregano

2 cups fresh tomatoes, diced

1 tablespoon tomato paste

1 tablespoon cider vinegar

2 teaspoons salt

1. Heat the oil in the pressure cooker over medium heat. Add the onions and bell pepper and sauté about 3 minutes. Add the burger crumbles and garlic and cook until the crumbles are heated.

2. Add all remaining ingredients. Lock the lid into place; bring to high pressure and maintain for 10 minutes. Remove from heat and allow pressure to release naturally.

3. If the desired consistency has not been reached, place the chili back on the burner over medium-low heat and simmer with the lid off.

PER SERVING
Calories: 310 | Fat: 9g | Protein: 24g | Sodium: 2180mg | Carbohydrates: 36g | Fiber: 12g

Vegan Beef

In addition to Boca Ground Crumbles there are other types of vegetarian ground beef on the market. Try Gimme Lean Ground Beef Style or Morningstar Farms Crumbles (not suitable for vegans) for a prepackaged option. Or try using rehydrated texturized vegetable protein (TVP).

Five Pepper Chili

Sound the alarm! This chili will set mouths aflame.

INGREDIENTS | SERVES 6

1 tablespoon vegetable oil

1 onion, diced

1 jalapeño, seeded and minced

1 habanero pepper, seeded and minced

1 bell pepper, diced

1 poblano pepper, seeded and diced

2 cloves garlic, minced

2 14½-ounce cans crushed tomatoes

2 cups fresh tomatoes, diced

2 tablespoons chili powder

1 tablespoon cumin

½ tablespoon cayenne pepper

⅛ cup vegan Worcestershire sauce

4 cups cooked Pinto Beans (page 129)

Salt and pepper, to taste

1. Add the vegetable oil to the pressure cooker and sauté the onion until it has caramelized. Add the jalapeño, habanero, bell, and poblano peppers and sauté for 1 minute more. Add the garlic, crushed tomatoes, fresh tomatoes, chili powder, cumin, cayenne pepper, Worcestershire, beans, salt, and pepper.

2. Lock the lid into place; bring to high pressure and maintain for 12 minutes. Remove from the heat and allow pressure to release naturally. Serve.

PER SERVING
Calories: 580 | Fat: 14g | Protein: 30g | Sodium: 1690mg | Carbohydrates: 90g | Fiber: 27g

Gumbo

Gumbo is a popular dish across Louisiana that is traditionally made with meat or seafood, but you can you use vegetables instead to create "gumbo z'herbes."

INGREDIENTS | SERVES 6

½ cup vegetable oil

½ cup flour

1 white onion, diced

1 bell pepper, diced

2 stalks celery, diced

4 cloves garlic, minced

4 cups water

2 cups Vegetable Stock (page 29)

1 tablespoon vegan Worcestershire sauce

1 16-ounce package frozen chopped okra

1 tablespoon Cajun seasoning

1 bay leaf

2 teaspoons salt

2 teaspoons black pepper

1 pound vegan chicken, chopped

½ cup flat leaf parsley, chopped

½ cup scallions, sliced

½ teaspoon filé powder

6 cups cooked white rice

1. Bring the oil and flour to medium heat in the pressure cooker. Stir continuously until the roux achieves a rich brown color, about 25 minutes.

2. Add the onion, bell pepper, celery, and garlic to the roux and sauté for 5 minutes. Add the water and bring to a boil over high heat for 20 minutes.

3. Add the stock, vegan Worcestershire sauce, okra, Cajun seasoning, bay leaf, salt, and pepper. Lock the lid into place; bring to low pressure and maintain for 1 hour. Allow pressure to release naturally.

4. Add all remaining ingredients except the rice and cook over low heat for 10 minutes.

5. Remove the bay leaf and serve over cooked white rice.

PER SERVING
Calories: 630 | Fat: 29g | Protein: 25g | Sodium: 1830mg | Carbohydrates: 69g | Fiber: 7g

Vegan Chicken

Major grocery store chains around the United States carry several varieties of vegan faux meats, making meat-free cooking easier than ever. Morningstar Farms Meal Starter Chik'n Strips are a fast-cooking option commonly sold in the frozen foods section, near breakfast items. Lightlife's Smart Menu Chick'n Strips are another delicious option, usually found near the produce or health foods sections.

Vegetable Étoufée

Onion, celery, and bell pepper, otherwise known as the "holy trinity"
of Creole and Cajun cuisines, are the foundation of many New Orleans dishes.

INGREDIENTS | SERVES 6

10 tablespoons butter, or vegan margarine, such as Earth Balance

1 cup white onion, finely diced

1 cup celery, finely diced

1 cup green bell pepper, finely diced

1 clove garlic, minced

2 tablespoons flour

2 ounces tomato paste

2 cups water

2 teaspoons salt

1 teaspoon black pepper

1 tablespoon vegan Worcestershire sauce

½ cup green onion, finely diced

¼ cup parsley, chopped

½ teaspoon cayenne pepper

1 bay leaf

6 cups cooked white rice

1. Melt the butter or margarine in the pressure cooker over medium-low heat. Add the onion, celery, and bell pepper and sauté for 45 minutes, stirring often. Add the garlic and sauté for 1 additional minute.

2. Stir in the flour to make a roux and cook for about 5 minutes. It should still be light in color.

3. Add all remaining ingredients except the rice. Lock the lid into place; bring to medium pressure and maintain for 10 minutes. Remove from heat and allow pressure to release naturally.

4. Remove the bay leaf and serve over cooked white rice.

PER SERVING
Calories: 420 | Fat: 20g | Protein: 6g | Sodium: 900mg | Carbohydrates: 54g | Fiber: 3g

Seitan Bourguignon

Better Than Bouillon's "No Beef Base"
is a vegetarian alternative to beef stock.

INGREDIENTS | SERVES 4

2 tablespoons olive oil

1 pound cooked seitan, cut into 2" cubes

2 carrots, sliced

1 onion, sliced

1 teaspoon salt

2 tablespoons flour

2 cups red wine

2 cups faux beef stock

1 tablespoon tomato paste

2 cloves garlic, minced

½ teaspoon dried thyme

1 bay leaf

¼ teaspoon pepper

1 tablespoon butter, or vegan margarine, such as Earth Balance

18 whole pearl onions, peeled

2 cups button mushrooms, sliced

Seitan

Seitan is made from wheat gluten and is often used as a vegetarian substitute for chicken. It's one of the easiest meat substitutes to make at home; see Chapter 13 for more recipes.

1. Bring the olive oil to medium heat in the pressure cooker. Add the seitan, carrots, and onion and sauté until soft, about 7 minutes. Stir in the salt and flour.

2. Add the red wine, faux beef stock, tomato paste, garlic, thyme, bay leaf, and pepper. Lock the lid into place; bring to high pressure and maintain for 30 minutes. Remove from heat and allow pressure to release naturally.

3. While the pressure is releasing, melt the butter in a small sauté pan over medium-low heat. Add the onions and mushrooms and sauté until just soft, about 15 minutes.

4. Once the pressure has released, add the cooked onions and mushrooms to the pressure cooker and stir.

5. Remove the bay leaf before serving.

PER SERVING
Calories: 880 | Fat: 12g | Protein: 91g | Sodium: 940mg | Carbohydrates: 67g | Fiber: 11g

Irish "Beef" Stew

Surprisingly, not all beers are safe for vegetarian consumption. Guinness is a popular Irish stout, but it is treated with isinglass finings made from fish, and should not be used in this stew.

INGREDIENTS | SERVES 5

2 tablespoons olive oil

1 pound cooked seitan, cut into 1" cubes

2 carrots, sliced

1 onion, diced

2 cloves garlic, minced

3 tablespoons flour

1 pound russet potatoes, cubed

6 cups faux beef stock

1 cup Irish stout beer

1 cup red wine

2 tablespoons tomato paste

1 tablespoon sugar

1 tablespoon dried thyme

1 tablespoon vegan Worcestershire sauce

1 bay leaf

1 teaspoon salt

½ teaspoon black pepper

1. Bring the olive oil to medium heat in the pressure cooker. Add the seitan, carrots, and onion and sauté until just soft, about 5 minutes. Stir in the garlic and flour and sauté an additional 30 seconds.

2. Add all remaining ingredients. Lock the lid into place; bring to high pressure and maintain for 30 minutes. Remove from heat and allow pressure to release naturally.

3. Remove the bay leaf before serving.

PER SERVING
Calories: 760 | Fat: 7g | Protein: 74g | Sodium: 1280mg | Carbohydrates: 75g | Fiber: 9g

Oyster Mushroom Stew

Any type of mushroom will work in this stew, but oyster mushrooms are recommended because of their delicate texture that mimics fish.

INGREDIENTS | SERVES 4

2 tablespoons butter, or vegan margarine, such as Earth Balance

½ cup onions, diced

½ cup celery, diced

1 clove garlic, minced

½ cup Béchamel Sauce (page 48), or vegan version of Béchamel Sauce

1 pound oyster mushrooms, chopped

½ cup white wine

2 cups heavy cream, or unsweetened soymilk

½ teaspoon dried thyme

1 teaspoon salt

1 teaspoon lemon juice

Optional: chopped parsley

1. Heat the butter in the pressure cooker over medium heat. Add the onions and celery and sauté for 5 minutes. Add the garlic and sauté an additional 30 seconds.

2. Add the Béchamel Sauce, mushrooms, white wine, cream, thyme, and salt. Lock the lid into place; bring to low pressure and maintain for 30 minutes. Remove from heat and allow pressure to release naturally.

3. Once the pressure has released remove the lid and check for consistency. If it is not thick enough return to the burner and simmer over low heat with the lid off. Stir in the lemon juice.

4. Stir in chopped parsley before serving, if desired.

PER SERVING
Calories: 590 | Fat: 54g | Protein: 9g | Sodium: 790mg | Carbohydrates: 18g | Fiber: 9g

Brunswick Stew

Original or hickory-smoked barbecue sauce works best in this recipe.

INGREDIENTS | SERVES 4

2 tablespoons olive oil

1 onion, chopped

2 stalks celery, sliced

1 bell pepper, diced

1 16-ounce package vegan chicken

1 28-ounce can crushed tomatoes

2 cups uncooked corn kernels

1 cup ketchup

½ cup barbecue sauce

1 tablespoon liquid smoke

1 tablespoon vegan Worcestershire sauce

1 teaspoon salt

½ teaspoon black pepper

1. Heat the olive oil in the pressure cooker over medium heat and sauté the onions, celery, and bell pepper until soft, about 5 minutes. Add the vegan chicken and cook until done according to package directions.

2. Add all remaining ingredients. Lock the lid into place; bring to high pressure and maintain for 30 minutes. Remove from heat and allow pressure to release naturally.

PER SERVING
Calories: 580 | Fat: 23g | Protein: 34g | Sodium: 2880mg | Carbohydrates: 69g | Fiber: 12g

Eggplant Stew

Large, purple eggplants are ideal for this dish,
but Japanese eggplants will work, too.

INGREDIENTS | SERVES 4

2 medium eggplants, cut into large cubes

1 russet potato, diced

1 14-ounce can chickpeas, drained

6 cups Vegetable Stock (page 29)

1 cup tomatoes, diced

1 tablespoon tomato paste

1 tablespoon lemon juice

1 bay leaf

1 teaspoon cumin

½ cup parsley, chopped

2 teaspoons salt

1. Add all of the ingredients to the pressure cooker and lock the lid into place.

2. Bring to low pressure and maintain for 30 minutes. Remove from heat and allow pressure to release naturally.

3. Remove bay leaf and adjust seasoning before serving, if necessary.

PER SERVING
Calories: 280 | Fat: 2g | Protein: 10g | Sodium: 2360mg | Carbohydrates: 60g | Fiber: 16g

Green Chili Stew

Jalapeños are the type of chilies typically used for canned chilies.

INGREDIENTS | SERVES 4

2 tablespoons olive oil

1 onion, diced

3 cloves garlic, minced

1 large russet potato, cubed

2 4-ounce cans green chilies, chopped

2 cups fresh tomatoes, diced

2 cups Vegetable Stock (page 29)

1 teaspoon vinegar

1 teaspoon cumin

1 teaspoon cayenne pepper

1 teaspoon salt

1 8-ounce package Morningstar Farms Meal Starter Chik'n Strips, defrosted and chopped

¼ cup cilantro, chopped

1. Bring the olive oil to medium heat in the pressure cooker. Add the onion and sauté for 5 minutes. Add the garlic and sauté an additional 30 seconds.

2. Add the potato, chilies, tomato, stock, vinegar, cumin, cayenne pepper, and salt to the pressure cooker. Lock the lid into place; bring to high pressure and maintain for 6 minutes. Remove from heat and allow pressure to release naturally.

3. Remove the lid, stir in the Chik'n Strips and cilantro, and bring the stew back to medium-high heat. Let simmer for 5 minutes, then serve.

PER SERVING
Calories: 270 | Fat: 9g | Protein: 14g | Sodium: 1400mg | Carbohydrates: 34g | Fiber: 7g

Faux Frogmore Stew

A 10- or 12-quart pressure cooker is recommended for this recipe.
If yours is smaller, just halve all of the ingredients to make sure they will fit.

INGREDIENTS | SERVES 6

12 cups water

¼ cup Old Bay seasoning

1 pound red potatoes, whole and unpeeled

6 ears corn on the cob, husked, cleaned, and halved

1 14-ounce package Tofurky sausage cut into 2" pieces

2 whole heads garlic

Old Bay Seasoning

Old Bay is a popular brand of seafood seasoning that comes in bags, liquid, or ground and loose. Any type of Old Bay will work in this recipe, just adjust the amount accordingly. A generic or homemade seafood blend will work just as well.

1. Add the water, Old Bay, and potatoes to the pressure cooker. Lock the lid into place; bring to high pressure and maintain for 5 minutes. Quick-release the pressure.

2. Remove the lid and add all remaining ingredients to the pressure cooker. Lock the lid into place; bring to high pressure and maintain for 5 more minutes. Remove from heat and allow pressure to release naturally.

3. Drain the liquid before serving or remove the vegetables and Tofurky sausage with a slotted spoon.

PER SERVING
Calories: 240 | Fat: 1.5g | Protein: 16g | Sodium: 730mg | Carbohydrates: 44g | Fiber: 7g

African Peanut Stew

West Africa is the home of this exotic peanut stew.

INGREDIENTS | SERVES 4

1 tablespoon peanut oil

1 cup onion, diced

1 red bell pepper, diced

2 cloves garlic, minced

2 tablespoons fresh ginger, minced

1 sweet potato, peeled and cubed

1 14-ounce can diced tomatoes, drained

1 14-ounce can chickpeas, drained

3 cups Vegetable Stock (page 29)

½ cup chunky peanut butter

1 tablespoon curry powder

1 teaspoon salt

½ teaspoon black pepper

½ cup coconut milk

1. Bring the peanut oil to medium heat in the pressure cooker. Add the onion and red bell pepper and sauté for 3 minutes. Add the garlic and ginger, and sauté an additional 30 seconds.

2. Add the sweet potato, tomatoes, chickpeas, stock, peanut butter, curry powder, salt, and pepper to the pressure cooker. Lock the lid into place; bring to high pressure and maintain for 10 minutes. Remove from heat and allow pressure to release naturally.

3. Stir in the coconut milk before serving.

PER SERVING
Calories: 510 | Fat: 27g | Protein: 16g | Sodium: 1540mg | Carbohydrates: 57g | Fiber: 12g

Potato-Kale Stew

Avoid using russet potatoes in this recipe because they become too mushy when overcooked.

INGREDIENTS | SERVES 4

3 cups kale, chopped

1 tablespoon olive oil

2 cloves garlic, minced

4 red potatoes, peeled and quartered

3 cups Vegetable Stock (page 29)

1 teaspoon salt

1 teaspoon black pepper

2 15-ounce cans cannellini beans, drained

1 14-ounce can whole tomatoes, drained

1. Trim the kale by removing the tough stalk end of each leaf, then chop the kale leaves into large pieces.

2. Bring the olive oil to medium heat in the pressure cooker. Add the garlic and sauté for 30 seconds.

3. Add all remaining ingredients. Lock the lid into place; bring to high pressure and maintain for 15 minutes. Remove from heat and allow pressure to release naturally.

PER SERVING
Calories: 500 | Fat: 5g | Protein: 22g | Sodium: 1080mg | Carbohydrates: 95g | Fiber: 15g

Korean Tofu Stew

A tablespoon of crushed red pepper may be a little too much for sensitive taste buds.
If so, reduce the amount to 1 teaspoon and add more as needed.

INGREDIENTS | SERVES 2–4

1 tablespoon sesame oil

½ onion, sliced

1 clove garlic, minced

1 teaspoon fresh ginger, minced

1 cup shredded green cabbage

1 cup shiitake mushrooms, sliced

1 12.3-ounce package soft silken tofu, drained and cubed

1 tablespoon crushed red pepper

1 teaspoon soy sauce

1 teaspoon rice wine vinegar

3" piece kombu

3 cups Vegetable Stock (page 29)

2 green onions, sliced

Kombu

Kombu is edible seaweed commonly used in Asian cuisine, and can help give salty flavor and nutrients to food. Be sure to remove large pieces of kombu from your recipes before serving.

1. Bring the sesame oil to medium heat in the pressure cooker. Add the onion and sauté for 3 minutes. Add the garlic and ginger and sauté an additional 30 seconds.

2. Add the cabbage, mushrooms, tofu, red pepper, soy sauce, vinegar, kombu, and stock to the pressure cooker. Lock the lid into place; bring to low pressure and maintain for 5 minutes. Remove from heat and allow pressure to release naturally.

3. Remove the lid. Discard the kombu and stir in the green onions before serving.

PER SERVING
Calories: 280 | Fat: 12g | Protein: 12g | Sodium: 1080mg | Carbohydrates: 34g | Fiber: 5g

CHAPTER 12

Tofu

Marinated Tofu Steaks

Tofu has very little flavor on its own and is best when marinated in a flavorful liquid before cooking.

INGREDIENTS | SERVES 2–4

1 16-ounce package extra-firm tofu
1 cup soy sauce
1 tablespoon white wine vinegar
1 teaspoon garlic, minced
1 teaspoon ginger, minced
2 tablespoons vegetable oil
1 cup water

1. Drain the tofu, pat dry with a towel or paper towel, and then cut into four equal-sized pieces. Place in a 1"-deep dish. Whisk together the soy sauce, vinegar, garlic, and ginger, and then pour over the tofu. Let stand for 10 minutes, being sure to turn the tofu often or spoon the excess liquid over the top.

2. Add the oil to the pressure cooker and sauté the tofu steaks until brown on each side. Remove the tofu steaks. Place the water in the pressure cooker along with the steamer tray. Place the tofu steaks on top of the steamer tray.

3. Lock the lid into place; bring to high pressure and maintain for 5 minutes. Remove from the heat and allow pressure to release naturally.

PER SERVING
Calories: 430 | Fat: 29g | Protein: 40g | Sodium: 8070mg | Carbohydrates: 11g | Fiber: 4g

Lemon Tofu Tacos

Tofu mimics the role of fish in these easy-to-make tacos. Kick up the flavor by adding a touch of cayenne or chipotle pepper to the tofu marinade.

INGREDIENTS | SERVES 4

1 16-ounce package extra-firm tofu
2 tablespoons lemon juice
½ tablespoon apple cider vinegar
2 tablespoons soy sauce
2 tablespoons olive oil
1 cup water
8 corn tortillas
1 tomato, diced
½ red onion, thinly sliced
2 teaspoons cilantro, chopped
Salt and pepper, to taste

Corn versus Flour Tortillas

There is no right or wrong answer as to which is better. It solely depends on your taste. Corn tortillas are more full-flavored than flour and they also have a grainier texture. Which variety you decide to use is up to you!

1. Wrap the block of tofu in paper towels and press for 5 minutes by adding weight on top. Remove the paper towels and cut the tofu into ½"-thick pieces. Place in a 1"-deep dish.

2. Whisk together the lemon juice, apple cider vinegar, soy sauce, and olive oil in a small bowl and pour it over the tofu. Let stand for 10 minutes, being sure to turn the tofu often or spoon the excess liquid over the top.

3. Place the water in the pressure cooker along with the steamer tray. Place the marinated tofu on top of the steamer tray. Lock the lid into place; bring to high pressure and maintain for 5 minutes. Remove from the heat and allow pressure to release naturally.

4. Serve the tofu on warm tortillas with tomato, red onion, and cilantro. Season with salt and pepper, to taste, if necessary.

PER SERVING
Calories: 310 | Fat: 16g | Protein: 17g | Sodium: 540mg | Carbohydrates: 29g | Fiber: 5g

Barbecue Tofu Sandwich

Not all bread is vegan, but a lot of it is. If you are making the vegan version of this recipe, be sure to read the label on your hamburger buns.

INGREDIENTS | SERVES 6

1 16-ounce package firm tofu, crumbled

1 cup mustard

½ cup sugar

¼ cup brown sugar

¾ cup apple cider vinegar

¼ cup water

2 tablespoons chili powder

½ teaspoon soy sauce

¼ teaspoon cayenne pepper

2 tablespoons butter, melted, or vegan margarine, such as Earth Balance

1 tablespoon liquid smoke

Salt and pepper, to taste

6 hamburger buns

1. Wrap the block of tofu in paper towels and press for 5 minutes by adding weight on top. Whisk the rest of the ingredients except buns in a medium bowl and pour them into the pressure cooker.

2. Crumble the tofu with your hands and mix it into the barbecue sauce in the pressure cooker. Lock the lid into place; bring to high pressure and maintain for 5 minutes. Remove from the heat and allow pressure to release naturally. Serve on hamburger buns.

PER SERVING
Calories: 340 | Fat: 14g | Protein: 14g | Sodium: 1210mg | Carbohydrates: 47g | Fiber: 3g

Blackened Tofu Sandwich

*Preparing blackened tofu on the grill is a delicious alternative
to using a pressure cooker on a warm summer day.*

INGREDIENTS | SERVES 6

1 16-ounce package extra-firm tofu

⅓ cup soy sauce

1 tablespoon apple cider vinegar

1 tablespoon garlic, minced

1 tablespoon paprika

2 teaspoons black pepper

1½ teaspoons salt

1 teaspoon garlic powder

1 teaspoon cayenne pepper

½ teaspoon dried oregano

½ teaspoon dried thyme

2 tablespoons vegetable oil

1 cup water

6 hamburger buns

1. Drain the tofu, pat dry with a towel or paper towel, and then cut into four equal-sized pieces. Place in a 1"-deep dish.

2. Whisk together the soy sauce, vinegar, and garlic, and then pour over the tofu. Let stand for 10 minutes, being sure to turn the tofu often or spoon the excess liquid over the top.

3. To make the blackened seasoning mixture, combine the paprika, pepper, salt, garlic powder, cayenne, oregano, and thyme in a small bowl. Remove the tofu from the soy marinade and dip each side into the blackened seasoning.

4. Add the oil to the pressure cooker and sauté the blackened tofu until brown on each side. Remove the blackened tofu. Place the water in the pressure cooker along with the steamer tray. Place the blackened tofu on top of the steamer tray.

5. Lock the lid into place; bring to high pressure and maintain for 5 minutes. Remove from the heat and allow pressure to release naturally. Serve on the hamburger buns.

PER SERVING
Calories: 210 | Fat: 11g | Protein: 13g | Sodium: 1610mg | Carbohydrates: 18g | Fiber: 2g

Coconut Green Curry Tofu

Coconut milk can range from thin and watery to something that is almost solid. Experiment with different types of coconut milk until you find the one you like most.

INGREDIENTS | SERVES 4–6

1 16-ounce package extra-firm tofu
2 green chilies, seeded and minced
4 scallions, chopped
2 cloves garlic, minced
1 teaspoon ginger, minced
1 tablespoon soy sauce
½ cup fresh cilantro, chopped
¼ cup fresh parsley, chopped
2 tablespoons water
2 tablespoons vegetable oil
1 13-ounce can coconut milk
Salt and pepper, to taste
4 cups cooked rice

1. Wrap the block of tofu in paper towels and press for 5 minutes by adding weight on top. Remove the paper towels and cut the tofu into ½"-thick pieces.

2. In a food processor, combine the chilies, scallions, garlic, ginger, soy sauce, cilantro, parsley, and water. Blend into a smooth paste, adding extra water if necessary.

3. Add the oil to the pressure cooker and sauté the tofu until it is light brown on all sides. Add the coconut milk and the green chili paste.

4. Lock the lid into place; bring to high pressure and maintain for 5 minutes. Remove from the heat and allow pressure to release naturally. Season with salt and pepper, if necessary. Serve with rice.

PER SERVING
Calories: 580 | Fat: 35g | Protein: 20g | Sodium: 280mg | Carbohydrates: 53g | Fiber: 4g

Panang Curry Tofu

Panang is a milder type of red curry and is made from chilies.

INGREDIENTS | **SERVES 4–6**

1 16-ounce package extra-firm tofu
1 13-ounce can coconut milk
1 tablespoon Panang curry paste
2 tablespoons soy sauce
1 tablespoon lime juice
2 tablespoons sugar
2 tablespoons olive oil
¼ onion, sliced
½ carrot, sliced diagonally
¼ red bell pepper, chopped
½ cup fresh basil, chopped
4 cups cooked rice

1. Wrap the block of tofu in paper towels and press for 5 minutes by adding weight on top. Remove the paper towels and cut the tofu into ½"-thick pieces. Place in a 1"-deep dish.

2. In a medium bowl combine the coconut milk, curry paste, soy sauce, lime juice, and sugar.

3. Add the oil to the pressure cooker and sauté the tofu until it is light brown on all sides. Add the onion, carrot, and red bell pepper and sauté for 1–2 minutes more. Add the Panang curry paste to the pressure cooker.

4. Lock the lid into place; bring to high pressure and maintain for 5 minutes. Remove from the heat and allow pressure to release naturally. Garnish with fresh basil. Serve with rice.

PER SERVING
Calories: 580 | Fat: 31g | Protein: 20g | Sodium: 540mg | Carbohydrates: 59g | Fiber: 4g

Tofu Stir-Fry with Vegetables

Mix and match the vegetables in this all-purpose stir-fry to make your own creation.

INGREDIENTS | SERVES 2–4

1 16-ounce package extra-firm tofu

1 red chili pepper, seeded and minced

2 garlic cloves, minced

1 teaspoon ginger, minced

1 tablespoon olive oil

3 tablespoons soy sauce

¼ cup water

1 tablespoon cornstarch

2 tablespoons vegetable oil

2 carrots, cut diagonally

1 red bell pepper, chopped

½ onion, sliced

2 cups head bok choy, chopped

½ cup yellow squash, chopped

4 cups cooked rice

Cooking with Cornstarch

To help thicken a sauce or stew, use cornstarch. To avoid lumps, combine cornstarch with a small amount of cold water, stir until dissolved, then slowly add it to your dish, stirring over low heat until thickened. If lumps do occur, try vigorous stirring to work them out.

1. Wrap the block of tofu in paper towels and press for 5 minutes by adding weight on top. Remove the paper towels and cut the tofu into ½"-thick pieces. Place in a 1"-deep dish.

2. In a medium bowl, combine the chili pepper, garlic, ginger, olive oil, soy sauce, water, and cornstarch. Pour it over the tofu. Let stand for 10 minutes, being sure to turn the tofu often or spoon the excess liquid over the top. Reserve the excess marinade for use later in the recipe.

3. Add the vegetable oil to the pressure cooker and sauté the tofu until it is light brown on all sides. Add the carrot, red bell pepper, onion, bok choy, and yellow squash and sauté for 1–2 minutes.

4. Pour the reserved marinade into the pressure cooker. Lock the lid into place; bring to high pressure and maintain for 5 minutes. Remove from the heat and allow pressure to release naturally. Serve with rice.

PER SERVING
Calories: 990 | Fat: 38g | Protein: 46g | Sodium: 1860mg | Carbohydrates: 125g | Fiber: 13g

Kung Pao Tofu

Kung Pao Chicken is a traditional Szechuan dish that can be made vegan easily.
Just replace the chicken with tofu.

INGREDIENTS | SERVES 2–4

1 16-ounce package extra-firm tofu

2 tablespoons white wine

2 tablespoons soy sauce

2 tablespoons sesame oil

2 tablespoons cornstarch, dissolved in 2 tablespoons water

½ tablespoon hot chili paste

1 teaspoon rice wine vinegar

2 teaspoons brown sugar

1 cup water

1 teaspoon olive oil

½ red bell pepper, chopped

1 clove garlic, minced

4 tablespoons peanuts

4 cups cooked rice

1. Wrap the block of tofu in paper towels and press for 5 minutes by adding weight on top. Remove the paper towels and cut the tofu into ½"-thick pieces. Place in a 1"-deep dish.

2. Whisk together the white wine, soy sauce, sesame oil, cornstarch, chili paste, rice wine vinegar, and brown sugar in a small bowl and pour it over the tofu. Let stand for 10 minutes, being sure to turn the tofu often or spoon the excess liquid over the top.

3. Place the water in the pressure cooker along with the steamer tray. Place the marinated tofu on top of the steamer tray. Lock the lid into place; bring to high pressure and maintain for 5 minutes. Remove from the heat and allow pressure to release naturally.

4. Add the oil to a wok or pan and sauté the red bell pepper for 1–2 minutes. Add the marinated tofu and garlic and sauté 1 minute more. Add the sauce and cook for 2–3 minutes more. Garnish with the peanuts and serve with rice.

PER SERVING
Calories: 980 | Fat: 42g | Protein: 40g | Sodium: 1060mg | Carbohydrates: 112g | Fiber: 7g

General Tso's Tofu

The combination of sweet and spicy is what makes this dish a hit at Chinese restaurants across the country.

INGREDIENTS | SERVES 2–4

1 16-ounce package of extra-firm tofu

2 cups water

2 tablespoons cornstarch

2 cloves garlic, minced

1 teaspoon ginger, minced

⅛ cup sugar

¼ cup soy sauce

⅛ cup white wine vinegar

⅛ cup sherry

2 teaspoons cayenne pepper

2 tablespoons vegetable oil

2 cups broccoli, blanched and chopped

4 cups cooked rice

Types of Rice

Options are diverse when choosing a rice or grain to serve with a Chinese or Chinese-inspired tofu dish. Long grain white rice is most commonly used, but you can also use brown rice, quinoa, or couscous. See Chapter 7 for recipes and cooking times.

1. Wrap the block of tofu in paper towels and press for 5 minutes by adding weight on top. Remove the paper towels and cut the tofu into ½"-thick pieces.

2. In a small bowl, whisk together 1 cup water, cornstarch, garlic, ginger, sugar, soy sauce, vinegar, sherry, and cayenne pepper. Set the sauce aside.

3. Add the oil to the pressure cooker and sauté the tofu until brown on all sides. Add the broccoli and saute for 1 minute more. Add the sauce.

4. Lock the lid into place; bring to high pressure and maintain for 5 minutes. Remove from the heat and allow pressure to release naturally. Serve with rice.

PER SERVING
Calories: 900 | Fat: 30g | Protein: 40g | Sodium: 2060mg | Carbohydrates: 119g | Fiber: 7g

Palak Tofu Paneer

*Paneer is a type of cheese, but many versions
of this popular recipe use tofu instead.*

INGREDIENTS | SERVES 2–4

1 16-ounce package extra-firm tofu

2 tablespoons vegetable oil

2 cloves garlic, minced

1 teaspoon ginger, minced

2 teaspoons dried red pepper flakes

½ onion, diced

1 tablespoon cumin

1 teaspoon coriander powder

1 teaspoon sugar

1 teaspoon turmeric

1 cup sour cream or soy sour cream

6 cups fresh spinach

⅛ cup cilantro, chopped

Salt and pepper, to taste

1. Wrap the block of tofu in paper towels and press for 5 minutes by adding weight on top. Remove the paper towels and cut the tofu into ½"-thick pieces.

2. Add the oil to the pressure cooker and sauté the tofu until brown on all sides. Add the garlic, ginger, red pepper flakes, onion, cumin, coriander, sugar, and turmeric. Saute for 1–2 minutes more.

3. Mix in the sour cream and fresh spinach. Lock the lid into place; bring to high pressure and maintain for 5 minutes. Remove from the heat and allow pressure to release naturally. Garnish with cilantro, adding salt and pepper to taste. Serve with rice.

PER SERVING
Calories: 660 | Fat: 55g | Protein: 33g | Sodium: 170mg |
Carbohydrates: 20g | Fiber: 7g

CHAPTER 13

Seitan and Tempeh

Homemade Seitan

When pressed for time, use packaged seitan instead of making it at home.

Seitan Variations

The taste and texture of seitan can vary greatly depending on the type of flour you use and the amount of time spent kneading the dough. Experiment with different combinations until you reach the consistency most pleasing to your palate.

1. Place the whole wheat and unbleached flour in a large mixing bowl and stir well to combine. While stirring, gradually pour enough water into the flour to form a sticky dough that can be kneaded. Knead for 15 minutes. Cover the dough with cold water, place in the refrigerator, and keep submerged for at least 30 minutes.

2. Transfer the dough from the bowl to a colander and place it in the sink. Under cold running water, carefully knead the dough, rinsing out the starch and bran. After several minutes of cold water rinsing and kneading, the gluten will start to stick together. Alternate between room temperature water and cold water rinses while continuing to knead the dough until it has a firm, rubbery texture.

3. Add the Vegetable Stock to the pressure cooker. Pull pieces of gluten into small billiard-sized balls. Drop the gluten into the liquid, one piece at a time, stirring occasionally to prevent sticking.

4. Lock the lid into place; bring to high pressure for 20 minutes. Remove from the heat and quick-release the pressure. Seitan can be refrigerated in the cooking liquid for 3–4 days.

PER RECIPE
Calories: 3280 | Fat: 15g | Protein: 128g | Sodium: 4150mg | Carbohydrates: 711g | Fiber: 62g

Shredded BBQ Seitan

Bottled barbecue sauce will work just as well in this recipe; just make sure it's vegetarian or vegan.

INGREDIENTS | SERVES 4–6

1¾ cups whole wheat flour

1¾ cups unbleached white flour

1¾ cups cold water

3½ cups Vegetable Stock (page 29)

1 cup prepared mustard

½ cup sugar

¼ cup brown sugar

¾ cup cider vinegar

2 tablespoons chili powder

¼ tablespoon cayenne pepper

1 teaspoon soy sauce

2 tablespoons butter, or vegan margarine, such as Earth Balance

1 tablespoon liquid smoke

Salt and pepper, to taste

1. Place the whole wheat and unbleached flour in a large mixing bowl and stir well to combine. While stirring, gradually pour enough water into the flour to form a sticky dough that can be kneaded. Knead for 15 minutes. Cover the dough with cold water, place in the refrigerator, and keep submerged for at least 30 minutes.

2. Transfer the dough from the bowl to a colander and place it in the sink. Under cold running water, carefully knead the dough, rinsing out the starch and bran. After several minutes of cold water rinsing and kneading, the gluten will start to stick together. Alternate between room temperature water and cold water rinses while continuing to knead the dough until it has a firm, rubbery texture.

3. Add the stock to the pressure cooker. Pull pieces of gluten into small billiard-sized balls. Drop the gluten into the liquid, one piece at a time, stirring occasionally to prevent sticking.

4. Lock the lid into place; bring to high pressure for 20 minutes. Remove from the heat and quick-release the pressure. Drain off the remaining liquid from the seitan.

5. Add the mustard, sugars, vinegar, chili powder, cayenne pepper, soy sauce, butter, liquid smoke, salt, and pepper to a medium pot. Shred the seitan by hand or with a knife and add to the barbecue sauce. Let simmer for about 10 minutes. Serve.

PER SERVING
Calories: 700 | Fat: 14g | Protein: 21g | Sodium: 2160mg | Carbohydrates: 136g | Fiber: 10g

Seitan Sloppy Joes

Add to the Sloppy Joes by tossing cheese (or vegan cheese) and diced onions onto this messy, delicious sandwich. Be sure to have extra napkins on hand!

INGREDIENTS | SERVES 4–6

1¾ cups whole wheat flour

1¾ cups unbleached white flour

1¾ cups cold water

3½ cups Vegetable Stock (page 29)

1 tablespoon olive oil

½ onion, diced

½ teaspoon garlic powder

2 teaspoons brown sugar

1 tablespoon mustard

¾ cup ketchup

1 tablespoon vegan Worcestershire sauce

Salt and pepper, to taste

6–8 hamburger buns

Seitan Alternatives

There are many alternatives to homemade seitan when making sloppy joes. Crumbled tofu or tempeh will work, as well as vegetarian beef substitutes, such as Boca Ground Crumbles.

1. Place the whole wheat and unbleached flour in a large mixing bowl and stir well to combine. While stirring, gradually pour enough water into the flour to form a sticky dough that can be kneaded. Knead for 15 minutes. Cover the dough with cold water, place in the refrigerator, and keep submerged for at least 30 minutes.

2. Transfer the dough from the bowl to a colander and place it in the sink. Under cold running water, carefully knead the dough, rinsing out the starch and bran. After several minutes of cold water rinsing and kneading, the gluten will start to stick together. Alternate between room temperature water and cold water rinses while continuing to knead the dough until it has a firm, rubbery texture.

3. Add the stock to the pressure cooker. Pull pieces of gluten into small billiard-sized balls. Drop the gluten into the liquid, one piece at a time, stirring occasionally to prevent sticking.

4. Lock the lid into place; bring to high pressure for 20 minutes. Remove from the heat and quick-release the pressure. Drain off the remaining liquid from the seitan.

5. Slice the seitan very thinly. Add the oil to a pan and sauté the onion until it caramelizes. Add the seitan and the rest of the ingredients except buns. Allow to simmer for 5–8 minutes. Serve on hamburger buns.

PER SERVING
Calories: 620 | Fat: 7g | Protein: 20g | Sodium: 1420mg | Carbohydrates: 127g | Fiber: 9g

Seitan with Sauerkraut and Onions

An ale, or another light beer, is recommended over dark beers in this recipe.

INGREDIENTS | SERVES 4–6

1¾ cups whole wheat flour

1¾ cups unbleached white flour

1¾ cups cold water

3½ cups Vegetable Stock (page 29)

¼ cup olive oil

3 onions, thinly sliced

2 teaspoons brown sugar

3 cups sauerkraut

2 cloves garlic, minced

2 bay leaves

4 red potatoes, quartered

2 carrots, roughly chopped

1 12-ounce beer of your choice

Salt and pepper, to taste

Optional: chopped parsley

1. Place the whole wheat and unbleached flour in a large mixing bowl and stir well to combine. While stirring, gradually pour enough water into the flour to form a sticky dough that can be kneaded. Knead for 15 minutes. Cover the dough with cold water, place in the refrigerator, and keep submerged for at least 30 minutes.

2. Transfer the dough from the bowl to a colander and place it in the sink. Under cold running water, carefully knead the dough, rinsing out the starch and bran. After several minutes of cold water rinsing and kneading, the gluten will start to stick together. Alternate between room temperature water and cold water rinses while continuing to knead the dough until it has a firm, rubbery texture.

3. Add the stock to the pressure cooker. Pull pieces of gluten into small billiard-sized balls. Drop the gluten into the liquid, one piece at a time, stirring occasionally to prevent sticking.

4. Lock the lid into place; bring to high pressure for 20 minutes. Remove from the heat and quick-release the pressure. Drain off the remaining liquid from the seitan.

5. Chop the seitan into bite-sized pieces. Add the seitan and all the remaining ingredients to the pressure cooker. Lock the lid into place; bring to high pressure for 10 minutes. Remove from the heat and quick-release the pressure. Serve.

PER SERVING
Calories: 820 | Fat: 16g | Protein: 22g | Sodium: 1620mg | Carbohydrates: 154g | Fiber: 14g

Veggie Pot Roast

*Throw potatoes, carrots, or other vegetables into
the mix to make this recipe a complete meal.*

INGREDIENTS | SERVES 4–6

1¾ cups whole wheat flour

1¾ cups unbleached white flour

1¾ cups cold water

3½ cups Vegetable Stock (page 29)

1 onion, sliced

1 cup mushrooms, sliced

2 tablespoons olive oil

1 tablespoon soy sauce

1 12-ounce beer of your choice

2 tablespoons all-purpose flour

Salt and pepper, to taste

1. Place the whole wheat and unbleached flour in a large mixing bowl and stir well to combine. While stirring, gradually pour enough water into the flour to form a sticky dough. Knead for 15 minutes. Cover with cold water and place in the refrigerator for 30 minutes.

2. Transfer the dough from the bowl to a colander and place it in the sink. Under cold running water, carefully knead the dough, rinsing out the starch and bran. After several minutes, the gluten will start to stick together. Alternate between room temperature water and cold water rinses while continuing to knead the dough until it has a firm, rubbery texture.

3. Add the stock to the pressure cooker. Pull pieces of gluten into small billiard-sized balls. Drop into the liquid one piece at a time, stirring occasionally to prevent sticking.

4. Lock the lid into place; bring to high pressure for 20 minutes. Remove from the heat and quick-release the pressure. Drain off the remaining liquid from the seitan.

5. Chop the seitan into bite-sized pieces. In the pressure cooker, sauté the onions and mushrooms in oil until they are tender. Add the seitan, soy sauce, and beer. Lock the lid into place; bring to high pressure for 10 minutes. Remove from the heat and quick-release the pressure.

6. Remove the seitan, onions, and mushrooms from the pressure cooker. Bring the remaining liquid to a simmer. Gradually stir in the all-purpose flour to create a gravy. Add salt and pepper to taste.

PER SERVING
Calories: 480 | Fat: 2g | Protein: 18g | Sodium: 780mg |
Carbohydrates: 99g | Fiber: 9g

Smoked Portobello and Seitan

*If you don't have red wine in the house or don't drink alcohol,
substitute extra Vegetable Stock (page 29).*

INGREDIENTS | SERVES 4–6

1¾ cups whole wheat flour

1¾ cups unbleached white flour

1¾ cups cold water

3½ cups Vegetable Stock (page 29)

1 tablespoon olive oil

1 onion, chopped

3 portobello mushroom caps, chopped

1 tablespoon soy sauce

¼ teaspoon liquid smoke

½ cup red wine

2–4 tablespoons flour

Salt and pepper, to taste

2 tablespoons parsley, chopped

1. Place the whole wheat and unbleached flour in a large mixing bowl and stir well to combine. While stirring, gradually pour enough water into the flour to form a sticky dough. Knead for 15 minutes. Cover with cold water and place in the refrigerator for 30 minutes.

2. Transfer the dough from the bowl to a colander and place it in the sink. Under cold running water, carefully knead the dough, rinsing out the starch and bran. After several minutes of cold water rinsing and kneading, the gluten will start to stick together. Alternate between room temperature water and cold water rinses while continuing to knead the dough until it has a firm, rubbery texture.

3. Add the stock to the pressure cooker. Pull pieces of gluten into small billiard-sized balls. Drop the gluten into the liquid, one piece at a time, stirring occasionally to prevent sticking.

4. Lock the lid into place; bring to high pressure for 20 minutes. Remove from the heat and quick-release the pressure. Remove the seitan and chop into bite-sized pieces.

5. Add the olive oil to a pan and sauté the onions and mushrooms until tender. Add the seitan, soy sauce, liquid smoke, and red wine and allow to simmer 2–3 minutes. Remove the seitan, onions, and mushrooms with a slotted spoon. Gradually add the flour to make a gravy. When the gravy is done, drizzle it over the seitan mixture. Add salt and pepper to taste and garnish with parsley. Serve.

PER SERVING
Calories: 510 | Fat: 5g | Protein: 19g | Sodium: 780mg |
Carbohydrates: 99g | Fiber: 10g

Indian Seitan Curry

*The combination of curry and cayenne give
this dish one healthy dose of spice.*

INGREDIENTS | SERVES 4–6

1¾ cups whole wheat flour

1¾ cups unbleached white flour

1¾ cups cold water

3½ cups Vegetable Stock (page 29)

2 tablespoons olive oil

½ onion, chopped

2 cloves garlic, minced

1 teaspoon fresh ginger, minced

3 tablespoons curry powder

1 teaspoon paprika

1 teaspoon sugar

½ teaspoon cayenne pepper

1 teaspoon soy sauce

1 14-ounce can coconut milk

Salt and pepper, to taste

1. Place the whole wheat and unbleached flour in a large mixing bowl and stir well to combine. While stirring, gradually pour enough water into the flour to form a sticky dough that can be kneaded. Knead for 15 minutes. Cover the dough with cold water, place in the refrigerator, and keep submerged for at least 30 minutes.

2. Transfer the dough from the bowl to a colander and place it in the sink. Under cold running water, carefully knead the dough, rinsing out the starch and bran. After several minutes of cold water rinsing and kneading, the gluten will start to stick together. Alternate between room temperature water and cold water rinses while continuing to knead the dough until it has a firm, rubbery texture.

3. Add the stock to the pressure cooker. Pull pieces of gluten into small billiard-sized balls. Drop the gluten into the liquid, one piece at a time, stirring occasionally to prevent sticking.

4. Lock the lid into place; bring to high pressure for 20 minutes. Remove from the heat and quick-release the pressure. Remove the seitan and chop into bite-sized pieces.

5. Add the olive oil to a pan and sauté the onion until it is caramelized. Add the garlic and ginger and sauté for 1 minute more. Add the seitan and the rest of the ingredients and allow to simmer for 20–25 minutes.

PER SERVING
Calories: 700 | Fat: 30g | Protein: 19g | Sodium: 620mg | Carbohydrates: 98g | Fiber: 11g

Black Pepper Seitan and Broccoli

Modeled after the popular Chinese dish,
this recipe can be served with white or brown rice.

INGREDIENTS | SERVES 4–6

1¾ cups whole wheat flour

1¾ cups unbleached white flour

1¾ cups cold water

3½ cups Vegetable Stock (page 29)

2 tablespoons vegetable oil

1 onion, sliced

2 cloves garlic, minced

2 cups broccoli, chopped and blanched

2 tablespoons soy sauce

1 teaspoon black pepper

½ teaspoon sugar

Spice It Up

The herbs and spices in this recipe are kept to a minimum, but you can add more flavor if you'd like. Add 1 teaspoon of cayenne pepper for a little kick, and ½ teaspoon of ginger or Chinese five-spice for added flavor.

1. Place the whole wheat and unbleached flour in a large mixing bowl and stir well to combine. While stirring, gradually pour enough water into the flour to form a sticky dough that can be kneaded. Knead for 15 minutes. Cover the dough with cold water, place in the refrigerator, and keep submerged for at least 30 minutes.

2. Transfer the dough from the bowl to a colander and place it in the sink. Under cold running water, carefully knead the dough, rinsing out the starch and bran. After several minutes of cold water rinsing and kneading, the gluten will start to stick together. Alternate between room temperature water and cold water rinses while continuing to knead the dough until it has a firm, rubbery texture.

3. Add the stock to the pressure cooker. Pull pieces of gluten into small billiard-sized balls. Drop the gluten into the liquid, one piece at a time, stirring occasionally to prevent sticking.

4. Lock the lid into place; bring to high pressure for 20 minutes. Remove from the heat and quick-release the pressure. Remove the seitan and chop into bite-sized pieces.

5. Add the oil to a wok or large pan and sauté the onions on high heat until browned. Add the garlic, seitan, and broccoli and sauté for 1 minute more. Add the soy sauce, black pepper, and sugar. Mix well and sauté for an additional 30 seconds before serving.

PER SERVING
Calories: 510 | Fat: 9g | Protein: 19g | Sodium: 1030mg | Carbohydrates: 96g | Fiber: 10g

Seitan and Dumplings

These are down-home dumplings that would
make any Southern grandmother proud.

INGREDIENTS | SERVES 4–6

1¾ cups whole wheat flour

1¾ cups unbleached white flour

1¾ cups cold water

3½ cups Vegetable Stock (page 29)

2 cups all-purpose flour

3 tablespoons butter, or vegan margarine, such as Earth Balance

1 teaspoon salt

¼ cup water

1. Place the whole wheat and unbleached flour in a large mixing bowl and stir well to combine flour. While stirring, gradually pour enough water into the flour to form a sticky dough. Knead for 15 minutes. Cover with cold water; place in the refrigerator for at least 30 minutes.

2. Transfer the dough from the bowl to a colander and place it in the sink. Under cold running water, carefully knead the dough, rinsing out the starch and bran. After several minutes of cold water rinsing and kneading, the gluten will start to stick together. Alternate between room temperature water and cold water rinses while continuing to knead the dough until it has a firm, rubbery texture.

3. Add the stock to the pressure cooker. Pull pieces of gluten into small billiard-sized balls. Drop the gluten into the liquid, one piece at a time, stirring occasionally to prevent sticking.

4. Lock the lid into place; bring to high pressure for 20 minutes. Remove from the heat and quick-release the pressure. With a slotted spoon, remove the seitan and chop into bite-sized pieces. Return the seitan to the pressure cooker. Add 1 cup of water and bring the seitan and stock to a simmer.

5. To make the dumplings, combine the flour, butter, salt, and water in a medium bowl. Form the mixture into a dough. Roll the dough very thin with a rolling pin. Cut into 1" squares and drop the dumplings into the simmering stock. Allow to cook for 15–20 minutes.

PER SERVING
Calories: 710 | Fat: 11g | Protein: 22g | Sodium: 1100mg | Carbohydrates: 137g | Fiber: 9g

Braised Seitan, Onion, and Pepper Subs

Mayonnaise and cheese, or vegan versions of them,
make delicious accompaniments to this sub sandwich.

INGREDIENTS | **SERVES 4–6**

1¾ cups whole wheat flour

1¾ cups unbleached white flour

1¾ cups cold water

3½ cups Vegetable Stock (page 29)

1 tablespoon olive oil

½ onion, sliced

½ green bell pepper, sliced

½ red bell pepper, sliced

1 jalapeño, minced

1 teaspoon soy sauce

Salt and pepper, to taste

4–6 hoagie buns, or vegan buns

1. Place the whole wheat and unbleached flour in a large mixing bowl and stir well to combine. While stirring, gradually pour enough water into the flour to form a sticky dough that can be kneaded. Knead for 15 minutes. Cover the dough with cold water, place in the refrigerator, and keep submerged for at least 30 minutes.

2. Transfer the dough from the bowl to a colander and place it in the sink. Under cold running water, carefully knead the dough, rinsing out the starch and bran. After several minutes of cold water rinsing and kneading, the gluten will start to stick together. Alternate between room temperature water and cold water rinses while continuing to knead the dough until it has a firm, rubbery texture.

3. Add the stock to the pressure cooker. Pull pieces of gluten into small billiard-sized balls. Drop the gluten into the liquid, one piece at a time, stirring occasionally to prevent sticking.

4. Lock the lid into place; bring to high pressure for 20 minutes. Remove from the heat and quick-release the pressure. Remove the seitan and slice into thin strips.

5. Add the oil to a pan and sauté the onion until it caramelizes. Add the seitan, green, red, and jalapeño peppers and saute for 2–3 minutes more. Stir in the soy sauce, salt, and pepper. Serve on hoagie buns.

PER SERVING
Calories: 670 | Fat: 10g | Protein: 24g | Sodium: 950mg |
Carbohydrates: 129g | Fiber: 11g

Seitan Au Jus Sandwich

This sandwich can be considered a vegan version of a roast beef sandwich.

INGREDIENTS | SERVES 4–6

1¾ cups whole wheat flour
1¾ cups unbleached white flour
1¾ cups cold water
3½ cups Vegetable Stock (page 29)
1 cup Au Jus (page 48)
8–12 slices bread

1. Place the whole wheat and unbleached flour in a large mixing bowl and stir well to combine. While stirring, gradually pour enough water into the flour to form a sticky dough that can be kneaded. Knead for 15 minutes. Cover the dough with cold water, place in the refrigerator, and keep submerged for at least 30 minutes.

2. Transfer the dough from the bowl to a colander and place it in the sink. Under cold running water, carefully knead the dough, rinsing out the starch and bran. After several minutes of cold water rinsing and kneading, the gluten will start to stick together. Alternate between room temperature water and cold water rinses while continuing to knead the dough until it has a firm, rubbery texture.

3. Add the stock to the pressure cooker. Pull pieces of gluten into small billiard-sized balls. Drop the gluten into the liquid, one piece at a time, stirring occasionally to prevent sticking.

4. Lock the lid into place; bring to high pressure for 20 minutes. Remove from the heat and quick-release the pressure. Remove the seitan and thinly slice.

5. In a medium sauté pan, warm the Au Jus sauce, then add the pieces of sliced seitan until warmed.

6. Place five slices of seitan on one piece of bread, top with extra sauce, and cover with an additional piece of bread. Serve any extra Au Jus on the side.

PER SERVING
Calories: 650 | Fat: 9g | Protein: 20g | Sodium: 1520mg |
Carbohydrates: 121g | Fiber: 9g

Spicy Tempeh Fajitas

Add a dollop of sour cream, or soy sour cream, and salsa to finish off each of your fajitas.

INGREDIENTS | SERVES 4

1 13-ounce package tempeh
6 cups water
2 cloves garlic, minced
1 teaspoon fresh ginger, minced
½ cup soy sauce
1 tablespoon olive oil
½ onion, sliced
½ green bell pepper, sliced
½ cup mushrooms sliced
1 jalapeño, minced
½ teaspoon chili powder
¼ teaspoon chipotle powder
Salt and pepper, to taste
1 tomato, diced
Optional: chopped cilantro
1 lime, cut into wedges
8–12 corn tortillas

Tricks of the Trade

It may seem like a surprising addition, but many restaurants add soy sauce to fajitas to give them an extra boost of flavor.

1. Cut the tempeh in half lengthwise, then cut the 2 slabs in half widthwise (as if you were slicing a roll), creating 4 squares that are nearly identical in size. Next, cut the tempeh into smaller strips, about 1" × 3".

2. Add the tempeh, water, garlic, ginger, and soy sauce to the pressure cooker. Lock the lid into place; bring to high pressure for 20 minutes. Remove from the heat and quick-release the pressure. Remove the tempeh.

3. Add the oil to a pan and sauté the onion, green pepper, mushrooms, and jalapeño until caramelized. Add the tempeh, chili powder, chipotle powder, salt, and pepper. Cook for 2–3 minutes more. Garnish with the tomato, cilantro, and lime. Serve on warmed tortillas.

PER SERVING
Calories: 380 | Fat: 12g | Protein: 28g | Sodium: 2040mg | Carbohydrates: 43g | Fiber: 13g

Hoisin-Glazed Tempeh

*Hoisin is a strongly flavored, slightly spicy,
and slightly sweet Chinese sauce.*

INGREDIENTS | SERVES 4

1 13-ounce package tempeh
6 cups water
4 cloves garlic, minced
2 teaspoons fresh ginger, minced
¾ cup soy sauce
½ cup hoisin sauce
2 tablespoons fresh lime juice
1 lime, cut into wedges
Salt and pepper, to taste

1. Cut the tempeh in half lengthwise, then cut the 2 slabs in half widthwise (as if you were slicing a roll), creating 4 squares that are nearly identical in size. Next, cut the tempeh into smaller strips, about 1" × 3".

2. Add the tempeh, water, 2 cloves minced garlic, 1 teaspoon ginger, and ½ cup of soy sauce to the pressure cooker. Lock the lid into place; bring to high pressure for 20 minutes. Remove from the heat and quick-release the pressure. Remove the tempeh.

3. Preheat the oven to 450°F. Place the tempeh in a casserole dish. In a medium bowl, mix the ¼ cup soy sauce, hoisin sauce, lime juice, 2 cloves minced garlic, and 1 teaspoon ginger. Pour the mixture onto the tempeh and marinate for 10 minutes.

4. Place the tempeh into the oven for 10 minutes, flipping one time. Garnish with the lime wedges and serve with rice. Taste and season with salt and pepper, if necessary.

PER SERVING
Calories: 290 | Fat: 8g | Protein: 26g | Sodium: 3530mg | Carbohydrates: 32g | Fiber: 9g

Lemon-Pepper Tempeh

*When fresh herbs are in season, add chopped curly
or flat leaf parsley to this dish before serving.*

INGREDIENTS | SERVES 4

1 8-ounce package tempeh

6 cups water

6 cloves garlic, minced

1 teaspoon fresh ginger, minced

½ cup soy sauce

¼ cup extra-virgin olive oil

2 tablespoons fresh lemon juice

1 teaspoon black pepper

Salt, to taste

Serving Suggestions

Make this tempeh dish the star of the show
and serve as a main course, with a vegetable and grain on the side. Or, place the
strips on a hoagie roll topped with mayonnaise or vegan mayonnaise and lettuce to
make a tasty sub sandwich.

1. Cut the tempeh in half lengthwise, then cut the 2 slabs in half widthwise (as if you were slicing a roll), creating 4 squares that are nearly identical in size. Next, cut the tempeh into smaller strips, about 1" × 3".

2. Add the tempeh, water, 2 cloves garlic, ginger, and soy sauce to the pressure cooker. Lock the lid into place; bring to high pressure for 20 minutes. Remove from the heat and quick-release the pressure. Remove the tempeh.

3. Preheat the oven to 450°F. In a bowl, mix the oil, lemon juice, remaining 4 garlic cloves, black pepper, and salt.

4. Place the tempeh in a casserole dish and pour the marinade over it. Allow the tempeh to marinate for 10 minutes. Place the dish in the oven and bake for about 15 minutes, turning once.

PER SERVING
Calories: 270 | Fat: 20g | Protein: 15g | Sodium: 2020mg |
Carbohydrates: 10g | Fiber: <1g

Tempeh Tamales

Be sure to use vegetable shortening in this recipe.
Plain shortening can be made from the fat of an animal.

INGREDIENTS | SERVES 4

1 13-ounce package tempeh
7½ cups water, divided use
2 cloves garlic, minced
1 teaspoon fresh ginger, minced
½ cup soy sauce
15 corn husks
2 Anaheim chilies
1¼ cups corn tortilla flour
½ cup fine cornmeal
¾ teaspoon baking powder
1 teaspoon salt
½ cup plus 1 tablespoon vegetable shortening
½ white onion, chopped
¾ cup fresh corn
½ red onion, thinly sliced
1 lime, cut into wedges
1 cup tomatillo salsa

Corn Husks

Dried corn husks are used as the casing for tamale fillings, but they have other uses in cooking. You can also use them to hold tofu, or other items, when grilling.

1. Cut the tempeh in half lengthwise, then cut the 2 slabs in half widthwise (as if you were slicing a roll), creating 4 squares that are nearly identical in size. Next, cut the tempeh into smaller strips, about 1" × 3".

2. Add tempeh, 6 cups water, garlic, ginger, and soy sauce to the pressure cooker. Lock the lid into place; bring to high pressure for 20 minutes. Remove from the heat and quick-release the pressure. Remove the tempeh.

3. Submerge the corn husks in hot water, placing a weight on top of them to keep them submerged. Let soak for 30 minutes and then rinse. Cover with a damp towel and set aside. Roast the chilies on medium-high heat until the skin is charred. Place the chilies in a plastic bag, twist closed, and let sit for 10 minutes. Gently remove the skins, the stem, and the seeds. Chop the pepper flesh and set aside.

4. Whisk together the corn tortilla flour, cornmeal, baking powder, and salt in a large bowl. Slowly pour in 1½ cups water, mix slightly, and then let stand for 5 minutes. Add ½ cup shortening and mix together using a spoon or an electric mixer. Set aside.

5. Heat the remaining tablespoon of shortening over medium heat. Add the white onion and sauté until tender. Add the tempeh, chopped chilies, and the corn and cook for about 6 minutes. Remove from the heat and let cool completely before adding to the corn flour mixture.

6. When ready to assemble, stir the cooled tempeh and vegetables into the corn flour mixture. Place one corn husk at a time on a flat work surface and scoop ¼ cup of the filling into the center. Fold the narrow end up to

the center, then fold both sides together to enclose the filling. Tie the tamales closed with strands of corn husk.

7. Stand the tamales up in a large steamer or colander with the open end up. Steam for 35 minutes, or until the filling is firm. To serve, slice open the corn husk (or completely remove the husk) and top the filling with sliced red onions, fresh lime juice, and tomatillo salsa.

PER SERVING
Calories: 730 | Fat: 37g | Protein: 31g | Sodium: 2710mg | Carbohydrates: 72g | Fiber: 14g

Carolina-Style Barbecue Tempeh

Vinegar-based barbecue sauce, as opposed to tomato-based, is popular across the South.

INGREDIENTS | SERVES 4

1 8-ounce package tempeh
6 cups water
2 cloves garlic, minced
1 teaspoon fresh ginger, minced
1 cup soy sauce
½ cup apple cider vinegar
½ cup maple syrup
½ cup olive oil
2 teaspoons chipotle powder
1 teaspoon dried thyme
1 teaspoon paprika
1 teaspoon cumin
Salt and pepper, to taste
4 hamburger buns

1. Cut the tempeh in half lengthwise, then cut the 2 slabs in half widthwise (as if you were slicing a roll), creating 4 squares that are nearly identical in size. Next, cut the tempeh into smaller strips, about 1" × 3".

2. Add the tempeh, water, garlic, ginger, and ½ cup of the soy sauce to the pressure cooker. Lock the lid into place; bring to high pressure for 20 minutes. Remove from the heat and quick-release the pressure. Remove the tempeh.

3. In a medium pot, add the rest of the soy sauce, cider vinegar, syrup, oil, chipotle, thyme, paprika, cumin, salt, and pepper. Bring to a simmer and add the tempeh. Let simmer for 15–20 minutes. Serve on a bun.

PER SERVING
Calories: 580 | Fat: 35g | Protein: 21g | Sodium: 4180mg | Carbohydrates: 52g | Fiber: 2g

Spicy Tempeh Tacos

Hard taco shells or soft taco shells both work for this recipe. The only difference is that each requires different cooking times and methods, so be sure to read the package directions.

INGREDIENTS | SERVES 4

1 13-ounce package tempeh

6½ cups water, divided use

2 cloves garlic, minced

1 teaspoon fresh ginger, minced

½ cup soy sauce

1 tablespoon chili powder

¼ teaspoon chipotle powder

¼ teaspoon garlic powder

¼ teaspoon crushed red pepper flakes

¼ teaspoon onion powder

2 teaspoons cumin

½ teaspoon paprika

1 teaspoon salt

1 teaspoon pepper

1 tablespoon olive oil

8 taco shells

1 cup shredded Cheddar cheese, or vegan Cheddar, such as Daiya Cheddar Style Shreds

1 cup lettuce, shredded

1 tomato, diced

1. Cut the tempeh in half lengthwise, then cut the 2 slabs in half widthwise (as if you were slicing a roll), creating 4 squares that are nearly identical in size. Next, cut the tempeh into smaller strips, about 1" × 3".

2. Add the tempeh, 6 cups water, garlic, ginger, and soy sauce to the pressure cooker. Lock the lid into place; bring to high pressure for 20 minutes. Remove from the heat and quick-release the pressure. Remove the tempeh.

3. In a bowl, mix all the dried spices together. Add the oil to the pan and sauté the tempeh for 2–3 minutes. Add the spice mixture and ½ cup water. Stir the tempeh in the pan until all of the liquid is absorbed. Serve the tempeh in taco shells and garnish with cheese, lettuce, and tomato.

PER SERVING
Calories: 570 | Fat: 30g | Protein: 35g | Sodium: 2950mg | Carbohydrates: 46g | Fiber: 13g

Simplify This Recipe

The only required spices for the tempeh are some type of pepper, cumin, and salt, so even if you don't have all of the ingredients listed, you can still create a delicious recipe.

Tempeh Bacon

*Save money by making your own tempeh bacon
instead of buying it prepackaged in stores.*

INGREDIENTS | SERVES 8

1 13-ounce package tempeh

6½ cups water

2 cloves garlic, minced

1 teaspoon fresh ginger, minced

¾ cup soy sauce

1 tablespoon maple syrup

½ teaspoon garlic powder

1 tablespoon liquid smoke

2 tablespoons vegetable oil

1. Cut the tempeh in half lengthwise, then cut the 2 slabs in half widthwise (as if you were slicing a roll), creating 4 squares that are nearly identical in size. Next, cut the tempeh into smaller strips, about 1" × 3".

2. Add the tempeh, 6 cups of water, garlic, ginger, and ½ cup soy sauce to the pressure cooker. Lock the lid into place; bring to high pressure for 20 minutes. Remove from the heat and quick-release the pressure. Remove the tempeh.

3. In a small bowl, mix ½ cup water, ¼ cup soy sauce, maple syrup, garlic powder, and liquid smoke. Place the tempeh in a small casserole dish and pour the marinade on top of it. Allow the tempeh to marinate for about 30 minutes.

4. Add the oil to a pan and sauté the "bacon" until it is brown on both sides.

PER SERVING
Calories: 150 | Fat: 7g | Protein: 13g | Sodium: 1510mg | Carbohydrates: 10g | Fiber: 4g

Thai-Style Tempeh

Serve Thai-Style Tempeh over rice or in cool, crisp lettuce leaves.

INGREDIENTS | SERVES 4

1 13-ounce package tempeh
6 cups water
2 cloves garlic, minced
1 teaspoon fresh ginger, minced
¾ cup soy sauce
1 tablespoon vegetable oil
1 13-ounce can coconut milk
1 tablespoon Sriracha sauce
¼ cup fresh basil, chopped

Sriracha

Sriracha is a very hot chili sauce, popular in many Thai dishes. The most commonly sold brand is made by Huy Fong Foods and is available at grocery and specialty stores around the country.

1. Cut the tempeh in half lengthwise, then cut the 2 slabs in half widthwise (as if you were slicing a roll), creating 4 squares that are nearly identical in size. Next, cut the tempeh into smaller strips, about 1" × 3".

2. Add the tempeh, water, garlic, ginger, and ½ cup soy sauce to the pressure cooker. Lock the lid into place; bring to high pressure for 20 minutes. Remove from the heat and quick-release the pressure. Remove the tempeh.

3. In a wok or large pan, add the oil and sauté the tempeh until it is browned on both sides. Add the remaining ¼ cup of soy sauce, coconut milk, and Sriracha sauce. Cook until all of the liquid has been absorbed. Toss in the fresh basil before serving.

PER SERVING
Calories: 430 | Fat: 30g | Protein: 27g | Sodium: 3120mg | Carbohydrates: 18g | Fiber: 9g

General Tso's Tempeh

*This recipe is very similar to General Tso's Tofu (page 197),
and would also be delicious if made with seitan.*

INGREDIENTS | SERVES 4

1 13-ounce package tempeh

7 cups water

4 cloves garlic, minced

3 teaspoons fresh ginger, minced

¾ cup soy sauce

¼ cup cornstarch

¼ cup sugar

⅛ cup white wine vinegar

⅛ cup sherry

2 tablespoons vegetable oil

2 cups broccoli, blanched and chopped

1. Cut the tempeh in half lengthwise, then cut the 2 slabs in half widthwise (as if you were slicing a roll), creating 4 squares that are nearly identical in size. Next, cut the tempeh into smaller strips, about 1" × 3".

2. Add the tempeh, 6 cups water, 2 cloves garlic, 1 teaspoon ginger, and ½ cup soy sauce to the pressure cooker. Lock the lid into place; bring to high pressure for 20 minutes. Remove from the heat and quick-release the pressure. Remove the tempeh.

3. In a small bowl, combine 1 cup water, ¼ cup soy sauce, 2 cloves garlic, 2 teaspoons ginger, cornstarch, sugar, vinegar, and sherry to create the sauce.

4. In a wok or large pan, add the oil and sauté the tempeh and broccoli for 1–2 minutes. Add the sauce and cook until it thickens, 2–3 minutes. Serve with rice.

PER SERVING
Calories: 370 | Fat: 14g | Protein: 26g | Sodium: 3030mg | Carbohydrates: 38g | Fiber: 9g

Fried Tempeh with White Gravy

*Fried and fatty foods should be kept to a minimum,
but the occasional indulgence probably won't hurt.*

INGREDIENTS | SERVES 4

1 13-ounce package tempeh

8 cups water

4 cloves garlic, minced

1 teaspoon fresh ginger, minced

¾ cup soy sauce

1 tablespoon plus ½ cup vegetable oil

¼ cup onion, diced

½ cup flour

2 tablespoons nutritional yeast

½ teaspoon sage

Salt and pepper, to taste

6–8 biscuits, or vegan biscuits

1. Cut the tempeh in half lengthwise, then cut the 2 slabs in half widthwise (as if you were slicing a roll), creating 4 squares that are nearly identical in size.

2. Add the tempeh, 6 cups water, 2 cloves garlic, ginger, and ½ cup soy sauce to the pressure cooker. Lock the lid into place; bring to high pressure for 20 minutes. Remove from the heat and quick-release the pressure. Remove the tempeh.

3. In a small frying pan over medium heat, heat 1 tablespoon vegetable oil and fry each piece of tempeh for 3 minutes on each side. Remove from the pan when cooked and set aside.

4. Add the remaining oil to a small pot. Sauté the remaining 2 garlic cloves and the onion for 2–3 minutes. Add ¼ cup soy sauce and slowly stir in the flour to create a roux. Slowly stir in the remaining 2 cups water and bring to a boil, stirring constantly for 2–3 minutes. Remove from heat and add the nutritional yeast, sage, salt, and pepper. Serve on top of the tempeh with biscuits.

PER SERVING
Calories: 850 | Fat: 50g | Protein: 35g | Sodium: 3540mg |
Carbohydrates: 71g | Fiber: 11g

Tempeh BLT Sandwich

Leave the pork off your fork with this
vegan version of the popular BLT sandwich.

INGREDIENTS | SERVES 4

1 13-ounce package tempeh

6½ cups water

2 cloves garlic, minced

1 teaspoon fresh ginger, minced

¾ cup soy sauce

1 tablespoon maple syrup

½ teaspoon garlic powder

1 tablespoon liquid smoke

2 tablespoons vegetable oil

8 slices bread, toasted

6–8 lettuce leaves

1 tomato, sliced

1. Cut the tempeh in half lengthwise, then cut the 2 slabs in half widthwise (as if you were slicing a roll), creating 4 squares that are nearly identical in size. Next, cut the tempeh into smaller strips, about 1" × 3".

2. Add the tempeh, 6 cups of water, garlic, ginger, and ½ cup soy sauce to the pressure cooker. Lock the lid into place; bring to high pressure for 20 minutes. Remove from the heat and quick-release the pressure. Remove the tempeh.

3. In a small bowl, mix ½ cup water, ¼ cup soy sauce, maple syrup, garlic powder, and liquid smoke. Place the tempeh in a small casserole dish and pour the marinade on top of it. Allow the tempeh to marinate for about 30 minutes.

4. Add the oil to a pan and sauté the "bacon" until it is brown on both sides.

5. Toast the bread in a toaster or broiler. Assemble the sandwiches using the tempeh "bacon," lettuce, and tomato slices. Serve.

PER SERVING
Calories: 440 | Fat: 16g | Protein: 30g | Sodium: 3360mg | Carbohydrates: 47g | Fiber: 10g

New Orleans–Style Po' Boy

*Po' boys, or poor boys, are Louisiana's most popular sub sandwich.
Eat it plain or "dressed" with lettuce, tomato, pickles, and mayo.*

INGREDIENTS | SERVES 4

1 13-ounce package tempeh

6 cups water

2 cloves garlic, minced

1 teaspoon fresh ginger, minced

½ cup soy sauce

2 eggs, beaten, or 4 teaspoons cornstarch combined with 4 tablespoons warm water

2 cups cornmeal

¼ cup flour

1 teaspoon Old Bay seasoning

1½ teaspoons salt

1 teaspoon pepper

3–4 cups vegetable oil, for deep frying

4–6 French bread rolls or a baguette cut into 4 pieces

Optional: 2 cups lettuce, shredded

Optional: 1 tomato, sliced

Optional: dill pickle slices

Optional: mayonnaise, or vegan mayonnaise

1. Cut the tempeh in half lengthwise, then cut the 2 slabs in half widthwise (as if you were slicing a roll), creating 4 squares that are nearly identical in size. Next, cut the tempeh into smaller strips, about 1" × 3".

2. Add the tempeh, water, garlic, ginger, and soy sauce to the pressure cooker. Lock the lid into place; bring to high pressure for 20 minutes. Remove from the heat and quick-release the pressure. Remove the tempeh.

3. Place the pieces of tempeh in the eggs. In a small bowl, mix the cornmeal, flour, Old Bay, salt, and pepper.

4. Heat the oil in a pot to 350°F. Pull the pieces of tempeh from the egg and coat them in the cornmeal mixture. Place the coated tempeh in the oil and fry until golden brown.

5. To assemble the sandwiches, place the fried tempeh on a French roll and top with lettuce, tomato, dill pickle slices, and mayonnaise, if desired.

PER SERVING
Calories: 870 | Fat: 41g | Protein: 36g | Sodium: 3150mg | Carbohydrates: 94g | Fiber: 14g

Philly Cheese Seitan Sandwich

The city of brotherly love extends its compassion to animals with this sandwich.

INGREDIENTS | SERVES 4

1 13-ounce package tempeh

6 cups water

3 cloves garlic, minced

1 teaspoon fresh ginger, minced

1 cup soy sauce

2 tablespoons olive oil

1 onion, sliced

½ green bell pepper, sliced

Salt and pepper, to taste

4–6 French rolls

4–6 slices Provolone cheese, or vegan mozzarella, such as Daiya Mozzarella Style Shreds

1. Cut the tempeh in half lengthwise, then cut the 2 slabs in half widthwise (as if you were slicing a roll), creating 4 squares that are nearly identical in size. Next, cut the tempeh into smaller strips, about 1" × 3".

2. Add the tempeh, water, garlic, ginger, and soy sauce to the pressure cooker. Lock the lid into place; bring to high pressure for 20 minutes. Remove from the heat and quick-release the pressure. Remove the tempeh.

3. Add the oil to a pan and sauté the onion and green bell peppers until they are caramelized. Add the tempeh, salt, and pepper.

4. Preheat the oven to 450°F. Place the tempeh mixture inside the French rolls and place 1–2 slices of the Provolone cheese on each. Place the tempeh sandwiches in the oven and bake for 3–5 minutes, or until the cheese has melted.

PER SERVING
Calories: 510 | Fat: 23g | Protein: 38g | Sodium: 4500mg | Carbohydrates: 41g | Fiber: 10g

Tempeh Sliders

Sliders are mini sandwiches, perfect as an appetizer or a snack.

INGREDIENTS | SERVES 4

1 13-ounce package tempeh

6 cups water

2 cloves garlic, minced

1 teaspoon fresh ginger, minced

½ cup soy sauce

1 tablespoon salt

1 teaspoon black pepper

½ teaspoon garlic powder

½ teaspoon onion powder

¼ teaspoon cumin

⅛ teaspoon cayenne pepper

3 tablespoons olive oil

½ red onion, sliced

6–8 slices American cheese or vegan cheddar

8 mini hamburger buns

1. Cut the tempeh in half lengthwise, then cut the 2 slabs in half widthwise (as if you were slicing a roll), creating 4 squares that are nearly identical in size.

2. Add the tempeh, water, garlic, ginger, and soy sauce to the pressure cooker. Lock the lid into place; bring to high pressure for 20 minutes. Remove from the heat and quick-release the pressure. Remove the tempeh.

3. In a small bowl, combine the salt, pepper, garlic powder, onion powder, cumin, and cayenne pepper. In a small pan, add 1 tablespoon of the olive oil and sauté the red onions until they have caramelized. Set them aside.

4. In a large pan, heat the remaining 2 tablespoons of olive oil and add the tempeh sliders. Season the tempeh with the spice mixture and cook until browned on each side. Melt a slice of American cheese on each piece of tempeh and top with the caramelized onions. Serve on a mini hamburger bun.

PER SERVING
Calories: 600 | Fat: 36g | Protein: 38g | Sodium: 4730mg | Carbohydrates: 32g | Fiber: 9g

Mojo Tempeh Cuban Sandwich

Mojo is a Cuban sauce made with garlic, olive oil, and citrus juice.

INGREDIENTS | SERVES 4

1 13-ounce package tempeh

6 cups water

3 cloves garlic, minced

1 teaspoon fresh ginger, minced

½ cup soy sauce

2 tablespoons orange juice

1 tablespoon lime juice

1 tablespoon lemon juice

2 tablespoons olive oil

3 tablespoons parsley, chopped

½ teaspoon dried oregano

½ teaspoon salt

¼ teaspoon pepper

4 Cuban rolls

6–8 slices Swiss cheese, or vegan mozzarella, such as Daiya Mozzarella Style Shreds

Optional: 2 cups lettuce, shredded

Optional: 1 tomato, sliced

Optional: dill pickle slices

Traditional Cuban Sandwiches

In the United States, Cuban sandwiches are typically identified by the type of bread (Cuban) and condiments on the sandwich. Common ingredients are pickles, mustard, and cheese.

1. Cut the tempeh in half lengthwise, then cut the 2 slabs in half widthwise (as if you were slicing a roll), creating 4 squares that are nearly identical in size. Next, cut the tempeh into smaller strips, about 1" × 3".

2. Add the tempeh, water, 2 cloves of garlic, ginger, and soy sauce to the pressure cooker. Lock the lid into place; bring to high pressure for 20 minutes. Remove from the heat and quick-release the pressure. Remove the tempeh.

3. In a small bowl, make the Mojo sauce by mixing the orange juice, lime juice, lemon juice, olive oil, 1 clove garlic, parsley, oregano, salt, and pepper. Let the tempeh marinate in the Mojo sauce for 10 minutes.

4. Preheat the oven to 450°F. Place the marinated tempeh on the Cuban rolls and drizzle a little more Mojo sauce on top of the tempeh. Place 1–2 slices of Swiss cheese on each sandwich. Place the sandwiches in the oven and cook for about 3–5 minutes, or until the cheese has melted.

5. Assemble the rest of the sandwich by adding lettuce, tomato, pickles, and more Mojo sauce. Press the sandwich before serving.

PER SERVING
Calories: 540 | Fat: 31g | Protein: 41g | Sodium: 2530mg | Carbohydrates: 30g | Fiber: 8g

Jams and Chutneys

Cranberry-Apple Chutney

*Chutney is an Indian dish that was introduced
to the rest of the world by the British.*

INGREDIENTS | SERVES 16

1 12-ounce bag cranberries

1 cup light brown sugar, packed

1 small sweet onion, peeled and diced

1 jalapeño pepper, seeded and minced

2 tablespoons fresh ginger, peeled and grated

1 clove garlic, minced

1 teaspoon yellow mustard seed

3" cinnamon stick

1 teaspoon lemon juice

¼ teaspoon salt

3 pounds tart cooking apples

Optional: ground ginger, to taste

Optional: ground cinnamon, to taste

For Best Results

Placing the apples over the cranberry mixture prevents the cranberries from foaming as they cook, which could clog the pressure cooker vent. Serve this chutney with roast pork or turkey. If you'd like to make cranberry-pear chutney, substitute 3 pounds of peeled and cored ripe Bartlett pears for the apples.

1. Rinse and pick over the cranberries. Add the cranberries, brown sugar, onion, jalapeño, ginger, garlic, mustard, cinnamon stick, lemon juice, and salt to a 5- to 7-quart pressure cooker. Cook over medium heat until the sugar dissolves, stirring occasionally.

2. Peel and core the apples; cut into strips, 1" in length. Place the apples in a layer over the cranberry mixture in the pressure cooker. Do not stir the apples into the mixture.

3. Lock the lid in place and bring to high pressure. Cook on high pressure for 1 minute. Remove from the heat and quick-release the pressure.

4. Remove the cinnamon stick. Taste for seasoning and add ground ginger and ground cinnamon if desired.

5. Store in a covered container in the refrigerator for up to 2 weeks. Serve heated or chilled.

PER SERVING

Calories: 110 | Fat: 0g | Protein: 0g | Sodium: 40mg | Carbohydrates: 28g | Fiber: 2g

Fresh Tomato Chutney

For a change of pace, you can spread this chutney over Indian chapati bread, flat bread, or pizza crust; top with goat cheese or vegan mozzarella; and bake.

INGREDIENTS | YIELDS 4 CUPS

4 pounds ripe tomatoes, peeled

1" piece fresh gingerroot

3 cloves garlic

1¾ cups white sugar

1 cup red wine vinegar

2 onions, diced

¼ cup golden raisins

¾ teaspoon ground cinnamon

½ teaspoon ground coriander

¼ teaspoon ground cloves

¼ teaspoon ground nutmeg

¼ teaspoon ground ginger

1 teaspoon chili powder

1 pinch paprika

1 tablespoon curry paste

1. Purée the peeled tomatoes and fresh ginger in a blender or food processor.

2. Pour the puréed tomato mixture into the pressure cooker. Stir in the remaining ingredients. Stir to mix, lock the lid into place, and cook at low pressure for 10 minutes. Remove from heat and allow pressure to release naturally. Refrigerate in a covered container until ready to use. Serve chilled or at room temperature.

PER CUP
Calories: 520 | Fat: 2g | Protein: 5g | Sodium: 30mg | Carbohydrates: 126g | Fiber: 6g

Peeling Fresh Vine-Ripened Tomatoes

Add enough water to a saucepan to cover the tomatoes; bring to a boil over medium-high heat. Use a slotted spoon to submerge the tomatoes in the boiling water for 1 minute, or until their skins begin to crack and peel. Use the slotted spoon to remove the tomatoes from the water and plunge them into ice water. The peelings will slip right off.

Green Tomato Chutney

If you prefer spicy chutney, you can substitute an Anaheim and 4 small red chili or jalapeño peppers for the red bell peppers.

INGREDIENTS | **YIELDS 5 CUPS**

2 pounds green tomatoes, diced, with stems removed

1 white onion, quartered lengthwise, and thinly sliced

2 red bell peppers, diced

¼ cup dried currants

2 tablespoons fresh ginger, grated

¾ cup dark brown sugar, firmly packed

¾ cup white wine or white distilled vinegar

Pinch sea salt

1. Put all ingredients in the pressure cooker; stir to mix. Lock on the lid and bring to low pressure. Cook on low pressure for 10 minutes. Remove from the heat and allow pressure to release naturally.

2. Cool and refrigerate overnight before serving. Can be stored in a covered container in the refrigerator for 2 months.

PER CUP
Calories: 210 | Fat: 0.5g | Protein: 3g | Sodium: 70mg | Carbohydrates: 53g | Fiber: 4g

Sweet Onion Relish

Use sweet onions like Vidalia, Candy, First Edition,
Maui, or Walla Walla for this relish.

INGREDIENTS | YIELDS 4 CUPS

4 medium sweet onions
Water, as needed
¾ cup golden raisins
1 cup agave nectar
1 tablespoon cider vinegar
Pinch salt

1. Peel and thinly slice onions. Add onions to the pressure cooker and pour in water to cover. Bring to a boil over high heat; drain immediately and discard water.

2. Return onions to pressure cooker; stir in raisins, agave nectar, vinegar, and salt until agave nectar is evenly distributed throughout onion slices.

3. Lock on lid, bring to high pressure, and cook for 5 minutes. Reduce heat and maintain low pressure for an additional 10 minutes. Remove from heat and allow pressure to release naturally.

4. Remove lid and stir relish. If relish needs thickening, return pan to heat; bring to a gentle boil for 5 minutes. Can be served warm or stored in a covered container in the refrigerator for up to 4 weeks.

PER CUP
Calories: 300 | Fat: 0g | Protein: 2g | Sodium: 45mg |
Carbohydrates: 75g | Fiber: 3g

Strawberry Jam

In addition to the usual uses for fruit spread, this jam is the perfect addition to some plain yogurt or soy yogurt.

INGREDIENTS | YIELDS 4 CUPS

4 cups strawberries

3 cups granulated cane sugar

¼ cup fresh lemon juice

1. Rinse and hull the strawberries, then quarter or halve them. Add to the pressure cooker. Stir in the sugar. Set aside for 1 hour or until the strawberries are juicy.

2. Use a potato masher to crush the fruit and mix in the sugar until the sugar is dissolved. Stir in the lemon juice.

3. Lock the lid in place. Bring the cooker to full pressure and cook for 7 minutes. Remove from the heat and allow pressure to release naturally.

4. Remove the lid. Return to heat and bring to a full boil over medium-high heat. Boil for 3 minutes or until jam reaches the desired gel state.

5. Skim off and discard any foam. Ladle into hot, sterilized glass containers or jars, leaving ½" of headspace. Seal the containers or jars. Cool and refrigerate for a week or freeze. (If you prefer, you can follow the instructions that came with your canning jars and process the jam for shelf storage.)

PER CUP
Calories: 620 | Fat: 0g | Protein: 1g | Sodium: 0mg | Carbohydrates: 154g | Fiber: 3g

Dried Apricot Preserves

*Never fill the pressure cooker more than half full when
making preserves, chutneys, or other fruit dishes.*

INGREDIENTS | YIELDS 7 CUPS

4 cups dried apricots, chopped

2 cups water

5 black peppercorns

5 cardamom pods

2 3" cinnamon sticks

2 star anise

½ cup lemon juice

4 cups granulated cane sugar

Determining the Gel Point

Test a small amount of preserves by spoon-
ing it onto an ice-cold plate. It's reached
the gel point when it's as thick as you
desire. A softer set is ideal for use in
sauces; if you prefer a firm, jam-like consistency, you may need to continue to boil the
mixture for up to 20 minutes.

1. Add the apricots to a bowl or to the pressure cooker.
   Pour in the water, cover, and let the apricots soak for
   24 hours.

2. Wrap the peppercorns, cardamom pods, cinnamon
   sticks, and star anise in cheesecloth and secure with a
   string. Add to the pressure cooker along with the apricots, soaking water, and lemon juice. Lock the lid into
   place. Bring to pressure and cook on low pressure for
   10 minutes. Remove from the heat and allow pressure
   to release naturally.

3. Uncover the pressure cooker. Remove and discard the
   cheesecloth spice bag and stir in the sugar.

4. Return the pressure cooker to the heat and bring to a
   rapid boil over medium-high heat. Boil covered for 2
   minutes and uncovered for 2 minutes or until the apri-
   cot mixture reaches the gel point.

5. Skim off and discard any foam. Ladle into hot, sterilized glass containers or jars, leaving ½" of headspace.
   Seal the containers or jars. Cool and refrigerate for a
   week or freeze. (If you prefer, you can follow the
   instructions that came with your canning jars and process the preserves for shelf storage.)

PER CUP
Calories: 630 | Fat: 0g | Protein: 3g | Sodium: 10mg |
Carbohydrates: 158g | Fiber: 6g

Mixed Citrus Marmalade

Jam sugar contains pectin, the soluble dietary fiber extracted from citrus fruits used as a gelling agent for jams, jellies, and marmalades.

INGREDIENTS | YIELDS 4 CUPS

1 large orange
1 lime
2 lemons
2 clementines or satsumas
1 pink grapefruit
3 cups water
4 pounds jam sugar

Sugar Crystals and the Gelling Process

After you've added sugar, putting the lid back on the pressure cooker once the mixture comes to a boil creates steam inside the cooker that will cause any sugar clinging to the sides of the pan to wash down into the mixture. Even one lone sugar crystal can set off a chain reaction that will cause the entire mixture to crystallize rather than remain in its gelled state.

1. Wash the fruit in hot water to remove any wax. Remove the zest from the orange, lime, and lemons; add to the pressure cooker. Quarter all fruit and place in a large (doubled) piece of cheesecloth; twist the cheesecloth to squeeze out the juice into the pressure cooker. Tie the cheesecloth over the fruit and seeds and add it to the pressure cooker along with half of the water. Lock the lid in place and bring the pressure cooker to high pressure; cook on high for 10 minutes. Remove from the heat and allow pressure to release naturally.

2. Remove the lid from the pressure cooker. Place the cooker over medium heat and add the remaining water and sugar. Bring to a boil, stirring continuously until all the sugar has dissolved.

3. While the mixture continues to boil, place the lid back on the cooker (but do not lock it into place). Leave the lid in place for 2 minutes, remove it, and then continue to let the mixture boil for 8 minutes or until the desire gel point is reached.

4. Skim off and discard any foam. Ladle into hot, sterilized glass containers or jars, leaving ½" of head space. Seal the containers or jars. Cool and refrigerate for a week or freeze until needed. (If you prefer, you can follow the instructions that came with your canning jars and process the preserves for shelf storage.)

PER SERVING
Calories: 230 | Fat: 0g | Protein: 0g | Sodium: 0mg | Carbohydrates: 59g | Fiber: 0g

Rainbow Bell Pepper Marmalade

*Serve Rainbow Bell Pepper Marmalade as a relish
for tempeh or seitan, or on top of cheese on crackers.*

INGREDIENTS | YIELDS 2 CUPS

1 large green bell pepper
1 large red bell pepper
1 large yellow bell pepper
1 large purple or orange bell pepper
1 small yellow, white, or sweet onion
Water, as needed
2 cups granulated cane sugar
Pinch salt
2 tablespoons balsamic vinegar

1. Wash, quarter, and seed the bell peppers; cut them into thin slices or dice them. Peel, quarter, and thinly slice the onion. Add the peppers and onion to the pressure cooker.

2. Add enough water to the pressure cooker to cover the peppers and onion. Bring to a boil over high heat; drain immediately and discard the water.

3. Return the peppers and onion to the pressure cooker. Stir in the sugar, salt, and vinegar. Bring to high pressure and cook for 5 minutes. Remove pan from the heat and let sit for 5 minutes.

4. Quick-release any remaining pressure. Remove the lid and return the pan to the heat. Simmer briskly over medium-high heat for 6 minutes or until the mixture is thickened. Once cooled, store in a covered container in the refrigerator overnight before using.

PER CUP
Calories: 860 | Fat: 0g | Protein: 2g | Sodium: 80mg | Carbohydrates: 212g | Fiber: 5g

Blueberry Jam

You can substitute a 6-ounce bottle of pectin for the dry pectin.

INGREDIENTS | YIELDS 4 CUPS

4 cups blueberries
4 cups granulated cane sugar
1 cup orange juice
1 teaspoon orange zest
Pinch freshly ground nutmeg
Pinch salt
1 1¾-ounce package dry pectin

1. Add the blueberries, sugar, orange juice, orange zest, nutmeg, and salt to the pressure cooker. Stir to combine.

2. Lock on the lid and bring to low pressure. Maintain pressure for 3 minutes. Remove from the heat and allow pressure to release naturally.

3. Remove the lid. Either process in a food mill to separate the pulp from the skins or push the blueberry mixture through a strainer.

4. Return the pulp to the pressure cooker. Place over medium-high heat, stir in the pectin, and bring mixture to a rolling boil, stirring constantly. Continue to boil and stir for 1 minute.

5. Skim off and discard any foam. Ladle into hot, sterilized glass containers or jars, leaving 1" of headspace. Seal the containers or jars. Cool and refrigerate for up to 5 weeks or freeze for up to 8 months. (If you prefer, you can follow the instructions that came with your canning jars and process the preserves for shelf storage.)

PER CUP
Calories: 920 | Fat: 0.5g | Protein: 2g | Sodium: 65mg | Carbohydrates: 228g | Fiber: 5g

Mincemeat

Use mincemeat as a condiment or in mincemeat pie.

INGREDIENTS | YIELDS 5 CUPS

2½ pounds pears

1 tart green apple

1 lemon, juiced and zested

1 orange, juiced and zested

1 cup golden raisins

½ cup dried cranberries or dried currants

½ cup light brown sugar, firmly packed

1 teaspoon ground cinnamon

½ teaspoon ground ginger

¼ teaspoon ground cloves

¼ teaspoon ground nutmeg

Pinch salt

½ cup walnuts or pecans, chopped and toasted

½ cup brandy or cognac

Mincemeat Seasoning

Seasoning is an arbitrary thing. You'll want to add some of the spices to the mincemeat before you cook it, but if you prefer to taste for seasoning and then increase the spices according to your taste, use half of the spices during the cooking process, and add more later if desired.

1. Peel, core, and dice the pears and apple. Wash the lemon and orange to remove any waxy coating. Add to the pressure cooker along with lemon zest and juice, orange zest and juice, raisins, cranberries or currants, brown sugar, cinnamon, ginger, cloves, nutmeg, and salt. Stir to combine.

2. Lock the lid into place and bring to high pressure; maintain pressure for 10 minutes. Remove from heat and allow pressure to release naturally.

3. Return to heat and bring to a simmer. Simmer for 10 minutes or until mixture is very thick. Stir in the nuts and brandy or cognac. Continue to simmer for an additional 5 minutes.

4. Ladle into hot, sterilized glass containers or jars, leaving ½" of headspace. Seal the containers or jars. Cool and then refrigerate for a week or freeze. (If you prefer, you can follow the instructions that came with your canning jars and process the preserves for shelf storage.)

PER CUP
Calories: 510 | Fat: 8g | Protein: 4g | Sodium: 50mg | Carbohydrates: 101g | Fiber: 11g

Peach and Toasted Almond Preserves

*Toasting the almonds is an important step that
enhances the rich flavor of these preserves.*

INGREDIENTS | YIELDS 4 CUPS

6 fresh ripe peaches

1 cup water

1 8-ounce package dried apricots, diced

½ cup toasted almonds

1¼ cups orange juice

¼ cup lemon juice

4½ cups granulated cane sugar

2 whole cloves

1 3" cinnamon stick

Pinch salt

1 1¾-ounce package pectin powder

Toasting Nuts

Preheat oven to 350°F. Place nuts in a shallow baking pan. Stirring occasionally, bake for 8 minutes or until the nuts are fragrant and golden brown. You can also toast nuts in a frying pan over medium-high heat. Stir and shake the pan constantly for 5 minutes or until nuts are golden brown.

1. Use a skewer or toothpick to poke several holes in each of the peaches. Place the peaches in the pressure cooker and pour the water over them. Lock the lid on the pressure cooker. Bring to high pressure and maintain for 3 minutes.

2. Quick-release the pressure and remove the lid. Use a slotted spoon to move the peaches to a large bowl of ice water or to a bowl under cold running water. Peel the peaches and then cut them into small pieces, discarding the pits.

3. Add the peaches, apricots, almonds, orange juice, lemon juice, sugar, cloves, cinnamon stick, and salt to water remaining in the pressure cooker. Stir to combine. Lock on the lid and bring to high pressure; maintain pressure for 2 minutes.

4. Remove the pressure cooker from the heat. Quick-release the pressure and remove the lid. Remove the cloves and cinnamon stick; discard. Stir the pectin into the fruit mixture. Return to the heat and bring to a rolling boil over medium-high heat, stirring constantly.

5. Skim off and discard any foam. Ladle into hot, sterilized glass containers or jars, leaving 1" of headspace. Seal the containers or jars. Cool and then refrigerate for up to 5 weeks or freeze for up to 8 months. (If you prefer, you can follow the instructions that came with your canning jars and process the preserves for shelf storage.)

PER CUP
Calories: 129 | Fat: 10g | Protein: 8g | Sodium: 110mg |
Carbohydrates: 301g | Fiber: 11g

Caribbean Relish

Think of this relish as hummus with a Caribbean flair.

INGREDIENTS | SERVES 12

1½ cups red or white kidney beans

7 cups water

2 teaspoons vegetable oil

Salt, to taste

2 tablespoons tahini paste

¾ cup crushed pineapple, drained

4 cloves garlic, minced

¼ teaspoon dried cumin

¼ teaspoon ground ginger

¼ teaspoon freshly ground white pepper

½ cup fresh cilantro, minced

Tomato Relish

Peel, seed, and dice 2 large tomatoes. Add to bowl and mix them together with ½ cup thawed frozen corn, ¼ cup extra-virgin olive oil, and 6 diced scallions. Season with salt, freshly ground black pepper, and fresh lime juice to taste.

1. Add the beans to the pressure cooker and pour 3 cups water over them or enough to cover the beans completely. Cover and let soak overnight. Drain and return to the pressure cooker. Pour 4 cups water over the beans. Add the oil. Lock the lid into place. Bring to high pressure; maintain pressure for 10 minutes. Remove from the heat and allow pressure to release naturally for 10 minutes.

2. Quick-release any remaining pressure. Remove the lid and, if the beans are cooked through, drain them. If additional cooking time is needed, lock the lid into place, return to high pressure, and cook for an additional 2–5 minutes.

3. Add the cooked beans, salt, tahini, pineapple, garlic, cumin, ginger, pepper, and cilantro to a blender or food processor. Pulse until mixed but still chunky. Transfer to a covered container and chill.

PER SERVING
Calories: 100 | Fat: 2.5g | Protein: 5g | Sodium: 0mg |
Carbohydrates: 16g | Fiber: 0g

Blackberry Jam

Experiment with the types of berries used to make homemade jam, or try a combination of a few.

INGREDIENTS | YIELDS 4 CUPS

4 cups blackberries
4 cups granulated cane sugar
1 cup orange juice
1 teaspoon lemon juice
Pinch salt
1 1¾-ounce package dry pectin

1. Add the blackberries, sugar, orange juice, lemon juice, and salt to the pressure cooker. Stir to combine.

2. Lock on the lid and bring to low pressure. Maintain pressure for 3 minutes. Remove from the heat and allow pressure to release naturally.

3. Remove the lid. Either process in a food mill to separate the pulp from the skins or push the blackberry mixture through a strainer.

4. Return the pulp to the pressure cooker. Place over medium-high heat, stir in the pectin, and bring mixture to a rolling boil, stirring constantly. Continue to boil and stir for 1 minute.

5. Skim off and discard any foam. Ladle into hot, sterilized glass containers or jars, leaving 1" of headspace. Seal the containers or jars. Cool and refrigerate for up to 5 weeks or freeze for up to 8 months. (If you prefer, you can follow the instructions that came with your canning jars and process the preserves for shelf storage.)

PER CUP
Calories: 890 | Fat: 1g | Protein: 2g | Sodium: 65mg | Carbohydrates: 221g | Fiber: 9g

Peach Jam

*In most states, peach season is during summer.
Using in-season fruit will result in the best flavor for homemade jams.*

INGREDIENTS | YIELDS 4 CUPS

4 cups peaches, peeled and chopped
4 cups granulated sugar
1 teaspoon lemon juice
1 1¾-ounce package dry pectin

1. Add the peaches, sugar, and lemon juice to the pressure cooker. Stir to combine. Lock on the lid and bring to low pressure. Maintain for 3 minutes. Remove from the heat and allow pressure to release naturally.

2. Remove the lid. Place over medium-high heat, stir in the pectin, and bring mixture to a rolling boil, stirring constantly. Continue to boil and stir for 1 minute. Skim off and discard any foam. Ladle into hot, sterilized glass containers, leaving 1" of headspace. Seal. Cool and refrigerate for up to 5 weeks or freeze for up to 8 months.

PER CUP
Calories: 880 | Fat: 0g | Protein: 2g | Sodium: 25mg | Carbohydrates: 228g | Fiber: 4g

Easy Grape Jelly

*A lunchbox staple can seem gourmet when
you're making the jelly yourself.*

INGREDIENTS | YIELDS 5 CUPS

5 cups grape juice
2 1¾-ounce packages dry pectin
½ cups sugar

Choosing Your Juice

For this recipe, avoid using any light or diet juices because they most likely have a higher water content or artificial sweeteners, and will result in less flavor.

1. Add grape juice and pectin to the pressure cooker and bring to medium-high heat. Stir to combine. Lock on the lid and bring to high pressure. Maintain pressure for 1 minute. Remove from the heat and quick-release the pressure. Remove the lid. Slowly stir in the sugar.

2. Skim off and discard any foam. Ladle into hot, sterilized glass containers, leaving 1" of headspace. Seal. Let cool at room temperature for 24 hours, then refrigerate for up to 5 weeks or freeze for up to 8 months.

PER CUP
Calories: 300 | Fat: 0g | Protein: 1g | Sodium: 45mg | Carbohydrates: 76g | Fiber: 2g

CHAPTER 15

Breakfast and Brunch

Steel-Cut Oats

Steel-cut oats, whole grain oats that have been cut into only two or three pieces, are sometimes referred to as Irish oatmeal. They are high in B-vitamins, calcium, protein, and fiber.

INGREDIENTS | SERVES 2

4 cups water

1 cup steel-cut oats, toasted

1 tablespoon butter, or vegan margarine, such as Earth Balance

Pinch salt

Toasting Steel-Cut Oats

Preheat the oven to 300°F. Place the steel-cut oats on a baking sheet. Bake for 20 minutes. Store toasted steel-cut oats in a covered container in a cool place. Toasting steel-cut oats will enhance the flavor and allow them to cook in half the time.

1. Place the rack in the pressure cooker; pour ½ cup water over the rack.

2. In a metal bowl that will fit inside the pressure cooker and rest on the rack, add the oats, butter, salt, and 3½ cups water. Lock the lid into place.

3. Bring to low pressure. For chewy oatmeal, maintain the pressure for 5 minutes. For creamy oatmeal, maintain pressure for 8 minutes.

4. Remove from the heat and allow pressure to release naturally. Use tongs to lift the metal bowl out of the pressure cooker.

5. Spoon the cooked oats into bowls; season and serve as you would regular oatmeal.

PER SERVING
Calories: 350 | Fat: 11g | Protein: 11g | Sodium: 75mg | Carbohydrates: 55g | Fiber: 7g

Banana Nut Bread Oatmeal

Skip instant oatmeal packets, which can be high in sugar, and make this homemade version instead.

INGREDIENTS | SERVES 2

¾ cup water

1 cup milk or soymilk

1 cup quick-cooking oats

2 bananas, sliced

2 tablespoons brown sugar

2 teaspoons cinnamon

2 tablespoons chopped walnuts

1. Place all of the ingredients in the pressure cooker.

2. Lock the lid into place. Bring to high pressure and maintain for 5 minutes. Remove from the heat and allow pressure to release naturally.

3. Remove the lid and stir the oatmeal, adding more milk if desired.

PER SERVING
Calories: 440 | Fat: 8g | Protein: 12g | Sodium: 60mg | Carbohydrates: 84g | Fiber: 11g

Apple Streusel Oatmeal

Get creative and turn any of your favorite desserts into a breakfast oatmeal.

INGREDIENTS | SERVES 2

¾ cup water

1 cup milk or soymilk

1 cup quick-cooking oats

2 apples, peeled, cored, and diced

2 tablespoons brown sugar

2 teaspoons cinnamon

2 tablespoons chopped pecans

1. Place all of the ingredients in the pressure cooker.

2. Lock the lid into place. Bring to high pressure and maintain for 5 minutes. Remove from the heat and allow pressure to release naturally.

3. Remove the lid and stir the oatmeal, adding more milk if desired.

PER SERVING
Calories: 410 | Fat: 9g | Protein: 11g | Sodium: 60mg | Carbohydrates: 77g | Fiber: 12g

Irish Oatmeal with Fruit

*You can substitute other dried fruit according to your tastes.
Try prunes, dates, and cherries for different flavors.*

INGREDIENTS | SERVES 2

3 cups water

1 cup toasted steel-cut oats

2 teaspoons butter, or vegan margarine, such as Earth Balance

1 cup apple juice

1 tablespoon dried cranberries

1 tablespoon golden raisins

1 tablespoon snipped dried apricots

1 tablespoon maple syrup

¼ teaspoon ground cinnamon

Pinch salt

Cooking Ahead

If you're not a morning person, you can make Irish Oatmeal with Fruit the night before. Once it's cooled, divide between two covered microwave-safe containers and refrigerate overnight. The next morning, cover each bowl with a paper towel to catch any splatters and then microwave on high for 1–2 minutes or until heated through.

1. Place the rack in the pressure cooker; pour ½ cup water over the rack.

2. In a metal bowl that will fit inside the pressure cooker and rest on the rack, add the 2½ cups water, oats, butter, apple juice, cranberries, raisins, apricots, maple syrup, cinnamon, and salt; stir to combine.

3. Lock the lid into place. Bring to low pressure. For chewy oatmeal, maintain the pressure for 5 minutes. For creamy oatmeal, maintain pressure for 8 minutes.

4. Remove from the heat and allow pressure to release naturally. Use tongs to lift the metal bowl out of the pressure cooker.

PER SERVING
Calories: 450 | Fat: 10g | Protein: 11g | Sodium: 85mg | Carbohydrates: 86g | Fiber: 9g

Maple-Pecan Oatmeal

Rolled oats or quick-cooking oats will work in this recipe.
Just be sure to adjust the cooking time accordingly.

INGREDIENTS | SERVES 2

¾ cup water
1 cup milk or soymilk
1 cup quick-cooking oats
2 tablespoons maple syrup
2 tablespoons chopped pecans

Syrup Substitutions

Maple syrup can be expensive. If you don't have any in your cupboards, use plain pancake syrup instead. Agave nectar is another type of sweetener that will also work in this recipe.

1. Place all of the ingredients in the pressure cooker.

2. Lock the lid into place. Bring to high pressure and maintain for 5 minutes. Remove from the heat and allow pressure to release naturally.

3. Remove the lid and stir the oatmeal, adding more milk if desired.

PER SERVING
Calories: 330 | Fat: 8g | Protein: 11g | Sodium: 55mg |
Carbohydrates: 53g | Fiber: 6g

Eggless "Eggs"

Build upon this basic recipe to create a variety of tofu scrambles.

INGREDIENTS | SERVES 2–4

16 ounces firm tofu, drained and mashed
1 teaspoon fresh lemon juice
1 teaspoon salt
½ teaspoon black pepper
½ teaspoon turmeric
1 tablespoon olive oil
¼ cup onion, diced
1 clove garlic, minced
¼ cup water

1. In a large bowl, mash the tofu with your hands or a fork, then stir in the lemon juice, salt, pepper, and turmeric.

2. Bring the olive oil to medium heat in the pressure cooker. Add the onion and sauté for 3 minutes. Add the garlic and sauté for an additional 30 seconds.

3. Add in the tofu mixture and water; stir, then lock the lid into place. Bring to medium pressure and maintain for 6 minutes. Remove from the heat and allow pressure to release naturally.

PER SERVING
Calories: 300 | Fat: 22g | Protein: 25g | Sodium: 1190mg |
Carbohydrates: 6g | Fiber: 3g

Garden Tofu Scramble

Go gourmet with this tofu scramble by substituting shiitake mushrooms and Japanese eggplant instead of the broccoli and button mushrooms.

INGREDIENTS | SERVES 2–4

16 ounces firm tofu, drained and mashed
1 teaspoon fresh lemon juice
1 teaspoon salt
½ teaspoon black pepper
½ teaspoon turmeric
1 tablespoon olive oil
½ cup broccoli florets, blanched
½ cup button mushrooms, sliced
½ cup tomato, diced
1 clove garlic, minced
¼ cup water
2 tablespoons parsley, chopped

1. In a large bowl, mash the tofu with your hands or a fork, then stir in the lemon juice, salt, pepper, and turmeric.

2. Bring the olive oil to medium heat in the pressure cooker. Add the broccoli and mushrooms and sauté for 5 minutes. Add the tomato and garlic, and sauté for an additional 30 seconds.

3. Pour in the tofu mixture and water; stir, then lock the lid into place. Bring to medium pressure and maintain for 6 minutes. Remove from the heat and allow pressure to release naturally.

4. Remove the lid and stir in the parsley before serving.

PER SERVING
Calories: 310 | Fat: 22g | Protein: 27g | Sodium: 1200mg | Carbohydrates: 7g | Fiber: 4g

Spicy Tofu Scramble

*Serve this spicy scramble on its own, or rolled up in a
flour tortilla to make a delicious breakfast burrito.*

INGREDIENTS | SERVES 2–4

16 ounces firm tofu, drained and mashed

1 teaspoon fresh lemon juice

1 teaspoon salt

½ teaspoon black pepper

½ teaspoon turmeric

1 tablespoon olive oil

¼ cup onion, diced

¼ cup red bell pepper, diced

¼ cup tomato

1 clove garlic, minced

1 teaspoon cumin

½ teaspoon chipotle powder

½ teaspoon chili powder

¼ cup water

2 tablespoons cilantro, chopped

1. In a large bowl, mash the tofu with your hands or a fork, then stir in the lemon juice, salt, pepper, and turmeric.

2. Bring the olive oil to medium heat in the pressure cooker. Add the onion and bell pepper and sauté for 3 minutes. Add the tomato, garlic, cumin, chipotle powder, and chili powder and sauté for an additional 30 seconds.

3. Pour in the tofu mixture and water; stir, then lock the lid into place. Bring to medium pressure and maintain for 6 minutes. Remove from the heat and allow pressure to release naturally.

4. Remove the lid and stir in the cilantro before serving.

PER SERVING
Calories: 320 | Fat: 22g | Protein: 26g | Sodium: 1210mg |
Carbohydrates: 9g | Fiber: 5g

Grits

*Slowly adding grits to boiling water, while gently stirring,
will help prevent clumping.*

INGREDIENTS | SERVES 4

4 cups water
1 teaspoon salt
½ teaspoon black pepper
1 cup stone-ground grits
1 tablespoon butter, or vegan
margarine, such as Earth Balance

Grits

Grits are a southern breakfast staple that
are served topped with butter or margarine, salt, pepper, and sometimes cheese.
It's very similar to polenta, especially when
polenta is served creamy.

1. Bring the water, salt, and pepper to a boil in the pressure cooker over high heat. Slowly stir in the grits.

2. Lock the lid into place. Bring to high pressure and
   maintain for 10 minutes. Remove from the heat and
   allow pressure to release naturally.

3. Remove the lid and stir in butter before serving.

PER SERVING
Calories: 170 | Fat: 3.5g | Protein: 3g | Sodium: 580mg |
Carbohydrates: 31g | Fiber: <1g

Red Pepper Grits

*Cooking grits in Vegetable Stock instead of water adds more depth
to the flavor and makes them more appropriate for dinner or lunch.*

INGREDIENTS | SERVES 4

4 cups Vegetable Stock (page 29)
1 teaspoon salt
¼ teaspoon dried thyme
1 cup stone-ground grits
½ tablespoon dried red pepper flakes

1. Bring the stock, salt, and thyme to a boil in the pressure cooker over high heat. Slowly stir in the grits.

2. Lock the lid into place. Bring to high pressure and
   maintain for 10 minutes. Remove from the heat and
   allow pressure to release naturally.

3. Remove the lid and stir in the red pepper flakes before
   serving.

PER SERVING
Calories: 170 | Fat: 0.5g | Protein: 4g | Sodium: 1170mg |
Carbohydrates: 37g | Fiber: <1g

Cornmeal Mush

*This recipe cooks into a thick cornmeal porridge.
It makes for a tasty and inexpensive breakfast food.*

INGREDIENTS | SERVES 6

1 cup yellow cornmeal

4 cups water

½ teaspoon salt

1 tablespoon butter, or vegan margarine, such as Earth Balance

1. In a bowl, whisk the cornmeal together with 1 cup water and salt. Set aside.

2. Add the remaining water to the pressure cooker. Bring to a boil over medium heat. Stir cornmeal and water mixture into the boiling water. Add butter and stir continuously until the mixture returns to a boil.

3. Lock the lid into place. Bring to low pressure; maintain for 10 minutes. Remove from heat and quick-release the pressure. Spoon into bowls and serve with a sweetener and milk or cream, like you would with oatmeal.

PER SERVING
Calories: 100 | Fat: 2.5g | Protein: 2g | Sodium: 190mg | Carbohydrates: 19g | Fiber: 1g

Home Fries

*Like hash browns, home fries can also be served with a variety
of toppings or plain with a side of ketchup.*

INGREDIENTS | SERVES 4

2 tablespoons olive oil

4 cups red potatoes, diced

1½ teaspoons paprika

1 teaspoon chili powder

1½ teaspoons salt

1 teaspoon black pepper

1. Bring the olive oil to medium heat in the pressure cooker. Add the potatoes and sauté for about 3 minutes.

2. Add all remaining ingredients and stir. Lock the lid in place and bring to high pressure; maintain pressure for 7 minutes. Remove from the heat and quick-release the pressure.

PER SERVING
Calories: 150 | Fat: 7g | Protein: 2g | Sodium: 890mg | Carbohydrates: 19g | Fiber: 3g

Hash Browns

Let Waffle House inspire you to serve these hash browns any way you'd like—scattered, covered, or smothered.

INGREDIENTS | SERVES 4

4 cups russet potatoes, peeled and grated

2 tablespoons olive oil

2 tablespoons butter, or vegan margarine, such as Earth Balance

Salt and freshly ground pepper, to taste

Preparing the Potatoes

Rinsing and thoroughly drying the grated potatoes will help you achieve a delicious crispy brown exterior on your hash browns. After grating the potatoes, pour them into a colander and let sit under running cold water for 1 minute. Once done, let the potatoes air dry or use a towel to remove excess water before cooking.

1. Prepare the potatoes and set aside.

2. Add the oil and butter to the pressure cooker and bring to temperature over medium heat.

3. Add the hash brown potatoes; sauté for 5 minutes, stirring occasionally, until they are just beginning to brown. Season with the salt and pepper.

4. Use a wide metal spatula to press the potatoes down firmly in the pan.

5. Lock the lid in place and bring to low pressure; maintain pressure for 6 minutes. Remove from the heat and quick-release the pressure.

PER SERVING
Calories: 200 | Fat: 13g | Protein: 2g | Sodium: 5mg | Carbohydrates: 20g | Fiber: 1g

Poblano Hash Browns

*Any type of pepper will do, such as poblano, jalapeño,
or bell pepper, in these spicy hash browns.*

INGREDIENTS | SERVES 4

4 cups russet potatoes, peeled and grated

2 tablespoons olive oil

2 tablespoons butter, or vegan margarine, such as Earth Balance

¼ cup onion, diced

1 poblano pepper, cored and diced

1 clove garlic, minced

Salt and freshly ground pepper, to taste

1 teaspoon cumin

1. Prepare the grated potatoes by rinsing in a colander, then air drying or using a towel to remove excess water.

2. Add the oil and butter to the pressure cooker and bring to temperature over medium heat. Add the onion and poblano pepper and sauté until just soft, about 5 minutes.

3. Add the garlic and potatoes; sauté for an additional 5 minutes, stirring occasionally, until they are just beginning to brown. Season with the salt, pepper, and cumin.

4. Use a wide metal spatula to press the potatoes down firmly in the pan.

5. Lock the lid in place and bring to low pressure; maintain pressure for 6 minutes. Remove from the heat and quick-release the pressure.

PER SERVING
Calories: 210 | Fat: 13g | Protein: 3g | Sodium: 10mg | Carbohydrates: 23g | Fiber: 2g

Three Pepper Vegan Frittata

*Frittatas are traditionally made with eggs, but you can use tofu
for a cholesterol-free breakfast dish instead.*

INGREDIENTS | SERVES 4

2 tablespoons olive oil
1 cup red potatoes, peeled and diced
½ cup onion, diced
½ cup red bell pepper, diced
½ cup green bell pepper, diced
1 teaspoon jalapeño, minced
1 clove garlic, minced
¼ cup chopped parsley
16 ounces firm tofu
½ cup unsweetened soymilk
4 teaspoons cornstarch
2 teaspoons nutritional yeast
1 teaspoon mustard
½ teaspoon turmeric
1 teaspoon salt

Make It a Scramble

To shorten the preparation time for this meal while keeping all of the flavors, try making this dish into a scramble by preparing the entire recipe in the pressure cooker. Skip the step of blending the tofu and omit the cornstarch. Add remaining ingredients, breaking apart tofu as you stir, and sauté until cooked through.

1. Preheat the oven to 400°F.

2. Bring the olive oil to medium heat in the pressure cooker. Add the potatoes, onion, peppers, garlic, and parsley, and sauté for 3 minutes. Lock the lid in place and bring to high pressure; maintain pressure for 6 minutes. Remove from the heat and quick-release the pressure.

3. Combine the tofu, soymilk, cornstarch, nutritional yeast, mustard, turmeric, and salt in a blender or food processor until smooth, then pour the tofu mixture into the cooked potato mixture.

4. Spoon the mixture into an oiled quiche or pie pan. Bake for 45 minutes, or until the frittata is firm, then remove from heat and let stand before serving.

PER SERVING
Calories: 250 | Fat: 15g | Protein: 16g | Sodium: 650mg | Carbohydrates: 18g | Fiber: 4g

Yeasty Tofu and Veggies

Nutritional yeast has a cheesy flavor and should not be replaced with other types of yeast.

INGREDIENTS | SERVES 4

1 16-ounce package extra-firm tofu
2 tablespoons vegetable oil
2 tablespoons soy sauce
1 cup water
½ onion, diced
1 cup broccoli, blanched and chopped
½ green bell pepper, chopped
½ zucchini, chopped
½ cup yellow squash, chopped
¼ cup nutritional yeast

1. Wrap the block of tofu in paper towels and press for 5 minutes by adding weight on top. Remove the paper towels and cut the tofu into ½"-thick pieces. Add 1 tablespoon of oil to the pressure cooker and sauté the tofu until it is light brown on all sides. Add 1 tablespoon of soy sauce and sauté for 10 seconds more. Remove the tofu.

2. Place the water in the pressure cooker along with the steamer tray. Place the tofu on top of the steamer tray. Lock the lid into place; bring to high pressure and maintain for 5 minutes. Remove from the heat and allow pressure to release naturally.

3. Add 1 tablespoon of oil to a large pan and sauté the onions, broccoli, bell pepper, zucchini, and squash until tender. Add the tofu and 1 tablespoon soy sauce and sauté for 1 minute more. Sprinkle the nutritional yeast on top and serve.

PER SERVING
Calories: 230 | Fat: 15g | Protein: 19g | Sodium: 530mg | Carbohydrates: 10g | Fiber: 5g

Tofu Ranchero

Bring Mexican cuisine to the breakfast table with an easy tofu ranchero.

INGREDIENTS | SERVES 4

16 ounces firm tofu, drained and mashed
1 teaspoon fresh lemon juice
1 teaspoon salt
½ teaspoon black pepper
½ teaspoon turmeric
2 tablespoons olive oil
¼ cup onion, diced
1 clove garlic, minced
8 corn tortillas
1 cup vegetarian refried beans, warmed
½ cup cheese or vegan cheese
½ cup chipotle salsa

Choosing Salsa

Salsa comes in many delicious and unique varieties. Most are clearly labeled mild, medium, and hot, but one's interpretation of those words can vary greatly. Chipotle salsa has a deep, earthy spice, but you can also use plain tomato salsa or tomatillo salsa in this recipe.

1. Preheat the oven to 350°F. In a large bowl, mash the tofu with your hands or a fork, then stir in the lemon juice, salt, pepper, and turmeric.

2. Bring 1 tablespoon olive oil to medium heat in the pressure cooker. Add the onion and sauté for 3 minutes. Add the garlic and sauté for an additional 30 seconds.

3. Pour in the tofu mixture and stir, then lock the lid into place. Bring to medium pressure and maintain for 6 minutes. Remove from the heat and allow pressure to release naturally.

4. Heat 1 tablespoon olive oil in a small sauté pan over medium heat. Cook the tortillas one at a time, until they begin to brown on each side.

5. Place all eight of the tortillas on one or two baking sheets. Divide the refried beans evenly among the tortillas, then top with the cooked tofu mixture. Sprinkle cheese over each of the tortillas, then bake until the cheese begins to melt.

6. Remove from the oven and top with salsa before serving.

PER SERVING
Calories: 410 | Fat: 21g | Protein: 22g | Sodium: 1200mg | Carbohydrates: 37g | Fiber: 8g

Spinach and Portobello Benedict

*If making this recipe vegan, read the label before purchasing
your English muffins. Some brands are not vegan.*

INGREDIENTS | SERVES 2

½ cup silken tofu
1 tablespoon lemon juice
1 teaspoon Dijon mustard
⅛ teaspoon cayenne pepper
⅛ teaspoon turmeric
1 tablespoon vegetable oil
Salt, to taste
1 tablespoon olive oil
4 small portobello mushroom caps
2 cups fresh spinach
2 English muffins, toasted

1. Add the silken tofu to a food processor and purée until smooth. Add the lemon juice, mustard, cayenne, and turmeric. Blend until well combined. With the food processor still running, slowly add the vegetable oil and blend until combined. Season with salt, to taste, to complete the vegan hollandaise.

2. Pour the hollandaise into a small sauce pan over low heat and cook until the sauce is warm. Keep warm until ready to serve.

3. Heat the olive oil in the pressure cooker over low heat. Add the mushroom caps and spinach and stir until coated with the oil.

4. Lock the lid into place. Bring to medium pressure and maintain for 3 minutes. Remove from the heat and quick-release the pressure.

5. Place two open-faced English muffins on each plate and top each half with one portobello cap and sautéd spinach. Drizzle with a spoonful of the warm vegan hollandaise to finish.

PER SERVING
Calories: 360 | Fat: 17g | Protein: 14g | Sodium: 390mg |
Carbohydrates: 39g | Fiber: 5g

Breakfast Burrito

To make this burrito vegetarian instead of vegan,
use cooked eggs instead of tofu.

INGREDIENTS | SERVES 4

2 tablespoons olive oil

16 ounces firm tofu, drained and diced

¼ cup red onion, diced

½ cup tomato, diced

¼ cup cilantro, chopped

¼ cup water

1 teaspoon salt

4 large flour tortillas

1 cup cooked black beans, warmed

1 avocado, peeled and sliced

Optional: sour cream or soy sour cream

Optional: shredded Cheddar cheese, or vegan Cheddar, such as Daiya Cheddar Style Shreds

Steaming Tortillas

For best results, steam tortillas on the stovetop using a steamer basket. If you're in a hurry, throw the tortillas into the microwave one at a time and heat for about 30 seconds.

1. Heat the olive oil in the pressure cooker over medium-high heat. Add the tofu, stir until well coated, and sauté until it begins to brown, about 5 minutes. Add the onion, tomato, cilantro, water, and salt.

2. Lock the lid into place. Bring to high pressure and maintain for 6 minutes. Remove from the heat and quick-release the pressure.

3. Steam or microwave the tortillas until softened, then lay one tortilla on a flat surface to build the burrito. Place one fourth of the tofu mixture, one fourth of the drained beans, and one fourth of the avocado slices in a line in the center of the tortilla.

4. Roll your burrito by first folding the sides of the tortilla over the filling. Then, while still holding the sides closed, fold the bottom of the tortilla over the filling. Next, roll the burrito from the bottom up, while still holding the sides closed and pushing the filling down into the burrito if it tries to spill out. Repeat for remaining burritos.

5. Top with sour cream and/or cheese, if desired.

PER SERVING
Calories: 520 | Fat: 27g | Protein: 22g | Sodium: 1320mg | Carbohydrates: 53g | Fiber: 10g

Breakfast Casserole

Yes, even casseroles can be made in a pressure cooker!

INGREDIENTS | SERVES 4

2 tablespoons vegetable oil

1 onion, diced

½ green bell pepper, chopped

1 8-ounce package Morningstar Farm Sausage Style Crumbles, or Gimme Lean Sausage

3 cups potatoes, peeled and shredded

6 eggs, beaten, or 16 ounces firm crumbled tofu

1 cup cottage cheese, or omit

2 cups Cheddar cheese, or 2 cups of vegan Cheddar, such as Daiya Cheddar Style Shreds

Salt and pepper, to taste

1. Add the vegetable oil to the pressure cooker and sauté the onion and bell pepper until tender. Add the crumbles and cook for 2–3 minutes more. Add the rest of the ingredients to the pressure cooker.

2. Lock the lid into place; bring to high pressure and maintain for 5 minutes. Remove from the heat and allow pressure to release naturally.

PER SERVING
Calories: 640 | Fat: 37g | Protein: 44g | Sodium: 880mg | Carbohydrates: 32g | Fiber: 4g

CHAPTER 16

Desserts

Savory Sun-Dried Tomato Cheesecake

You can freeze this cheesecake for up to 3 months, so it makes the perfect make-ahead addition for a cheese plate. Thaw a wedge of the cheesecake in the refrigerator and then serve at room temperature to spread on crackers or thin slices of crusty bread.

INGREDIENTS | YIELDS 7" CHEESECAKE

3 tablespoons butter, melted, or vegan margarine, such as Earth Balance

⅓ cup bread crumbs or savory cracker crumbs

½ cup sun-dried tomatoes in oil

6 cloves garlic, peeled and minced

1 teaspoon dried oregano

3 large eggs, or 3 ounces silken soft tofu

3 tablespoons all-purpose flour

2 8-ounce packages cream cheese, or 18 ounces vegan cream cheese

¾ cup sour cream, or omit

½ cup scallion, diced

2 cups hot water

1. Coat the sides and bottom of a 7" springform pan with melted butter. Evenly distribute the crumbs over the bottom and sides. Place a 16" × 16" piece of plastic wrap on top of an equal-sized piece of aluminum foil. Put the pan in the center of the plastic wrap–topped foil; form and crimp the foil around the pan to seal the bottom.

2. Drain the tomatoes, leaving 1 tablespoon oil, and add to a food processor along with the garlic, oregano, eggs, flour, cream cheese, and ¼ cup sour cream. Purée until smooth. Stir in the scallions. Pour into the springform pan. Cover with foil; crimp to seal.

3. Place a trivet or rack on the bottom of the pressure cooker. Pour in the hot water. Use two 24" lengths of aluminum foil folded in half lengthwise twice to create 24" × 2" strips of foil. Crisscross the foil strips on the counter and place the springform pan in the center. Bring the ends of the foil strips up over the springform pan; hold on to the strips and use to lower the pan into the pressure cooker until it rests on the rack or trivet.

4. Lock the lid into place and bring to high pressure; maintain for 20 minutes. Remove from the heat and let rest for 7 minutes before quick-releasing any remaining pressure. Remove the lid and cool in the pressure cooker until all of the steam has dissipated.

5. Use the foil strips to lift the pan from the pressure cooker. Remove the foil lid. Sop up any moisture with a paper towel. Cool. Spread the remaining ½ cup sour cream over the top.

PER 1" SERVING
Calories: 410 | Fat: 36g | Protein: 10g | Sodium: 300mg | Carbohydrates: 13g | Fiber: 1g

Cranberry Applesauce

*Make sure that the ingredients don't go above
the halfway mark on the pressure cooker.*

INGREDIENTS | SERVES 8

4 medium tart apples

4 medium sweet apples

1 cup cranberries

Zest and juice from 1 large orange

½ cup dark brown sugar

½ cup granulated cane sugar

1 tablespoon unsalted butter, or vegan margarine, such as Earth Balance

2 teaspoons ground cinnamon

½ teaspoon ground cloves

¼ teaspoon freshly ground black pepper

⅛ teaspoon salt

1 tablespoon fresh lemon juice

1. Peel, core, and grate the apples. Wash the cranberries. Add the cranberries to the pressure cooker and top with grated apples. Add the remaining ingredients.

2. Lock the lid into place and bring to low pressure; maintain pressure for 5 minutes. Remove from heat and allow pressure to release naturally. Remove the lid; lightly mash the apples with a fork. Stir well. Serve warm or chilled.

PER SERVING
Calories: 210 | Fat: 1.5g | Protein: 0g | Sodium: 45mg | Carbohydrates: 51g | Fiber: 6g

Coconut Rice

*The combination of coconut, currants, and spices transforms this rice into a succulent dish.
It is especially good served after a curry entrée.*

INGREDIENTS | SERVES 4

2 tablespoons butter or vegetable oil

1 cup extra long-grain white rice, rinsed and drained

½ cup unsweetened coconut, flaked or grated

2¼ cups water

¼ cup currants

½ teaspoon ground cinnamon

1 teaspoon anise seeds

⅛ teaspoon ground cloves

½ teaspoon salt

1. Bring the butter or oil to temperature in the pressure cooker over medium heat. Add the rice, stirring well. Add the coconut, water, currants, cinnamon, anise seeds, cloves, and salt. Lock the lid and bring to high pressure; maintain for 3 minutes. Turn off the heat and let the pressure drop naturally for 7 minutes.

2. Quick-release any remaining pressure and remove the lid. Fluff the rice with a fork. Drain off any excess moisture. Taste for seasoning and adjust if necessary. Serve.

PER SERVING
Calories: 320 | Fat: 14g | Protein: 5g | Sodium: 300mg | Carbohydrates: 47g | Fiber: 3g

Basic Unsweetened Applesauce

*There's no need to core the apples to remove the seeds when you'll be
using a food mill to process the cooked apples.*

INGREDIENTS | YIELDS 5 CUPS

1 cup water

12 medium apples (about 3 pounds)

Applesauce Notes

This recipe's instructions are for a 6-quart
pressure cooker. For a yield of 3 cups in a
4-quart pressure cooker, reduce the apples
to 2 pounds and the water to ⅔ cup. For a
yield of 6½ cups of applesauce in an
8-quart pressure cooker, increase the
apples to 5 pounds and the water to 1⅔
cups.

1. Add the water to the pressure cooker. If using organic apples, rinse and quarter the apples. If not, rinse, peel, and quarter the apples. Add to the pressure cooker. Lock the lid, bring to high pressure, and remove from the heat; let the pressure release naturally for 10 minutes. Quick-release any remaining pressure.

2. Once the apples have cooled slightly, pass the apples and cooking liquid through a food mill, or blend in batches in a food processor or blender. Refrigerate covered for up to 10 days or freeze for up to 4 months.

PER CUP
Calories: 190 | Fat: 0g | Protein: 0g | Sodium: 0mg |
Carbohydrates: 53g | Fiber: 12g

Spiced Peaches

*To make spiced peach butter, after Step 2, process the peaches and liquid in a blender
or food processor until smooth, and return to the pressure cooker. Simmer and stir over
low heat for 30 minutes or until thickened enough to coat the back of a spoon.*

INGREDIENTS | SERVES 6

2 15-ounce cans sliced peaches in syrup

¼ cup water

1 tablespoon white wine vinegar

⅛ teaspoon ground allspice

1 cinnamon stick

4 whole cloves

½ teaspoon ground ginger

Pinch cayenne pepper

Optional: 1 tablespoon candied ginger,
minced

Optional: 3 whole black peppercorns

1. Add all of the ingredients to the pressure cooker. Stir to mix. Lock the lid into place and bring to low pressure; maintain pressure for 3 minutes. Remove the pressure cooker from the heat, quick-release the pressure, and remove the lid. Remove and discard the cinnamon stick, cloves, and peppercorns if used.

2. Return to medium heat. Simmer and stir for 5 minutes to thicken the syrup. Serve warm or chilled. To store, allow to cool and then refrigerate for up to a week.

PER SERVING
Calories: 70 | Fat: 0g | Protein: 0g | Sodium: 10mg |
Carbohydrates: 17g | Fiber: 1g

Special Occasion Chunky Applesauce

*To sweeten the applesauce, stir in sugar or maple syrup, to taste,
after you remove the lid from the pressure cooker.*

INGREDIENTS | SERVES 6

8 Granny Smith apples

1 cup apple juice or cider

2 tablespoons fresh lemon juice

¼ cup sugar

⅓ cup light brown sugar, packed

½ teaspoon ground nutmeg

¼ teaspoon ground cinnamon

⅓ cup cinnamon hearts candy

1. Rinse, peel, core, and dice the apples. Add to the pressure cooker with apple juice or cider, lemon juice, sugar, brown sugar, nutmeg, and cinnamon. Stir well. Lock the lid into place and bring to low pressure; maintain for 4 minutes. Remove from heat and allow pressure to release naturally for 10 minutes.

2. Quick-release any remaining pressure. Stir in the candy until it's melted and blended, mashing the apples slightly as you do so. Serve warm or chilled. Can be stored for several days in the refrigerator.

PER SERVING
Calories: 200 | Fat: 0g | Protein: 1g | Sodium: 10mg |
Carbohydrates: 53g | Fiber: 4g

Cranberry Sauce

For additional flavor, stir in some orange liqueur, bourbon, or brandy.

INGREDIENTS | SERVES 6

1 12-ounce bag fresh cranberries

1 cup sugar

½ cup water, apple juice, or pineapple juice

Pinch salt

1 tablespoon frozen orange juice concentrate

Optional: cinnamon and ground cloves, to taste

1. Rinse and drain the cranberries. Remove and discard any stems or blemished cranberries. Add to the pressure cooker along with the sugar, water, and salt. Lock the lid and bring to high pressure; maintain for 6 minutes.

2. Remove from heat and allow pressure to release naturally for 10 minutes. Remove the lid. Stir in the orange juice concentrate. Stir well, breaking the cranberries apart with a spoon.

3. Taste for seasoning, stirring in additional sugar and cinnamon and cloves if desired. Serve warm or chilled.

PER SERVING
Calories: 160 | Fat: 0g | Protein: 0g | Sodium: 25mg |
Carbohydrates: 41g | Fiber: 3g

Apple Butter

Serve on toast or as a sandwich spread.

INGREDIENTS | YIELDS ABOUT 2 CUPS

1 cup apple juice or cider
12 medium apples (about 3 pounds)
1½ teaspoons ground cinnamon
½ teaspoon ground allspice
⅛ teaspoon ground cloves
1½ cups sugar
Optional: 1 or 2 drops oil of cinnamon

1. Add the apple juice or cider to the pressure cooker. Wash, peel, core, and dice the apples. Lock the lid into place, bring to high pressure, and immediately remove from heat; let the pressure release naturally for 10 minutes. Quick-release any remaining pressure.

2. Press cooled apples through a fine sieve or food mill, or process in a food processor or blender. Return apples and liquids to pressure cooker, add the cinnamon, allspice, cloves, sugar, and oil of cinnamon, if using.

3. Return the pan to medium heat and bring to a simmer. Simmer uncovered and stir until the sugar is dissolved. Reduce heat, simmer, and stir for 1 hour. Note that it's important that you frequently stir the apple butter from the bottom of the pan to prevent it from burning.

PER CUP
Calories: 1130 | Fat: 0g | Protein: 0g | Sodium: 5mg | Carbohydrates: 299g | Fiber: 32g

Dried Fruit Compote

If you plan to add sugar to the dried fruit compote, do so before the fruit has cooled so that it can be stirred into the fruit mixture until it dissolves.

INGREDIENTS | SERVES 6

1 8-ounce package dried apricots

1 8-ounce package dried peaches

1 cup golden raisins

1½ cups orange juice

1 cinnamon stick

4 whole cloves

Optional: sugar

1. Cut the dried apricots and peaches into quarters and add them to the pressure cooker along with the raisins, orange juice, cinnamon stick, and cloves. Lock the lid into place and bring to high pressure; maintain pressure for 3 minutes. Remove from heat and allow pressure to release naturally. Remove the lid.

2. Remove the cinnamon stick and cloves. Return to medium heat and simmer for several minutes. Serve warm or allow to cool, then add sugar to taste, if using. Cover and store in the refrigerator until needed, up to 1 week.

PER SERVING
Calories: 320 | Fat: 0g | Protein: 4g | Sodium: 10mg | Carbohydrates: 74g | Fiber: 6g

Fruit Compote

Serve as a topping for plain or soy yogurt.

INGREDIENTS | SERVES 6

1 cup apple juice

1 cup dry white wine

2 tablespoons sugar

1 cinnamon stick

¼ teaspoon ground nutmeg

Zest of 1 lemon

Zest of 1 orange

3 apples

3 pears

½ cup dried cherries, cranberries, or raisins

1. Add the apple juice and wine to the pressure cooker over medium-high heat. Bring to a boil. Stir in the sugar until dissolved. Add the cinnamon stick, nutmeg, lemon zest, and orange zest. Reduce heat to maintain a simmer.

2. Wash, peel, core, and chop the apples and pears. Add to the pressure cooker. Stir. Lock the lid into place and bring to high pressure; maintain pressure for 1 minute. Remove the pressure cooker from heat, quick-release the pressure, and remove the lid.

3. Use a slotted spoon to transfer the cooked fruit to a serving bowl. Return the pressure cooker to the heat and bring to a boil; boil and stir until reduced to a syrup that will coat the back of a spoon. Stir the dried cherries, cranberries, or raisins in with the cooked fruit in the bowl and pour the syrup over the fruit mixture. Stir to mix. Allow to cool slightly, then cover with plastic wrap and chill overnight in the refrigerator.

PER SERVING
Calories: 190 | Fat: 0.5g | Protein: 1g | Sodium: 0mg | Carbohydrates: 42g | Fiber: 5g

Spiced Chocolate Cake

Serve with icing, powdered sugar, or ice cream on top.

INGREDIENTS | SERVES 10–12

1½ cups all-purpose flour

4 tablespoons cocoa powder

1 teaspoon cinnamon

1 teaspoon cayenne pepper

1 teaspoon sugar

¼ teaspoon salt

1 teaspoon baking powder

2 eggs, beaten, or 2 mashed bananas

4 tablespoons butter, melted, or vegan margarine, such as Earth Balance

1 cup milk, or soymilk

2 cups hot water

1. In a medium bowl, mix the flour, cocoa powder, cinnamon, cayenne, sugar, salt, and baking powder. In a large bowl, beat the eggs. Add the dry ingredients to the eggs. Slowly stir in the melted butter and the milk. Pour the cake mixture into an 8" round pan.

2. Add the steaming rack to the pressure cooker and pour in the hot water. Place the cake in the pressure cooker and lock the lid into place. Bring to high pressure, then reduce to low and cook for 30 minutes.

3. Remove the pressure cooker from the heat, quick-release the steam, and carefully remove the cake.

PER SERVING
Calories: 140 | Fat: 6g | Protein: 5g | Sodium: 135mg |
Carbohydrates: 18g | Fiber: 1g

Stuffed Apples

You can replace the sugar with maple syrup or brown sugar if desired.
Serve as dessert, with a scoop of vanilla ice cream or soy ice cream.

INGREDIENTS | SERVES 4

½ cup apple juice

¼ cup golden raisins

¼ cup walnuts, toasted and chopped

2 tablespoons sugar

½ teaspoon grated orange rind

½ teaspoon ground cinnamon

4 cooking apples

4 teaspoons butter, or vegan margarine, such as Earth Balance

1 cup water

1. Put the apple juice in a microwave-safe container; heat for 1 minute on high or until steaming and hot. Pour over the raisins. Soak the raisins for 30 minutes. Drain, reserving the apple juice. Add the nuts, sugar, orange rind, and cinnamon to the raisins and stir to mix.

2. Rinse and dry the apples. Cut off the top fourth of each apple. Peel the cut portion and chop it, then stir the diced apple pieces into the raisin mixture. Hollow out and core the apples by cutting to, but not through, the apple bottoms.

3. Place each apple on a piece of aluminum foil that is large enough to wrap the apple completely. Fill the apple centers with the raisin mixture.

4. Top each with a teaspoon of the butter. Wrap the foil around each apple, folding the foil over at the top and then pinching it firmly together.

5. Pour the water into the pressure cooker. Place the rack in the cooker. Place the apples on the rack. Lock the lid into place and bring to high pressure; maintain pressure for 10 minutes.

6. Remove pressure cooker from heat, quick-release the pressure, and remove the lid. Carefully lift the apples out of the pressure cooker. Unwrap and transfer to serving plates. Serve hot, at room temperature, or chilled.

PER SERVING
Calories: 230 | Fat: 9g | Protein: 1g | Sodium: 0mg |
Carbohydrates: 41g | Fiber: 6g

Pears Poached in Wine

Use Bartlett, Anjou, or Bosc pears. If you prefer, replace the cinnamon stick, ginger, and orange zest with a whole split and scraped vanilla bean.

INGREDIENTS | SERVES 4

4 ripe, but still firm pears
2 tablespoons fresh lemon juice
1¼ cups dry wine
½ cup cream sherry
¼ cup sugar
3" cinnamon stick, halved
¼ teaspoon ground ginger
2 teaspoons orange zest, grated

Recipe Alternatives

Make this dessert alcohol-free by replacing the wine and sherry with fruit juice; adjust the sugar accordingly. If you prefer to serve whole pears, peel the pears and cut off some of the bottom so they'll stand upright. After you've dissolved the sugar into the sauce, insert the rack into the pressure cooker and stand the pears upright.

1. Rinse and peel the pears and cut them in half. Use a spoon or melon baller to remove the cores. Brush the pears with the lemon juice.

2. Combine the wine, sherry, sugar, cinnamon, ginger, and orange zest in the pressure cooker. Bring to a boil; stir to blend and dissolve the sugar. Carefully place the pears cut-side down in the pressure cooker. Lock the lid into place and bring to low pressure; maintain pressure for 3 minutes. Remove the pressure cooker from the heat, quick-release the pressure, and remove the lid.

3. Use a slotted spoon to transfer the pears to a serving bowl or to place them on dessert plates. If desired, return the pressure cooker to medium heat and simmer uncovered for several minutes to thicken the sauce. Remove and discard the cinnamon stick pieces. Spoon the sauce over the pears. Serve.

PER SERVING
Calories: 220 | Fat: 1g | Protein: 1g | Sodium: 5mg | Carbohydrates: 40g | Fiber: 4g

Vanilla-Spice Pear Butter

Bartlett pears are light green and are especially prevalent in the Pacific Northwest.
Serve on scones or toasted English muffins.

INGREDIENTS | YIELDS ABOUT 2 CUPS

6 medium Bartlett pears
¼ cup dry white wine
1 tablespoon fresh lemon juice
¾ cup sugar
2 orange slices
1 lemon slice
2 whole cloves
1 vanilla bean, split lengthwise
1 cinnamon stick
¼ teaspoon ground cardamom
Pinch salt

1. Rinse, peel, and core the pears, and cut them into 1" dice. Add the pears, wine, and lemon juice to the pressure cooker. Lock the lid into place and bring to low pressure; maintain pressure for 8 minutes.

2. Remove from heat and allow pressure to release naturally for 10 minutes. Quick-release any remaining pressure and remove the lid. Transfer the fruit and juices to a blender or food processor and purée.

3. Return the purée to the pressure cooker. Add the sugar. Stir and cook over low heat until sugar dissolves. Stir in the remaining ingredients. Increase the heat to medium and boil gently, cooking and stirring for about 30 minutes or until mixture thickens and mounds slightly on a spoon.

4. Remove and discard the orange and lemon slices, cloves, and cinnamon stick. Remove the vanilla pod; use the back of a knife to scrape away any vanilla seeds still clinging to the pod and stir them into the pear butter. Cool and refrigerate covered for up to 10 days or freeze for up to 4 months.

PER CUP
Calories: 610 | Fat: 1g | Protein: 2g | Sodium: 80mg |
Carbohydrates: 155g | Fiber: 16g

Banana Pudding Cake

This is a delicious way to use up ripe bananas. You'll need to use a pressure cooker large enough to hold a 1-quart or 6-cup Bundt or angel food cake pan to make this recipe.

INGREDIENTS | SERVES 12

1 18¼-ounce package yellow cake mix, or vegan cake mix

1 3½-ounce package instant banana pudding mix, or vegan pudding mix

4 eggs, or 4 ounces silken tofu

4 cups water

¼ cup vegetable oil

3 small ripe bananas, mashed

2 cups powdered sugar, sifted

2 tablespoons milk, or soymilk

1 teaspoon vanilla extract

½ cup walnuts, toasted and chopped

1. Treat a 1-quart or 6-cup Bundt or angel food cake pan with nonstick spray. Set aside.

2. Add the cake mix and pudding mix to a large mixing bowl; stir to mix. Make a well in the center and add the eggs and pour in 1 cup water, oil, and mashed banana.

3. Beat on low speed until blended. Scrape bowl and beat another 4 minutes on medium speed. Pour the batter into the prepared pan. Cover tightly with a piece of heavy-duty aluminum foil.

4. Pour 3 cups water into the pressure cooker and add the rack. Lower the cake pan onto the rack.

5. Lock the lid into place and bring to high pressure; maintain pressure for 35 minutes.

6. Remove the pressure cooker from the heat, quick-release the pressure, and remove the lid.

7. Lift the cake pan out of the pressure cooker and place on a wire rack to cool for 10 minutes, then turn the cake out onto the wire rack to finish cooling.

8. To make the glaze, mix together the powdered sugar, milk, and vanilla in a bowl. Drizzle over the top of the cooled cake. Sprinkle the walnuts over the glaze before the glaze dries.

PER SERVING
Calories: 420 | Fat: 15g | Protein: 5g | Sodium: 370mg | Carbohydrates: 68g | Fiber: 1g

Chocolate-Berry Bread Pudding

You can somewhat cut the fat in Chocolate-Berry Bread Pudding by replacing the milk and cream with skim or 2% milk, but add one more egg to the batter if you do.

INGREDIENTS | SERVES 6

6 slices day-old challah or brioche, or vegan white bread

½ cup raspberry preserves

½ cup dried strawberries or prunes, diced

½ cup hazelnuts, chopped

½ cup cocoa powder

½ cup sugar

Pinch salt

2 tablespoons butter, melted, or vegan margarine, such as Earth Balance

3 large eggs, or 2 mashed bananas

2 cups whole milk, or 2 cups soymilk

2 cups heavy cream, or 2 cups soymilk

1 tablespoon vanilla

1 cup water

1. If the crusts on the bread are dark, remove them. If using fresh bread, lightly toast it. Spread raspberry preserves over the bread. Treat a 5-cup heatproof soufflé dish with nonstick spray.

2. Tear the bread into chunks. Layer half the bread in the bottom of the soufflé dish. Sprinkle with dried fruit and chopped hazelnuts. Add remaining bread with preserves.

3. Whisk the cocoa, sugar, and salt together. Add butter and eggs; whisk to mix. Whisk in milk, cream, and vanilla. Pour half the cocoa mixture over the bread. Tap down the dish and wait several minutes for the bread to absorb the liquid. Pour in remaining cocoa mixture.

4. Tear off 2 large pieces of heavy-duty aluminum foil. Lay one piece of the foil over the top of the dish, crimping it slightly around the edges, and wrap it around the dish, folding it and tucking it under. Set the dish in the middle of the remaining piece of foil; bring it up and over the top of the dish and crimp to seal.

5. Pour water into the pressure cooker and add rack. Crisscross 2 long doubled pieces of foil over the rack. Place the covered soufflé dish over the crossed strips.

6. Lock lid into place and bring to high pressure; maintain for 15 minutes. Remove from heat and allow pressure to release naturally. Remove the dish from the pressure cooker, remove the foil, and place on a rack until ready to serve or until it's cool enough to cover and refrigerate.

PER SERVING
Calories: 740 | Fat: 47g | Protein: 14g | Sodium: 310mg | Carbohydrates: 71g | Fiber: 5g

Lemon Cheesecake

*Serve this rich, popular dessert topped with cherry pie filling
or sugared fresh blueberries, raspberries, or strawberries.*

INGREDIENTS | SERVES 8

12 gingersnaps or vanilla wafers

1½ tablespoons almonds, toasted

½ tablespoon butter, melted, or vegan margarine, such as Earth Balance

2 8-ounce packages cream cheese, room temperature, or vegan cream cheese

½ cup sugar

2 large eggs, or 2 ounces silken tofu

Zest of 1 lemon, grated

1 tablespoon fresh lemon juice

½ teaspoon natural lemon extract

1 teaspoon vanilla

2 cups water

1. Use a pressure cooker with a rack that's large enough to hold a 7" × 3" springform pan. Treat the inside of the pan with nonstick spray.

2. Add the cookies and almonds to a food processor. Pulse to create cookie crumbs and chop the nuts. Add the melted butter and pulse to mix.

3. Transfer the crumb mixture to the springform pan and press down into the pan. Wipe out the food processor bowl.

4. Cut the cream cheese into cubes and add it to the food processor along with the sugar; process until smooth. Add the eggs, lemon zest, lemon juice, lemon extract, and vanilla. Process for 10 seconds.

5. Scrape the bowl and then process for another 10 seconds or until the batter is well mixed and smooth.

6. Place the springform pan in the center of two 16" × 16" pieces of aluminum foil. Crimp the foil to seal the bottom of the pan.

7. Transfer the cheesecake batter into the springform pan. Treat one side of a 10" square of aluminum foil with nonstick spray; lay over the top of the springform pan and crimp around the edges.

8. Bring the bottom foil up the sides so that it can be grasped to raise and lower the pan into and out of the pressure cooker.

9. Pour the water into the pressure cooker. Insert the rack. Set the springform pan holding the cheesecake batter on the rack.

Lemon Cheesecake (*continued*)

10. Lock the lid into place and bring to high pressure; maintain pressure for 8 minutes. Remove from heat and allow pressure to release naturally. Remove the lid.

11. Lift the covered springform pan out of the pressure cooker and place on a wire rack. Remove the top foil.

12. If any moisture has accumulated on top of the cheesecake, dab it with a piece of paper towel to remove it. Let cool to room temperature and then remove from the springform pan.

PER SERVING
Calories: 330 | Fat: 23g | Protein: 7g | Sodium: 250mg | Carbohydrates: 23g | Fiber: <1g

Creamy Coconut Rice Pudding

Garnish this pudding with a sprinkling of ground cinnamon and serve with a dollop of whipped cream or soy whip.

INGREDIENTS | SERVES 6

1½ cups Arborio rice, rinsed and drained

2 cups whole milk or soymilk

1 14-ounce can coconut milk

1 cup water

½ cup sugar

2 teaspoons ground cinnamon

½ teaspoon salt

1½ teaspoons vanilla

1 cup dried cherries, dried strawberries, or golden raisins

1. Add the rice, milk, coconut milk, water, sugar, cinnamon, and salt to the pressure cooker. Cook and stir to dissolve the sugar over medium-high heat and bring to a boil. Lock the lid into place and bring to low pressure; maintain for 15 minutes.

2. Turn off the heat, quick-release the pressure, and remove the lid. Stir in the vanilla and dried fruit. Replace the cover, but do not lock into place. Let stand for 15 minutes. Stir and serve.

PER SERVING
Calories: 400 | Fat: 17g | Protein: 6g | Sodium: 240mg | Carbohydrates: 57g | Fiber: 2g

Molten Fudge Pudding Cake

Serve warm with a scoop of vanilla bean ice cream or soy ice cream and garnish with fresh fruit or dust with powdered sugar.

INGREDIENTS | SERVES 6

4 ounces semisweet chocolate chips

¼ cup cocoa powder

⅛ teaspoon salt

3 tablespoons butter, or vegan margarine, such as Earth Balance

2 large eggs, separated, or 2 ounces silken tofu

¼ cup sugar, plus extra for the pan

1 teaspoon vanilla

½ cup pecans, chopped

¼ cup plus 2 tablespoons all-purpose flour

2 teaspoons instant coffee granules

2 tablespoons coffee liqueur

1 cup water

Vegan Chocolate Chips

Some popular brands of chocolate chips are "accidentally vegan." Check the label of grocery store brands to find a vegan option or order them online. See Appendix C for a list of online stores.

1. Add the chocolate chips, cocoa, salt, and 2 tablespoons butter to a microwave-safe bowl. Microwave on high for 1 minute; stir well. Microwave in additional 20-second segments if necessary, until the butter and chocolate are melted. Set aside to cool.

2. Add the egg whites to a medium-size mixing bowl. Whisk or beat with a mixer until the egg whites are foamy. Gradually add ¼ cup of sugar, continuing to whisk or beat until soft peaks form; set aside.

3. Add the egg yolks and vanilla to a mixing bowl; use a whisk or handheld mixer to beat until the yolks are light yellow and begin to stiffen. Stir in the cooled chocolate mixture, pecans, flour, instant coffee, and coffee liqueur.

4. Transfer a third of the beaten egg whites to the chocolate mixture; stir to loosen the batter. Gently fold in the remaining egg whites.

5. Treat the bottom and sides of a 1-quart metal pan with 2 teaspoons of the remaining butter. Add about a tablespoon of sugar to the pan; shake and roll to coat the buttered pan with the sugar.

6. Dump out and discard any extra sugar. Transfer the chocolate batter to the buttered pan.

7. Treat one side of a 15" piece of aluminum foil with the remaining teaspoon of butter. Place the foil butter-side down over the top of the pan; crimp around the edges of the pan to form a seal.

Molten Fudge Pudding Cake (*continued*)

8. Pour the water into the pressure cooker. Place the rack in the cooker. Create handles to use later to remove the pan by crisscrossing long, doubled strips of foil over the rack.

9. Place the metal pan in the center of the rack over the foil strips. Lock the lid into place and bring to low pressure; maintain pressure for 20 minutes.

10. Remove pressure cooker from heat, quick-release pressure, and remove the lid. Lift the pan out of the pressure cooker and place on a wire rack. Remove foil cover.

11. Let rest for 10–15 minutes. To serve, either spoon from the pan or run a knife around the edge of the pan, place a serving plate over the metal pan, and invert to transfer the cake.

PER SERVING
Calories: 320 | Fat: 21g | Protein: 5g | Sodium: 75mg | Carbohydrates: 33g | Fiber: 3g

Plum Pudding with Brandy Sauce

*This traditional steamed Christmas pudding can be made up to a month in advance
if you refrigerate it in a brandy-soaked cheesecloth in a covered container.
If made ahead, steam it or heat it gently in the microwave before serving it with the brandy sauce.*

INGREDIENTS | SERVES 10

1 cup prunes, snipped
1 cup dried currants
1 cup dried cranberries
1 cup raisins
1 cup candied lemon peel, minced
½ cup dark rum
1 cup butter, partially frozen, or vegan margarine, such as Earth Balance
1½ cups all-purpose flour
1 cup dried bread crumbs
½ cup pecans, chopped
1 tablespoon candied ginger, minced
1 teaspoon baking soda
½ teaspoon salt
1 teaspoon ground cinnamon
¼ teaspoon ground nutmeg
¼ teaspoon ground cloves
3 eggs, or 3 ounces silken tofu
2 cups light brown sugar, packed
3 cups water
1 cup heavy cream, or soymilk
¼ cup brandy

1. Add the prunes, currants, cranberries, raisins, candied lemon peel, and rum to a bowl. Stir to mix. Cover and let stand at room temperature for 8 hours.

2. Partially freeze ¾ cup butter. Add the flour, bread crumbs, pecans, ginger, baking soda, salt, cinnamon, nutmeg, and cloves to a large mixing bowl. Stir to mix.

3. Grate the butter into the flour mixture. Add the marinated fruit. Toss grated butter and fruit into flour mixture. Add eggs and 1 cup of brown sugar to a separate bowl; whisk to mix. Pour into the flour-butter-fruit mixture. Combine the two mixtures together.

4. Wrap the base of a 7" or 8" springform pan with heavy-duty aluminum foil.

5. Transfer the batter to the springform pan, pressing it down into the pan to eliminate any air pockets.

6. Tear off a 25"-long piece of heavy-duty aluminum foil and treat one side of one 8" end of the foil with nonstick spray. Place the nonstick spray-treated side of the foil over the top of the springform pan and then wrap the remaining foil under and over the pan again; crimp to seal.

7. Pour the water and place the rack into the pressure cooker. Crisscross long doubled strips of foil over the rack to create handles to use later to remove the pan.

8. Place springform pan on rack, over foil strips. Lock lid into place and bring to high pressure; maintain for 1 hour.

Plum Pudding with Brandy Sauce (*continued*)

9. Remove from heat and allow pressure to release naturally. Remove lid. Lift pan from the pressure cooker and cool. Remove foil cover.

10. Let rest and cool for 15 minutes, then run a knife around the edge of the pudding to loosen it from the sides of the pan. Unmold the pudding and transfer it to a plate.

11. To make the brandy sauce, add remaining cup of brown sugar, cream, and remaining ¼ cup butter to a saucepan placed over medium-high heat. Simmer and stir until sugar dissolves; stir in the brandy. Simmer and stir for 10 minutes. Serve over the warm pudding.

PER SERVING
Calories: 810 | Fat: 34g | Protein: 8g | Sodium: 380mg | Carbohydrates: 117g | Fiber: 6g

Peanut Butter and Fudge Cheesecake

Adults and kids alike love peanut butter and chocolate,
so this dessert will be a hit with everyone.

INGREDIENTS | SERVES 8

1 cup toasted, unsalted peanuts

½ cup vanilla wafers

1 tablespoon cocoa powder

3 tablespoons butter, melted, or vegan margarine, such as Earth Balance

1 cup peanut butter

2 8-ounce packages cream cheese, softened, or vegan cream cheese

½ cup light brown sugar, packed

½ cup powdered sugar, sifted

2 tablespoons cornstarch

2 large eggs, or 2 ounces silken tofu

¼ cup sour cream, or soy sour cream

1 12-ounce package semisweet chocolate chips

2 cups water

1. Add the peanuts, vanilla wafers, and cocoa to a food processor. Pulse to grind the peanuts and turn the vanilla wafers into crumbs. Add the butter. Pulse to mix. Press into the bottom of a 7" springform pan. Set aside. Wipe out the food processor.

2. Add the peanut butter, cream cheese, and brown sugar to the food processor. Process until smooth. Add the powdered sugar and cornstarch to a small bowl; stir to mix well. Add to the food processor with the eggs and sour cream. Process until smooth. Remove the lid and stir in the chocolate chips. Transfer the batter to the springform pan.

4. Wrap the base of the pan with heavy-duty aluminum foil. Tear off a 25"-long piece of heavy-duty aluminum foil and treat one side of one 8" end of the foil with nonstick spray. Place the spray-treated side of the foil over the top of the pan and then wrap the remaining foil under and then over the pan again; crimp to seal.

5. Pour the water and place the rack into the pressure cooker. Crisscross long, doubled strips of foil over the rack to create handles to use later to remove the pan. Place the springform pan on the rack over the foil strips. Lock the lid into place and bring to high pressure; maintain pressure for 22 minutes.

6. Remove from heat and allow pressure to release naturally. Remove the lid. Lift the pan from the pressure cooker and place it on a wire rack. Allow to cool slightly. Refrigerate at least 4 hours before serving.

PER SERVING
Calories: 870 | Fat: 65g | Protein: 20g | Sodium: 360mg | Carbohydrates: 63g | Fiber: 6g

Glazed Lemon Poppy Seed Cake

Make this cake ahead of time. The flavor improves if you wrap it in plastic wrap and store it for a day or two before you serve it.

INGREDIENTS | SERVES 8

½ cup butter, softened, or vegan margarine, such as Earth Balance

1 cup sugar

2 eggs, separated, or 2 ounces silken tofu

1 teaspoon vanilla

2 lemons

1¼ cups all-purpose flour

1 teaspoon baking soda

1 teaspoon baking powder

¼ teaspoon salt

⅔ cup whole milk, or soymilk

⅓ cup poppy seeds

2 cups water

½ cup powdered sugar, sifted

1. Add the butter and sugar to a mixing bowl; beat until light and fluffy. Beat in the egg yolks, vanilla, grated zest from 1 lemon, and juice from 1 lemon.

2. Mix together the flour, baking soda, baking powder, and salt. Add the flour and milk in 3 batches to the butter mixture, mixing after each addition. Stir in the poppy seeds. Add the egg whites to a chilled bowl. Whisk or beat until stiff. Fold the egg whites into the poppy seed batter.

3. Treat a 4-cup soufflé dish or Bundt pan with nonstick spray. Transfer the batter to the pan. Treat a 15" square of heavy-duty aluminum foil with nonstick spray. Place the foil, treated-side down, over the pan; crimp around the edges to seal.

4. Pour the water and place the rack into the pressure cooker. Crisscross long, doubled strips of foil over the rack to create handles to use later to remove the pan. Place the pan on the rack over the foil strips. Lock the lid into place and bring to low pressure; maintain pressure for 40 minutes.

5. Remove from heat and allow pressure to release naturally. Remove the lid. Lift the pan from the pressure cooker and place it on a cooling rack. Remove foil cover.

6. To make the glaze, whisk the juice and grated zest from the remaining lemon together with the powdered sugar. Transfer the cake to a serving platter and drizzle the glaze over the top.

PER SERVING
Calories: 360 | Fat: 16g | Protein: 5g | Sodium: 320mg | Carbohydrates: 51g | Fiber: 1g

Date Pudding

*This is a rich, decadent dessert in the tradition
of an English sticky toffee pudding.*

INGREDIENTS | SERVES 8

2½ cups dates, pitted and snipped

1½ teaspoons baking soda

1⅔ cups boiling water

2 cups dark brown sugar, packed

½ cup butter, softened, or vegan margarine, such as Earth Balance

3 large eggs, or 3 ounces firm tofu

2 teaspoons vanilla

3½ cups all-purpose or cake flour

4 teaspoons baking powder

Pinch salt

2 cups water

1. Add the dates to a mixing bowl and toss them together with the baking soda. Pour the boiling water over the dates. Set aside.

2. Add the brown sugar and butter to a food processor. Process to cream them together, and then continue to process while you add the eggs and vanilla. Use a spatula to scrape the brown sugar mixture into the bowl with the dates. Stir to mix.

3. Add the flour, baking powder, and salt to a bowl; stir to mix. Fold into the date and brown sugar mixture.

4. Wrap the base of a 7" or 8" springform pan with heavy-duty aluminum foil. Treat the pan with nonstick spray.

5. Press the batter into the springform pan. Tear off a 25"-long piece of heavy-duty aluminum foil and treat one side of one 8" end of the foil with nonstick spray. Place the treated side of the foil over the top of the spring-form pan and then wrap the remaining foil under and then over the pan again; crimp to seal.

6. Pour the water and place the rack into the pressure cooker. Crisscross long, doubled strips of foil over the rack to create handles to use later to remove the pan. Place the springform pan on the rack over the foil strips. Lock the lid into place and bring to low pressure; maintain pressure for 50 minutes.

7. Remove from heat and allow pressure to release naturally. Remove the lid. Lift the pan from the pressure cooker and place it on a cooling rack.

PER SERVING
Calories: 690 | Fat: 14g | Protein: 9g | Sodium: 550mg | Carbohydrates: 136g | Fiber: 5g

Cornmeal Cake

Serve warm with maple syrup or make a maple-infused butter by whisking pats of chilled butter or vegan margarine into heated maple syrup.

INGREDIENTS | SERVES 6

2 cups milk or soymilk

¼ cup light brown sugar, packed

1 teaspoon orange zest, grated

½ cup fine yellow cornmeal

2 large eggs or 2 ounces silken tofu

2 tablespoons butter, melted, or vegan margarine, such as Earth Balance

2 tablespoons orange marmalade

1 cup water

1. Bring milk to a simmer over medium heat. Stir in the brown sugar; simmer and stir until the milk is at a low boil. Whisk in the orange zest and cornmeal. Simmer and stir for 2 minutes. Remove from heat. Whisk together the eggs, butter, and orange marmalade. Stir into the cornmeal mixture. Treat a 1-quart soufflé or heatproof glass dish with nonstick spray. Add batter.

2. Pour water into the pressure cooker and add rack. Place soufflé dish on the rack. Lock lid into place and bring to low pressure; maintain pressure for 12 minutes. Remove from heat and allow pressure to release naturally for 10 minutes. Quick-release any remaining pressure and remove the lid. Transfer to a wire rack.

PER SERVING
Calories: 170 | Fat: 6g | Protein: 6g | Sodium: 210mg | Carbohydrates: 26g | Fiber: <1g

Piña Colada Bread Pudding

If desired, you can add 1 tablespoon butter and 2 tablespoons brown sugar to the juice drained from the pineapple. Simmer and stir over medium-low heat until it thickens, and then serve over the bread pudding.

INGREDIENTS | SERVES 8

1 16-ounce can cream of coconut

1 cup heavy cream, or soymilk

3 large eggs, or 3 ounces silken tofu

½ cup butter, melted, or vegan margarine, such as Earth Balance

¾ cup sugar

1½ teaspoons rum flavoring

¼ teaspoon ground nutmeg

1 20-ounce can pineapple chunks, drained

1¼ cups coconut

8 cups French bread, torn into 2" cubes

1½ cups water

1. Add the cream of coconut, cream, eggs, butter, sugar, rum flavoring, and nutmeg to a large bowl. Whisk to mix thoroughly. Stir in the drained pineapple and coconut. Fold in the bread cubes.

2. Treat a 5-cup soufflé dish with nonstick spray. Transfer the bread pudding mixture into the dish. Pour in the water and place the rack into the pressure cooker.

3. Crisscross long, doubled strips of foil over the rack to create handles to use later to remove the pan.

4. Treat one side of a 15"-square piece of heavy-duty aluminum foil with nonstick spray. Lay the foil, treated-side down, over the soufflé dish and crimp the edges to seal.

5. Tear off another piece of heavy-duty foil to completely wrap the soufflé dish to ensure the seal. Place over the crisscrossed pieces of foil.

6. Lock the lid into place and bring to high pressure; maintain pressure for 12 minutes. Remove pressure cooker from heat, quick-release pressure, and remove lid.

7. Remove pan from the pressure cooker, uncover, and place on a wire rack to cool. Serve warm, at room temperature, or chilled.

PER SERVING
Calories: 650 | Fat: 44g | Protein: 8g | Sodium: 360mg | Carbohydrates: 61g | Fiber: 4g

Tapioca Pudding

Add another dimension to this dish by combining it with other flavors.
You can stir in some toasted pecans, chocolate chips, or coconut.

INGREDIENTS | SERVES 4

½ cup small pearl tapioca

1¾ cups water

⅓ cup sugar

1 tablespoon butter, or vegan margarine, such as Earth Balance

2 large eggs or 2 ounces firm tofu

⅛ teaspoon salt

1½ cups milk, or soymilk

1 cup heavy cream, or soymilk

1 teaspoon vanilla

1. Combine the tapioca and ¾ cup water in a small bowl; cover and let soak overnight.

2. Add the sugar, butter, eggs, and salt to a bowl; beat until smooth. Stir in the milk, cream, and vanilla. Drain the tapioca and stir into the milk mixture.

3. Treat a 1-quart stainless steel bowl with nonstick spray. Pour the tapioca mixture into the bowl. Cover the bowl tightly with heavy-duty aluminum foil.

4. Pour the remaining cup of water into the pressure cooker and add the rack. Crisscross long, doubled strips of foil over the rack to create handles to use later to remove the pan. Center the covered pan holding the tapioca mixture on the foil strips on the rack.

5. Lock the lid into place and bring to low pressure; maintain pressure for 12 minutes. Remove the pressure cooker from the heat, quick-release the pressure, and remove the lid.

6. Lift the pudding out of the pressure cooker. Let rest for 15 minutes and then remove the foil cover. Stir. Taste for flavor and add more vanilla if desired. Chill until ready to serve.

PER SERVING
Calories: 430 | Fat: 27g | Protein: 8g | Sodium: 170mg | Carbohydrates: 40g | Fiber: 0g

Steamed Dessert Bread

Toast leftovers by placing slices on the oven rack
or a cookie sheet in a 350°F oven for 5 minutes.

INGREDIENTS | SERVES 8

½ cup unbleached all-purpose flour

½ cup stone-ground cornmeal

½ cup whole wheat flour

½ teaspoon baking powder

¼ teaspoon fine salt

¼ teaspoon baking soda

½ cup maple syrup

½ cup buttermilk, or ½ cup soymilk plus 1 tablespoon vinegar

1 large egg, or 1 ounce silken tofu

Butter, as needed; or vegan margarine, such as Earth Balance

2 cups water

1. Add the flour, cornmeal, whole wheat flour, baking powder, salt, and baking soda to a mixing bowl. Stir to combine.

2. Add the maple syrup, buttermilk, and egg to another mixing bowl. Whisk to mix, then pour into the flour mixture. Mix until a thick batter is formed.

3. Butter the inside of a 6-cup heatproof pudding mold or baking pan. Add enough batter to fill ¾ full.

4. Butter one side of a piece of heavy-duty aluminum foil large enough to cover the top of the baking dish. Place butter-side down over the pan and crimp to seal.

5. Pour the water and place the rack into the pressure cooker. Crisscross long, doubled strips of foil over the rack to create handles to use later to remove the pan. Place the pan on the rack over the foil strips. Lock the lid into place and bring to low pressure; maintain pressure for 1 hour.

6. Remove from heat and allow pressure to release naturally. Remove lid. Lift pan from pressure cooker and place on a cooling rack. Remove foil.

7. Test the bread with a toothpick; if the toothpick comes out wet, place the foil over the pan and return it to the pressure cooker for 5 more minutes, repeating if necessary. If the bread is done, use a knife to loosen the bread and invert it onto the cooling rack. Serve the bread warm.

PER SERVING
Calories: 150 | Fat: 1g | Protein: 4g | Sodium: 170mg | Carbohydrates: 31g | Fiber: 2g

Port-Poached Figs

Serve the figs on top of soy ice cream—
or simply on their own—with the syrup.

INGREDIENTS | SERVES 4

3 cups tawny port

1½ cups sugar

1 vanilla bean, split and scraped

½ teaspoon cinnamon

¼ cup orange juice

8 whole black peppercorns

12 dried black mission figs

1. Combine the port, sugar, vanilla pods and seeds, cinnamon, orange juice, and peppercorns in the pressure cooker over high heat. Bring to a boil and reduce the heat. Simmer for 20 minutes.

2. Add the figs. Lock the lid into place and bring to high pressure; maintain pressure for 6 minutes. Remove from the heat and allow pressure to release naturally.

PER SERVING
Calories: 710 | Fat: 0g | Protein: 2g | Sodium: 15mg | Carbohydrates: 130g | Fiber: 4g

Basic Yellow Cake

Serve this staple dessert any way you'd like—topped with icing,
a dollop of whip cream or soy whip, or a sprinkling of powdered sugar.

INGREDIENTS | SERVES 10–12

1½ cups all-purpose flour

1 teaspoon baking powder

1 cup sugar

½ teaspoon salt

2 eggs, beaten, or 2 mashed bananas

½ cup butter, melted, or vegan margarine, such as Earth Balance

1 teaspoon vanilla extract

1 cup milk, or soymilk

1. In a medium bowl, mix the flour, baking powder, sugar, and salt. In a large bowl, beat the eggs. Add the dry ingredients to the eggs. Slowly stir in the melted butter, vanilla extract, and the milk.

2. Pour the cake mixture into an 8" round pan. Place the cake in the pressure cooker and lock the lid into place. Cook the cake for 30 minutes over a low flame without the weight in place.

3. Remove the pressure cooker from the heat and carefully remove the cake. Serve with whatever topping that you like.

PER SERVING
Calories: 250 | Fat: 10g | Protein: 4g | Sodium: 190mg | Carbohydrates: 36g | Fiber: <1g

Vegan Flan

*To remove flan from the ramekins, dip the bottom in hot water
for about 15 seconds, then turn over onto a plate.*

INGREDIENTS | SERVES 6

½ cup plus 1½ tablespoons sugar, divided

2 cups plain soymilk

1 tablespoon agar-agar flakes

½ cup extra-firm silken tofu

1 tablespoon vanilla extract

¼ teaspoon salt

1. Place ½ cup sugar in a saucepan over medium-low heat. Stir and melt until golden. Pour into the bottom of ramekins.

2. Pour the soymilk into the pressure cooker and sprinkle with the agar flakes. Let sit for 10 minutes. Bring to a boil over high heat, then reduce the heat to low. Lock the lid into place and maintain pressure for 3 minutes. Remove from the heat and allow pressure to release naturally.

3. Blend the tofu, remaining sugar, vanilla, salt, and soymilk mixture in a blender or large food processor until very smooth.

4. Pour the tofu mixture into the ramekins over the syrup, then cover with plastic wrap and refrigerate for at least 2 hours.

PER SERVING
Calories: 140 | Fat: 1.5g | Protein: 4g | Sodium: 160mg | Carbohydrates: 26g | Fiber: 0g

Glossary of Terms and Ingredients

Adzuki beans: A sweet, reddish-brown bean, popular in Asian recipes.

Agar-agar: A type of dried seaweed used to thicken liquids and to replace gelatin.

Aloo gobi: A spicy dish using potatoes, cauliflower, and Indian spices.

Braising: A cooking method that consists of browning a protein or vegetable and then simmering it in liquid to finish it.

Caponata: A popular Italian dish made with eggplant and tomato.

Chorizo: A spicy, Spanish sausage commonly made with pork.

Chutney: A spicy, fruit-based condiment served in Indian cuisine.

Compote: A dessert consisting of fresh fruit cooked to a syrup.

Coulis: A sauce consisting of puréed vegetables or fruits.

Edamame: Baby soybeans in the pod, often eaten as an appetizer.

Gauge pressure: The point at which the cooker has achieved full pressure and from which the time in all pressure cooker recipes begin.

Gnocchi: An Italian pasta shaped like a dumpling and usually made from potatoes.

Interlock: Safety device in modern pressure cookers that prevents the lid from being opened while internal pressure exceeds atmospheric pressure.

Lemongrass: A thick, lemon-scented grass often used in Thai cooking.

Maque choux: A Cajun dish that includes corn and tomato.

Masala: An Indian curry that often includes cardamom, coriander, pepper, fennel, and nutmeg.

Orzo: A rice-shaped pasta.

Paella: A Spanish rice dish seasoned with saffron.

Pilaf: A cooking technique in which the rice is first sautéed and then simmered in stock.

Plantain: A starchy, banana-like fruit.

Polenta: An Italian porridge made from cornmeal.

Quinoa: A tiny grain, similar to couscous, high in protein and nutrients.

Ratatouille: A vegetable stew often consisting of tomatoes, bell peppers, zucchini, squash, and onions.

Relief valve: A device that allows the release of steam from inside a pressure cooker.

Risotto: An Italian dish prepared by slowly stirring hot stock into rice.

Sauté: To fry briefly with a small amount of fat over high heat.

Seitan: A meat substitute made from wheat gluten.

Succotash: A vegetable stew made from tomatoes, lima beans, and corn.

Tempeh: An Indonesian food made from fermented soybeans and fungus.

Tofu: A cheese-like food made from soybeans.

TVP: Texturized vegetable protein; a meat substitute, similar to ground beef, made from soybeans.

Substitutions

Bacon
Soy bacon pieces, such as Bacos, or tempeh bacon

Butter
Non-dairy vegan margarine, such as Earth Balance

Buttermilk
Combine 1 cup soymilk with 1 tablespoon vinegar

Cheese
Rice milk, soymilk, or non-dairy cheese, such as Daiya or Follow Your Heart

Chicken stock
Vegetable stock or faux chicken stock, such as Better Than Bouillon No Chicken Base

Cream cheese
Non-dairy cream cheese, such as Toffuti Better Than Cream Cheese or Vegan Gourmet Cream Cheese Alternative

Eggs
Ener-G Egg Replacer, cornstarch (2 teaspoons cornstarch plus 2 tablespoons warm water equals 1 egg), mashed banana (1 banana equals 1 egg), tofu, ground flaxseed (1 tablespoon of ground flaxseed plus 3 tablespoons hot water equals 1 egg)

Gelatin
Agar agar

Ground beef
Texturized vegetable protein (TVP), or soy beef, such as Gimme Lean Beef or Boca Ground Crumbles

Heavy cream
Soy cream, such as Silk Original Creamer, or Mimic-Cream Cream Subsitute

Honey
Agave nectar, maple syrup, or brown rice syrup

Ice cream
Soy ice cream, such as Tofutti or Purely Decadent, or coconut milk ice cream, such as Purely Decadent Made with Coconut Milk

Marshmallows
Gelatin-free marshmallows, such as Sweet and Sara

Milk
Sweetened or unsweetened soymilk, almond milk, or rice milk

Pork
Vegan Ground Pork by Match, Lightlife's Smart Bacon, or Smart Deli Baked Ham Style

Ricotta cheese
Crumbled firm tofu

Sausage
Meat-free sausage links, such as Tofurky Kielbasa, Beer Brats, or Sweet Italian

Sour cream
Non-dairy sour cream, such as Vegan Gourmet Sour Cream Alternative or Tofutti Sour Supreme

Whipped cream
Soy whipped cream, such as Soyatoo Soy Whip

Yogurt
Soy yogurt, such as Silk Live! Soy Yogurt; or coconut milk yogurt, such as So Delicious Coconut Milk Yogurt

Vegetarian/Vegan Internet Resources

Vegetarian/Vegan Information

PETA.org
A comprehensive resource provided by the world's largest animal rights group. Contains information on animal rights, a free vegetarian starter kit, vegan recipes, cruelty-free shopping guide, "accidentally vegan" shopping list, games, contests, celebrity ads, and more.
www.peta.org

Vegan Online Stores

Cosmo's Vegan Shoppe
100% vegan specialty store based in Atlanta, Georgia. Sells food, clothing, home products, cosmetics, media, and beauty and health care products.
www.cosmosveganshoppe.com

The Vegan Store
The first vegan store that started as a mail order catalog is now online. Sells food, clothing, home products, cosmetics, media, and beauty and health care products.
www.veganstore.com

Food Fight! Vegan Grocery
A vegan food store based in Portland, Oregon. Sells vegan meats, cheeses, sweets, beverages, and vitamins.
www.foodfightgrocery.com

Recipes

PETA.org
Free vegan recipes for breakfast, lunch, dinner, dessert, and snacks, covering almost all global cuisines.
www.peta.org

VegWeb.com
Over 13,000 vegetarian recipes and photos provided by registered users. The site also contains forums, a meal planner, articles, and coupons.
www.vegweb.com

Fat-Free Vegan Recipes
Low-fat and no-fat vegan recipes. The site also contains a popular blog, forum, and additional information on fat-free cooking.
http://fatfreevegan.com

Post Punk Kitchen
Vegan cooking with an edge. Free recipes, including categories for low-fat, no refined sugar, and wheat-free.
www.theppk.com/recipes

Pressure Cooker Cook Times

Miss Vickie's
A one-stop shop for beginner basics, cooking times, recipes, helpful hints, information on canning, and more.
http://missvickie.com

FastCooking.ca
Everything you need to know about pressure cookers, including cooking times, recipes, tips and tricks, and more.
www.fastcooking.ca

Index

Note: Page numbers in **bold** indicate recipe category lists.

We Have

EVERYTHING®

on Anything!

With more than 19 million copies sold, the Everything® series has become one of America's favorite resources for solving problems, learning new skills, and organizing lives. Our brand is not only recognizable—it's also welcomed.

The series is a hand-in-hand partner for people who are ready to tackle new subjects—like you!

For more information on the Everything® series, please visit *www.adamsmedia.com*

The Everything® list spans a wide range of subjects, with more than 500 titles covering 25 different categories:

Business

Careers

Children's Storybooks

Computers

Cooking

Crafts and Hobbies

Education/Schools

Games and Puzzles

Health

History

Home Improvement

Everything Kids

Languages

Music

New Age

Parenting

onal Finance

Pe

Reference

Religion

Self-Help

Sports & Fitness

Travel

Wedding

Writing